ART, MYTH, AND RITUAL IN CLASSICAL GREECE

What do Greek myths mean, and how was their meaning created for the ancient viewer? In *Art, Myth, and Ritual in Classical Greece*, Judith Barringer considers the use of myth on monuments at several key sites – Olympia, Athens, Delphi, and Trysa – showing that myth was neither randomly selected nor purely decorative. The mythic scenes on these monuments had meaning, the interpretation of which depended on context. Barringer explains how the same myth can possess different meanings and how, in a monumental context, the mythological image relates to the site and often to other monuments surrounding it, which redouble, resonate, or create variations on a theme. The architectural sculpture examined here is discussed in a series of five case studies, which are chronologically arranged and offer a range of physical settings, historical and social circumstances, and interpretive problems. Providing new interpretations of familiar monuments, this volume also offers a comprehensive way of seeing and understanding Greek art and culture as an integrated whole.

Judith M. Barringer is Professor of Greek Art and Archaeology at the University of Edinburgh. The author of *The Hunt in Ancient Greece* and *Divine Escorts: Nereids in Archaic and Classical Greek Art*, she has received awards and fellowships such as the National Endowment for the Humanities at the American School of Classical Studies in Athens and the British Academy Larger Research Grant, as well as awards from the Loeb Classical Library Foundation and the Carnegie Trust for the Universities of Scotland.

ART, MYTH,
AND RITUAL
IN CLASSICAL GREECE

JUDITH M. BARRINGER
University of Edinburgh

CAMBRIDGE
UNIVERSITY PRESS

CAMBRIDGE UNIVERSITY PRESS
Cambridge, New York, Melbourne, Madrid, Cape Town, Singapore, São Paulo, Delhi

Cambridge University Press
32 Avenue of the Americas, New York, NY 10013-2473, USA

www.cambridge.org
Information on this title: www.cambridge.org/9780521646475

First published 2008

Printed in the United States of America

A catalog record for this publication is available from the British Library.

Library of Congress Cataloging in Publication Data

Barringer, Judith M.
Art, myth, and ritual in classical Greece / Judith M. Barringer.
    p.   cm.
Includes bibliographical references and index.
ISBN: 978-0-521-64134-0 (hardback) – ISBN: 978-0-521-64647-5 (pbk.)
1. Mythology, Greek, in art.   2. Art and religion – Greece.
3. Sculpture, Greek.   I. Title.
NB160.B37   2008
733'.30938–dc22   2007041635

ISBN   978-0-521-64134-0 hardback
ISBN   978-0-521-64647-5 paperback

CONTENTS

Illustrations		*page* vii
Acknowledgments		xiii
Note on Abbreviations		xv
	Introduction	1
1	The Temple of Zeus at Olympia, Heroic Models, and the Panhellenic Sanctuary	8
2	The Athenian Akropolis, Female Power, and State Religion	59
3	Making Heroes in the Athenian Agora	109
4	Myth and Religion at Delphi	144
5	The Cult of the Individual and the Realm of the Dead	171
	Conclusion	203
Notes		213
Works Cited		241
Index of Ancient Citations		255
Object Index		258
Subject Index		259

ILLUSTRATIONS

1. Map of the Mediterranean region.   *page* 9
2. Map of the Greek mainland.   10
3. Aerial view of Olympia.   11
4. Olympia, east side of Temple of Zeus.   11
5. Olympia, plan, fifth century B.C.   12
6. Olympia, model of Altis.   12
7. Olympia, Temple of Zeus, east pediment sculptures.   13
8. Olympia, Temple of Zeus, east pediment reconstruction
   by A. F. Stewart.   13
9. Olympia, ash altar reconstruction by F. Adler.   14
10. Olympia, Temple of Zeus, west pediment sculptures.   15
11. Olympia, Temple of Zeus, west pediment reconstruction
    by A. F. Stewart.   15
12. Olympia, Temple of Zeus, cutaway drawing of pronaos.   16
13. Olympia, Temple of Zeus, metopes reconstruction.   17
14. Olympia, Temple of Zeus, Herakles v. Cretan bull metope.   18
15. Olympia, Temple of Zeus, cutaway drawing of cella.   18
16. Olympia, Temple of Zeus, Augean stables metope.   21
17. Olympia, Temple of Zeus, west pediment, central figures.   23
18. Olympia, Temple of Zeus, west pediment, struggling
    figures.   24
19. Tyrannicides (Roman copy).   25
20. Detail of Attic black-figure volute krater (François Vase) by
    Kleitias and Ergotimos: Theseus on Delos, Centauromachy.   26
21. Aigina, Temple of Aphaia, east pediment.   26
22. Delphi, Temple of Apollo, c. 510 B.C., east pediment
    reconstruction by A. F. Stewart.   27

23. Olympia, Megarian Treasury, c. 510 B.C., pediment sculptures. — 28

24. Olympia, Megarian Treasury, c. 510 B.C., pediment reconstruction by G. Treu. — 28

25. Olympia, Temple of Zeus, west pediment, Lapith Q. — 29

26. Olympia, Temple of Zeus, west pediment, female Lapith R. — 31

27. Olympia, Temple of Zeus, east pediment, central figures F, I, H, G, K. — 33

28. Attic black-figure lekythos attributed to the Sappho Painter, Chariot race of Pelops and Oinomaos. — 35

29. Attic black-figure lekythos, Chariot race of Pelops and Oinomaos. — 36

30. Olympia, Temple of Zeus, east pediment, Figure N. — 38

31. Olympia, Temple of Zeus, east pediment, Figure L. — 39

32. Olympia, Zanes bases. — 39

33. Bronze helmet from Olympia. — 41

34. Argive shield band from Olympia. — 42

35. Statue base of Poulydamas from Olympia. — 47

36. Statue base of Poulydamas from Olympia. — 48

37. Statue base of Poulydamas from Olympia. — 48

38. Silver tetradrachm minted by Alexander. — 56

39. Silver tetradrachm minted by Alexander. — 57

40. Athens, Akropolis, aerial view. — 61

41. Athens, Akropolis, view from west. — 61

42. Athens, Akropolis, reconstruction by M. Korres, fifth century B.C. — 62

43. Athens, Akropolis, Parthenon, view from northwest. — 63

44. Athens, Akropolis, plan, fifth century B.C. — 64

45. Athens, Akropolis, Parthenon, cross-section to show friezes. — 65

46. Athens, Akropolis, Parthenon, west pediment and Ionic frieze reconstruction by E. Berger. — 67

47. Athens, Akropolis, Parthenon, west pediment, Figures B–C. — 68

48. Athens, Akropolis, Parthenon, west metopes, reconstruction by M. Cox. — 68

49. Athens, Akropolis, Parthenon, east pediment and Ionic frieze reconstruction by E. Berger. — 70

50. Athens, Akropolis, Parthenon, east metopes, reconstruction by M. Cox. — 71

51. Delphi, Temple of Apollo, west pediment, reconstruction by A. F. Stewart. — 72

52. Athens, Akropolis, Old Temple of Athena, pediment sculptures. — 72

53. Athens, Akropolis, Parthenon, north metopes,
reconstruction by M. Cox. 73
54. Mykonos, Cycladic clay relief pithos. 74
55. Athens, Akropolis, Parthenon, south metopes,
reconstruction by M. Cox. 75
56. Athens, Akropolis, Parthenon, south metope 12. 76
57. Athens, Akropolis, Parthenon, south metope 29. 77
58. Athens, Akropolis, Parthenon, south metope 28. 78
59. Athens, Akropolis, Parthenon, west frieze VIII.15,
horseman. 81
60. Attic red-figure hydria attributed to the Kleophrades
Painter (Vivenzio Hydria), Ilioupersis. 84
61. Athens, Akropolis, Parthenon, north frieze XL.109–111,
horsemen. 86
62. Athens, Akropolis, Parthenon, north frieze XXIII.63–65,
apobatai. 87
63. Athens, Akropolis, Parthenon, north frieze VI.16–19,
hydriaphoroi. 88
64. Athens, Akropolis, Parthenon, south frieze XLIV.133–136,
sacrificial animals. 89
65. Athens, Akropolis, Parthenon, east frieze IV.20–23,
eponymous heroes. 90
66. Athens, Akropolis, Parthenon, east frieze V.29–37,
peplos scene flanked by gods. 90
67. Varvakeion Athena. 92
68. Athena Parthenos statue in the Parthenon, Reconstruction
by A. K. Orlandos. 93
69. Athens, Akropolis, Prokne and Itys. 97
70. Athens, Akropolis, Erechtheion, west side. 99
71. Athens, Akropolis, Erechtheion, south porch. 99
72. Attic white-ground lekythos attributed to the Bonsanquet
Painter, Man and woman at grave. 100
73. Athens, Akropolis, kore. 104
74. Athens, Akropolis, Parthenon, east frieze I.4–6, phialai
bearers. 105
75. Krateriskoi from Brauron. 106
76. View of Athenian Agora from Akropolis. 110
77. Athens, Agora, plan at the end of the fifth century B.C. 111
78. Athens, Agora, Hephaisteion, east façade. 112
79. Athens, Agora, Hephaisteion, south side. 113
80. Athens, Agora, Hephaisteion, east metopes. 113

81. Athens, Agora, Hephaisteion, east metopes reconstruction
by M. Cox.   114
82. Athens, Agora, Hephaisteion, north metopes.   115
83. Athens, Agora, Hephaisteion, north and south metopes
reconstruction by M. Cox.   115
84. Athens, Agora, Hephaisteion, plan.   116
85. Delphi, Athenian Treasury, east façade.   117
86. Delphi, Athenian Treasury, south and west sides.   118
87. Delphi, Athenian Treasury, Theseus metopes.   119
88. Delphi, Athenian Treasury, Theseus metopes.   119
89. Delphi, Athenian Treasury, Herakles metopes.   120
90. Delphi, Athenian Treasury, Herakles metopes.   120
91. Delphi, Athenian Treasury, metope of Herakles and
Keryneian hind.   121
92. Athens, Agora, Hephaisteion, east metope, Herakles
and Athena.   122
93. Athens, Agora, Hephaisteion, west frieze.   123
94. Athens, Agora, Hephaisteion, west frieze reconstruction by
M. Cox.   123
95. Athens, Agora, Hephaisteion, west frieze, Kaineus, and
Centaurs, Theseus.   124
96. Athens, Agora, Hephaisteion, east frieze composed from
casts.   124
97. Athens, Agora, Hephaisteion, east frieze reconstruction by
M. Cox.   125
98. Athens, Agora, Hephaisteion, east frieze, central figure. 126
99. Athena and Hephaistos, fragmentary Attic red-figure cup
attributed to the Foundry Painter, tondo.   127
100. Athens, Agora, Hephaisteion, reconstruction of cult statues
by S. Papaspyridi-Karusu.   128
101. Athens, Agora, view from Hephaisteion to east.   129
102. Athens, Agora, reconstruction of west side by W. Dinsmoor. 129
103. Athens, Agora, Hephaisteion, south metope: Theseus and
Minotaur.   132
104. Map of ancient Athens.   134
105. Athens, Agora, Stoa Basileus, reconstruction
by W. Dinsmoor.   135
106. Athens, Agora, Hephaisteion, east frieze, Hephaistos.   139
107. Delphi, aerial view.   145
108. Delphi, Temple of Apollo from northwest.   146
109. Delphi, Sanctuary of Apollo, plan.   147

110. Delphi, Temple of Apollo, c. 330 B.C., east pediment,
     reconstruction by F. Croissant. 148
111. Delphi, Temple of Apollo, c. 330 B.C., east pediment. 148
112. Delphi, Temple of Apollo, c. 330 B.C., west pediment,
     reconstruction by F. Croissant. 150
113. Delphi, Temple of Apollo, c. 330 B.C., west pediment. 150
114. Epidauros, Temple of Asklepios, west pediment,
     Amazonomachy. 152
115. Epidauros, Temple of Asklepios, east pediment,
     Ilioupersis, Priam. 152
116. Tegea, Temple of Athena Alea, east pediment. 153
117. Tegea, Temple of Athena Alea, west pediment. 153
118. Attic red-figure kalyx krater, Apollo and Dionysos. 154
119. Delphi, Temple of Apollo, c. 330 B.C., west pediment,
     Dionysos. 156
120. Delphi, Temple of Apollo, c. 330 B.C., west pediment,
     Thyiad. 157
121. Delphi, Temple of Apollo, c. 510 B.C., east pediment. 158
122. Delphi, Temple of Apollo, c. 510 B.C., west pediment. 158
123. Delphi, Stoa of the Athenians. 164
124. Delphi, Daochos Monument. 165
125. Delphi, Daochos Monument reconstruction
     by A. F. Stewart. 165
126. Delphi, Model of Apollo sanctuary. 166
127. Delphi, Akanthos Monument. 167
128. Delphi, Akanthos Monument reconstruction by
     Ph. Collet. 167
129. Model of Trysa Heroon. 172
130. Drawing of temenos and frieze themes, Trysa heroon. 173
131. Reconstruction of Trysa ruler's sarcophagus by
     T. Marksteiner. 174
132. Trysa Heroon, exterior south wall, Amazonomachy above
     Centauromachy. 175
133. (a–b) Trysa Heroon, exterior south wall, Seven against
     Thebes, battle. 176
134. (a–c) Trysa Heroon, interior south wall, chariot scene,
     abduction, Bellerophon fighting the Chimaira. 177
135. (a–b) Trysa Heroon, interior south wall, Odysseus
     slaughtering the suitors, Kalydonian boar hunt. 178
136. Trysa Heroon, west wall, southern portion, battle. 179
137. Trysa Heroon, west wall, city siege. 180

138. Trysa Heroon, west wall, northern portion,
     Amazonomachy.   181
139. Trysa Heroon, east wall, deeds of Theseus.   183
140. Trysa Heroon, east wall, banqueting and dancing.   183
141. Trysa Heroon, exterior lintel of the doorway.   184
142. Trysa Heroon, interior doorway.   185
143. Bassai, Temple of Apollo, Centauromachy.   189
144. Xanthos, Nereid Monument.   191
145. Xanthos, Nereid Monument, city-siege and battle friezes. 194
146. Xanthos, Nereid Monument, hunt frieze.   194
147. Xanthos, Nereid Monument, east pediment.   194
148. Xanthos, Nereid Monument, banqueting frieze.   195
149. Xanthos, Nereid Monument, banqueting frieze.   195
150. (a–b) Nereid Monument, sacrifice frieze.   197
151. Figurine of Alexander the Great.   200
152. Statuette of Demetrios Poliorcetes.   201
153. Dying Gaul, Roman copy.   206
154. Pergamon, Altar of Zeus.   208
155. Pergamon, Altar of Zeus, model.   208
156. Pergamon, Altar of Zeus, Telephos frieze.   209
157. Pergamon, Altar of Zeus, east frieze.   209
158. Sperlonga, Polyphemos group reconstruction.   210
159. Rome, Temple of Apollo Sosianus, pediment,
     Amazonomachy.   211

ACKNOWLEDGMENTS

I am indebted to a number of institutions, colleagues, and friends for their support and assistance as this book took shape. A Blegen Research Fellowship from Vassar College enabled me to begin work on this project, and subsequent funding came from the State University of New York at New Paltz and the University of Edinburgh. Without the resources of the Blegen Library at the American School of Classical Studies in Athens, this book would have taken even longer than it did.

Preliminary versions of various portions of this work were presented to numerous audiences in the form of scholarly lectures and conference papers in the United States, Canada, Europe, and Great Britain; comments, criticisms, and suggestions from my listeners were enormously productive in challenging and shaping my thinking, and the remarks of Andrew Stewart and Cambridge University Press's readers also bettered the final product. Bernard Andreae in Rome, Charles Arnold and Ken Evans at the British Museum, Norbert Eschbach in Göttingen, Jean-Robert Gisler in Basel, Mario Iozzo at the Soprintendenza Archeologica per la Toscana in Florence, Michael Krumme at the Deutsches Archäologisches Institut in Athens, Tomas Lochman in Vienna, and Andrew Stewart at the University of California, Berkeley were all helpful in obtaining photographs. The First Ephorate in Athens and the Ephorate at Olympia, together with the staff of the Olympia Museum and Klaus Herrmann, deserve thanks for their kind assistance and cooperation in studying and photographing sculpture on the Hephaisteion and in the Olympia Museum, respectively.

Michael Anderson, Douglas Cairns, Stephen Colvin, Eve D'Ambra, Corinne Pache, Jerry Pollitt, and Alan Shapiro offered support and encouragement along the way. Nancy Bookidis provided inspiration and companionship in the last phases of this book, and Shilpa Raval's enthusiasm and warmth are still with me though she is no longer with us. I offer my heartfelt thanks to all of the above, who bear no responsibility for any errors in the final product.

Greg Barringer never fails me, however far I roam, and for that and so much more, I am profoundly grateful. I commend the forbearance, good humor, and Job-like patience of Beatrice Rehl, who never seemed to give up hope on this project, and special thanks are due to Mary Paden at Aptara Inc., who was enormously patient and conscientious in the final editing stages. Finally, I owe a tremendous debt to Hans Rupprecht Goette, who happily provided most of the photographs for this volume. Our discussions, often on site, about much of the content of this book gave me much to think about, and our differences in interpretation forced me to sharpen my arguments. His encouragement and support are deeply appreciated.

NOTE ON ABBREVIATIONS

Abbreviations of ancient authors and texts are those used by the *Oxford Classical Dictionary*, 3rd ed., edited by Simon Hornblower and Antony Spawforth, Oxford, 1996. Journal and monograph abbreviations follow the guidelines set forth by the *American Journal of Archaeology*, which are available online at http://www.ajaonline.org/index.php?ptype=page&pid=8.

INTRODUCTION

Perhaps the most alluring and delightful characteristic of ancient Greek art is the pervasiveness of myth and mythological narratives as subjects for visual representation. The familiarity yet remoteness of the deities and mythological figures of this past society, combined with skillful narrative depictions, often in aesthetically pleasing form, make Greek art and myth nearly irresistible to layman and specialist alike. But what charms us in Greek art often was regarded with much greater seriousness by ancient Greek viewers, who understood such myths as part of their past history and whose gods, often the subject of myth, had complete control of their daily lives – weather phenomena were manifestations of the god Zeus, for example, and plagues and other illnesses were caused by some slight to a deity and could only be cured by making amends. Agriculture and the productivity of the land fell under the realm of Demeter; if the crops failed, it was clearly due to an offense to the goddess. A successful childbirth could only be accomplished with the help of Artemis, and those about to be married made offerings to Artemis and to Aphrodite to ensure a successful outcome of the transition from their unmarried to married state. Religious practice, for example, sacrificial ritual, and the need to respect and honor the gods were often explained in terms of myth, and narratives about deities are usually placed in the category of "myth." Yet not all myths concerned religion, and not all religious practices had mythological narratives attached to them.

Until the Hellenistic period (c. 323–31 B.C.), Greek sculpture is almost entirely religious in nature and, in the case of architectural sculpture and

large-scale free-standing sculpture, primarily composed of mythological figures (including Greek divinities) and/or mythological narratives.
Indeed, myth and religion were the raisons d'être for much of Greek art
throughout its history, although politics certainly played a critical role
in most public projects. Standing at a distance of nearly two and a half
millennia and situated in another, very different culture, how can we
understand what myth meant for the ancient Greeks?

Myths express and reveal cultural values; they offer messages, but the
modern viewer can only decipher or decode the "language" of the myth
and the monument if the myth and art are considered in their original
cultural context. In the case of ancient Greece, we are fortunate to have
written accounts by viewers of Greek art, such as Pausanias (fl. c. 150
A.D.) and Pliny (c. 23/24–79 A.D.), but we do not possess contemporary
interpretations of Greek art and myth. What do Greek myths mean, and
how was meaning created for the ancient viewer? This book considers
the use of myth as architectural sculpture in Classical Greece (c. 480–
323 B.C.) and argues that myth is not randomly selected and does not
serve a purely decorative function but has meaning (the same is true
for small-scale works, such as vase painting), and the interpretation of a
given myth depends on context. The same myth, such as the ubiquitous
Centauromachy, can mean different things in different contexts, and in
a monumental context, the mythological image relates to the site and
often to other monuments surrounding it, which redouble, resonate, or
create variations on a theme. Different facets or variants of a given myth
can be emphasized depending on context. Although the concentration
here is on architectural sculpture, that is, major monuments, the text
also, by necessity, examines if and how the meaning of a given myth
differs when an object, such as a funerary monument, is invested with
personal, not public, importance.

The architectural sculpture examined here is discussed in a series of
five case studies, chronologically arranged, which offer a range of physical
settings, historical and social circumstances, and interpretive problems.
While western Greece and many islands had a rich tradition of architectural sculpture in the Archaic (c. 600–480 B.C.) and Classical periods, this
book is confined to four mainland Greek sites and a fifth in Asia Minor.
Comparanda from elsewhere are adduced when useful. Throughout this
study, the methodology depends on visual semiotics – context determines

the meaning of images (in this case, mythological images), and meaning is malleable – and viewer response, that is, how an ancient viewer (who requires definition) might have interpreted these images. Reconstructing that context relies on using all available evidence – visual and written – to establish how a site appeared at any given moment, what occurred at the site (which determines who the intended viewers were likely to be), and the current political, religious, and historical situation.

The Temple of Zeus at Olympia (Chapter 1), a Panhellenic sanctuary and site of the ancient Olympic games, presents a rich array of architectural sculpture that addressed the athletes and visitors to Olympia. The myths used on the temple are clearly specific to the site, but also exhibit dramatic innovations, as well as variations on a theme, the labors of Herakles, already familiar from architectural sculpture at other sites. The sculptures of the Parthenon on the Athenian Akropolis (Chapter 2) are well known to modern viewers and have been studied extensively by scholars. However, a consideration of one aspect of the myths depicted, the role of women, together with religious rituals that occurred at the site facilitates a different interpretation of the sculptures available to one set of viewers, the girls and women who were so critical to the city's continuity and to the populace at large. Moreover, the Centauromachy that appears on the Parthenon offers an opportunity to compare this rendition to that at Olympia. In the Athenian Agora below the Akropolis, the Hephaisteion (Chapter 3) sits above the buildings central to the workings of the Athenian democracy, yet is carefully integrated into this larger political landscape. Its sculptures are spatially apportioned to emphasize their relationship to the surrounding structures, to which they have a thematic relationship, and were clearly addressed to Athenian citizens moving through the Agora. Both the labors of Herakles and the Centauromachy recur here, where they take on different significance as a result of their setting. Like the Temple of Zeus at Olympia, the Temple of Apollo at Delphi (Chapter 4) is set in a Panhellenic sanctuary but one with a different orientation; while Olympia was renowned first and foremost for its athletic games, it was Apollo's oracle that dominated at Delphi (although it is important to note that Olympia *also* had an oracle, and Delphi *also* had Panhellenic athletic games). Our study focuses on the temple's fourth-century B.C. incarnation, when the political situation in Greece was undergoing a critical upheaval as a result of encounters with the Macedonians. Unlike the architectural sculpture discussed in preceding chapters, that on the Temple of Apollo does not present mythological narratives but emblematic mythological figures, which were meant to recall past images on the same site in an effort to trumpet current political affiliations. The final case study takes us to Lycia in Asia Minor, where Greek myths appear on the Heroon at Trysa, a tomb and hero shrine for the local dynast, who served as a satrap for the Persian king. The dynast's tomb enclosure was extensively decorated with sculptured reliefs depicting Greek mythological themes, as well as narrative images apparently drawn from the life of the ruler. The reuse of familiar mythological themes from mainland architectural sculpture and monumental painting, together with the use of myths not commonly found in such monumental contexts, reveals differing aims: to reach a non-Greek audience and to exalt a mere mortal to the status of hero, a practice that persists and develops in the subsequent Hellenistic period. Finally, as an epilogue, the text briefly looks at the Altar of Zeus from Pergamon, which revives the use of the Gigantomachy in monumental form and combines it with a local myth to address the concerns of a monarch eager to promote the idea of Pergamon as a new Athens. In sum, specific and varied contexts – Panhellenic sanctuary, tomb, mainland, Asia Minor, private, public, time period – shape the patron's choice of myth, available meanings, and targeted audiences.

Although the myths examined in this book decorate temples and tombs among other structures, their meaning or deployment is not always religious, and this book will explore (though not exhaust) the complicated relationship and interaction among myth, religion, ritual, and art. Some myths clearly have nothing to do with religion, such as the Centauromachy and Amazonomachy, yet they decorate religious buildings and are demonstrably linked to their sites and monuments, most often because of historical, social, or topographical concerns. Other myths clearly have connections with religion and ritual, such as myths concerning Dionysos and his followers and resistors, which appear very rarely in monumental contexts, or those about Athena or Apollo, which frequently are used as architectural decoration. In many cases, however, the connection or disjunction between myth and religion is not so distinct. The relationship of the mythical followers of Dionysos to the real-life worshippers of the god and what practices each engages in are difficult to discern. If there are real-life counterparts to Bacchae, what about Satyrs? The problems multiply when we consider visual representations of myth and religion. To take only one example: at the Heroon of Gjölbaschi-Trysa, mythological images suggest the heroization of the deceased ruler, who was worshipped at the site. Why are particular myths chosen for this purpose, and how do they make the analogy between historical ruler and hero? Do the myths in some way justify the worship of the ruler as a hero, and if so, which myths do so? Is a heroic pedigree necessary for worship, or would the ruler have been worshipped if there were no visual images decorating the structure? Many questions cannot be answered with the present state of our evidence (the Trysa heroon is especially tricky because we have no ancient written evidence concerning it), but they should be borne in mind.

Even before one tackles these complex issues, other, more basic problems arise: how do we recognize Greek myth when it appears, and how is it distinguished from nonmythological depictions? For example, armed combat is a subject that frequently occurs in sixth-century vase painting and sculpture, yet some of these scenes represent a specific mythological battle (although the figures wear contemporary armor) as indicated by inscribed names, attributes, or accompanying figures, while others bear no inscriptions, no apparent indicators of myth. Are the latter also mythological, and if there is ambiguity, is it intentional, designed to blur the boundary between myth and actuality, or simply the modern viewer's failure to comprehend what s/he sees? Also important to consider is the intended viewers of architectural depictions of myth; differences in gender, social status (e.g., citizen, metic, slave), age, and social or civic circumstance (e.g., athlete competitor at Olympia v. female participant in the Panathenaia) affect perception of the myths depicted. In some instances, the targeted audience can be defined with some specificity, such as at Olympia, where the temple's sculptures seem to specifically address athletes, but in other instances, at the Parthenon in Athens, for example, varying messages seem to address a plurality of viewers, male and female, citizen and foreigner. Although public monuments and their myths are usually geared to aristocratic, even monarchical ideas, they also reflect popular beliefs and ideology and often incorporate elements of "real life" so that one can categorize them as monuments of popular culture, as well.

Ancient written accounts, however short on actual interpretations, are invaluable in deciphering visual material and provide vast amounts of information about religious, social, political, topographical, and historical matters that enable us to build a framework in which to contextualize monuments and to formulate interpretations. One of the most indispensable ancient authors for any Greek archaeologist is the travel writer Pausanias, though it must be borne in mind that he, and others such as Pliny or Strabo (born c. 64 B.C.), were writing centuries after the works they describe were created, so their accuracy is sometimes worth questioning (though I would not go so far as some scholars and largely or wholly discount their texts). In their favor, however, is the fact that they actually *saw* much of what they describe; they are first-hand witnesses to monuments, rituals, and events that, in some cases, would be entirely unknown to us were it not for their attestation. One frustration experienced by modern readers is that these writers were not always recording what we want to know or what we find most compelling, but what struck *them* as significant or what their guides prized. To give one notable example: although Pausanias mentions the Parthenon and describes the subjects of its pediments, he makes no mention of the frieze, which is an obsession of modern archaeologists! In the case of travel writers, such as Pausanias, or encyclopedists, such as Pliny, it is likely that they were not composing their texts on the spot as they walked through a particular site, but assembled texts some time, perhaps months, later from notes and memory. That details are omitted or sometimes in error should not vitiate the value of the entire text; it is sometimes the case that these texts, as flawed as they may be, provide the only means of identifying a myth portrayed on a building, or are the most complete source for a religious ritual known otherwise only from a brief tantalizing mention in other, sometimes fragmentary, texts.

In addition to these writers, who aimed to record the world around them, much can be derived from a sensitive interpretation of other literary genres – drama, lyric poetry, epinician, comedy, and the like. This can be tricky because writers such as Pindar, Euripides, and Aristophanes are not writing to transmit data, as Pausanias does (though this does not mean that his material is not artfully arranged or designed to elicit certain responses), but for different, often more dramatically motivated ends, such as theatrical productions. Their texts can be mined for cultural information about a number of topics – social relations, religious belief and practice, gender relations, and daily life matters, to name just a few. Again, care must be taken with writers of later date and also to separate out what can be designated as "information" from "literary device" or "artistic freedom." Some of the same precautions apply for writers of legal speeches and rhetoric, whose motivations or political agendas shape their prose.

A third category of written material is inscriptions – on stone, on metal, on terracotta, on precious stones, votive inscriptions, epitaphs, public decrees, inventory lists, and so on. This nonliterary information is immensely valuable, often a direct line to the ancient world and its thinking (as opposed to literature, which has different motivations), and for this study, it is especially useful for learning about which deities or mythological figures receive what kinds of dedications, about what mythological motives might be appropriate for a given situation, about how the ancient Greeks conceived of various mythological figures or sites or actions, and so on.

Finally, aside from the pure pleasure of looking at Greek architectural sculpture and myth, such a study is instructive in illuminating the complicated relationship of myth to reality and yields valuable information about ancient Greek culture, specifically ideas about some of man's most vexing questions: the nature of what it is to be human, the relationship of men and gods, gender and sexuality, man's relationship to the natural world, the role of the individual in his community, death, and human relationships. What we learn is that the Greeks were as troubled and perplexed about such matters as we are and that their means of addressing, explaining, and coping with them was sometimes similar but more often quite different from ours.

CHAPTER ONE

THE TEMPLE OF ZEUS AT OLYMPIA, HEROIC MODELS, AND THE PANHELLENIC SANCTUARY

These case studies begin with the Temple of Zeus at Olympia, which allows us to examine a Panhellenic sanctuary, a place of enormous renown, at an early point in the Classical period, shortly after the Battle of Plataia in 479, which we now categorize as the conclusion of the Persian Wars (Figs. 1-4).[*] The Greeks, however, did not know that and consequently were vigilant in their preparations for further conflicts on their own soil and beyond. The sculptures of the Temple of Zeus clearly were designed to be seen and understood in *this* location, in this context, which makes this site an especially good place to begin this study. They offer the first examples of several myths in monumental form - in some instances, the first depictions of a myth altogether - and offer innovations in conceptions of myth and architectural sculpture that signal the sculptures' close connections to the site. As is evident from the following chapters, the sculptures on the Temple of Zeus had a lasting impact not only at Olympia but also in Athens and elsewhere.

Legend held that the Olympic games, celebrated every four years at Olympia in the Peloponnese, were founded in c. 776 B.C. These Panhellenic athletic competitions were one of a series of four "crown" games, athletic contests open to all Greeks for which the victory prizes were vegetal crowns - olive in the case of Olympia. The Olympic games were unquestionably the most prestigious of this series, which also included games

---

[*] Part of the material in this chapter was published in *Hesperia* 74 (2005) 211-241 and is reproduced here by permission.

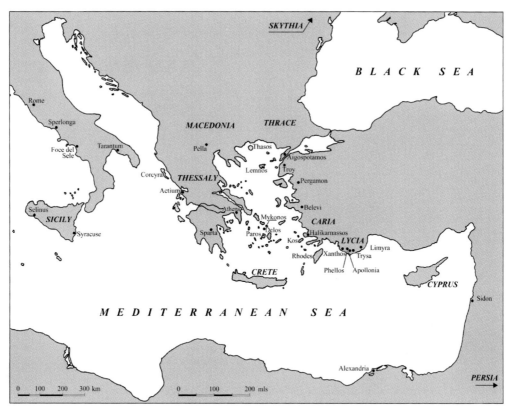

1. Map of the Mediterranean region. Drawing: H. R. Goette.

at Isthmia, Nemea, and Delphi (the Pythian Games). While the Olympic games were the earliest, the other three were founded in the sixth century B.C., perhaps as a result of the development of hoplite warfare and the consequent necessity for trained bodies. Athletic games had long been part of Greek culture (recall Homer's description of the funeral games in honor of Patroklos, organized by his bereaved companion Achilles, described in *Iliad* 23) and were consonant with the highly agonistic nature of Greek society.

The foundation of the Olympic games was variously attributed to Herakles (Pind. *Ol.* 6.67–69, 10.24–25, 57–59; Paus. 5.7.6–10), Zeus in honor of his victory over his father Kronos (Paus. 5.7.10), and most commonly, Pelops, the hero who gave his name to the Peloponnese (Pind. *Ol.* 1.67–88; Paus. 5.8.2).[1] Pelops accepted the challenge of Oinomaos, the king of nearby Pisa, to compete in a chariot race against him to win the hand of Oinomaos' daughter Hippodameia, thus becoming the heir to

2. Map of the Greek mainland. Drawing: H. R. Goette.

the throne. Equipped with special horses, Oinomaos had already defeated thirteen suitors, who paid with their lives: after giving the suitor a head start, Oinomaos overtook his opponent and as he did so, he planted a spear, a gift from his father Ares, in the suitor's back.[2] Aided by winged horses given to him by his erstwhile lover Poseidon, Pelops was able to defeat Oinomaos, thus winning the daughter and the kingdom. This race was regarded as the founding event of the Olympic games, according to Pindar, who composed his first *Olympian* ode in 476 B.C. (1.67–88).[3] An alternate tradition, not attested until c. 440 B.C. (Pherekyd. *FGrH* 3 F 37),

3. Aerial view of Olympia. Photo: A. Loxias, Athens.

4. Olympia, east side of Temple of Zeus, c. 470–456 B.C. Photo: H. R. Goette.

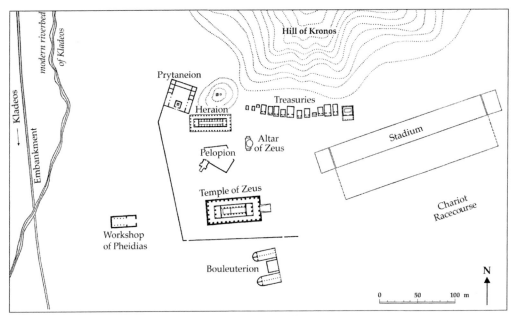

5. Olympia, plan, fifth century B.C. Reproduced and adapted with permission from H-V. Herrmann, *Olympia: Heiligtum und Wettkampfstätte* (Munich 1972) 158.

claims that Pelops won by bribing Oinomaos' charioteer to replace the metal linchpins in the king's chariot with pins made of wax; when the race began, the friction and heat created by the moving chariot melted the linchpins, causing the chariot to fall apart, and the king to fall to

6. Olympia, model of Altis. Photo: H. R. Goette.

7. Olympia, Temple of Zeus, c. 470–456 B.C., east pediment sculptures. Photo: H. R. Goette.

his death.[4] In this account, Pelops wins the race by cheating, hardly an auspicious beginning of the famed games.[5]

This myth, so central to Olympia, was depicted on the east pediment of the sanctuary's Temple to Zeus, as we learn from the second-century A.D. travel writer Pausanias (5.10.6–8; Figs. 5–8), who identifies the subjects of the temple's sculptures.[6] The Doric temple is firmly dated to 470–c. 456 B.C. on the basis of historical events. Pausanias 5.10.2 relates that the temple was erected by the city of Elis from the spoils of its conquest of neighboring Pisa (Oinomaos' city), which was captured by Elis c. 470,[7] thus yielding a *terminus post quem*. The Spartans dedicated a gold shield decorated with an image of Medusa at the temple of Zeus as a victory dedication for their defeat of the Athenians and others at the battle of Tanagra (Paus. 5.10.4), an event that took place in 457. Because the Spartans placed their shield at the center of the temple's apex, the temple had to have been finished by this time. Although scholars cannot pinpoint the exact date of inception of the construction, the temple's creation followed general improvements to the site, including a renovation and enlargement of the *stadion* in the 470s, and the introduction of a new roster of events and expansion of the athletic

A   B   C   D   B   K   G   H   I   F O M   N   E   P

8. Olympia, Temple of Zeus, east pediment reconstruction by A. F. Stewart, drawing by C. Smith.

9. Olympia, ash altar reconstruction by F. Adler reproduced from *Olympia* 2, Taf. 132.

games from three to five days, innovations that seem to have taken place c. 472.[8]

The temple was by no means the first monumental structure at Olympia. Significant to this discussion are the nearby Temple of Hera (perhaps originally dedicated only to Zeus then later to Hera) of c. 600 B.C., the ancient ash altar of Zeus at which sacrifices and offerings already had been made to the god for several centuries at the time that the temple to Zeus was constructed, and the Pelopion or hero shrine to Pelops, which also precedes the temple of Zeus by centuries (Figs. 5, 6, 9).[9] An earlier temple to Zeus may have occupied the site of its fifth-century successor, and of course, the racetrack or stadion existed prior to the temple's construction; its first incarnation, in fact, terminated close to the Pelopion. A row of treasuries also lined the northern boundary of the Altis, the sacred area at Olympia; most were constructed in the sixth century B.C. by cities in Magna Graecia, the Greek mainland, and elsewhere, which were eager to thank the god for various favors and to demonstrate a polis' wealth and power.

It was the temple of Zeus, however, that would have excited the greatest attention of athletes as they arrived at the Altis in the second half of the fifth century since it was the most prominent structure and was decorated

10. Olympia, Temple of Zeus, c. 470–456 B.C., west pediment sculptures. Photo: H. R. Goette.

with remarkably large, dynamic, and innovative marble sculptures (Figs. 7, 8, 10, 11). Athletes and other visitors to Olympia first would have encountered the west pediment of the temple of Zeus, which was ornamented with the story of the fight between the Lapith Greek men and the Centaurs, the Centauromachy,[10] overseen by the central figure of Apollo (Figs. 10, 11).[11] The fight took place in Thessaly, during the wedding of the Lapith Perithoos to his bride Hippodameia. The Centaurs were invited guests but they became drunk and began to attack the Lapith women. The Lapith men, led by Perithoos and his friend Theseus, rushed to the defense of the women and fought off the Centaurs, who were routed. Unlike the myth of Pelops' race against Oinomaos, which, purportedly the founding event of the games, is specifically suited to Olympia, the myth of the Centauromachy has no immediate or apparent associations with Olympia; we will return to the choice of myths for the temple later in this chapter.

Entering the Altis, the sacred area of Olympia, athletes and visitors would have proceeded to the east façade of the temple, whose pediment, as noted above, was filled with figures depicting the moment before the

11. Olympia, Temple of Zeus, west pediment reconstruction by A. F. Stewart, drawing by C. Smith.

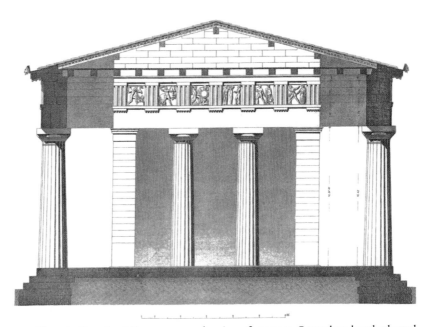

12. Olympia, Temple of Zeus, cutaway drawing of pronaos. Reproduced and adapted from *Olympia* 2, Taf. 10.

chariot race between Pelops and Oinomaos (Figs. 7, 8). All around the competitors were votive dedications in the form of bronze and marble monuments and objects from successful athletes and cities grateful for divine favor in athletics or battle, respectively. Passing beyond the outer colonnade at the short ends of the building, visitors encountered sculptured metopes, 1.6 m square, adorning the Doric frieze above the pronaos and opisthodomos of the temple, six per side (Figs. 12, 13, 14).[12] The metopes were devoted to the twelve labors of Herakles, a hero with numerous connections to Olympia. Within the cella was a 12.2-m-high chryselephantine cult statue of Zeus created by Pheidias and dedicated after c. 430 B.C. (Fig. 15). Described by ancient writers as one of the seven wonders of the ancient world, the god sat upon an enormous throne, elaborately decorated with numerous mythical themes. Crowning the temple as akroteria were bronze cauldrons and gilt Nikai (Paus. 5.10.4), but these are thought to have been later additions and are known only from their mention in written texts (Figs. 8, 11).

Why does this particular group of sculptures appear on the temple of Zeus, which was constructed by the city of Elis from war spoils in the years 470–456, at Olympia, a Panhellenic sanctuary and site of the

13. Olympia, Temple of Zeus, metopes, reconstruction. Reproduced from *Olympia* 3, Taf. 45.

famous Olympic games? How should we understand the sculptures in this agonistic context? The connection between Pelops, founder of the games and hero of Elis, portrayed in the east pediment, and Olympia is clear, but how were ancient viewers, particularly the athletes who came to compete at the games, meant to understand the sculptures? Although some of the earliest scholars to work on this material viewed Pelops' representation in the east pediment as a positive one, such an interpretation was largely discarded by later scholars, who propose that the east pediment refers to the cheating version of the myth and often point to parallels in Attic tragedy to support this reading. Accordingly, the two pediments together – and sometimes the metopes – are admonitory statements about hubris or justice evidenced in the recent Persian Wars, or declarations about various types of *dike*, *ethos*, and *arête* represented by all categories of beings in the temple's sculptures.[13] The east pediment is commonly read as a warning to the athletes of Olympia not to cheat as Pelops did and bring disaster on one's family and city as a result of hubris. Such an interpretation clearly assumes that the "cheating" version of the myth is operative. Alternately, Oinomaos is seen as a source of hubris because he did not wish his daughter to marry and/or tried to keep his daughter for himself (and we might add that Oinomaos' fatal attacks on the suitors from the rear could be regarded as cheating or at least as bad sportsmanship). Zeus distributes dike on the east pediment while a centrally placed Apollo restores order and defends marriage on the west pediment,[14] which has also been interpreted as an illustration of hubris, of civilized forces – the Greek Lapiths – fighting barbaric, uncontrolled creatures. Again, this would be a negative paradigm to instruct athletes against hubristic behavior. Such an interpretation is joined to the metopes and east pediment, which are all seen in terms of hubris and justice and sometimes given a historical slant: the Lapiths, symbolizing Greeks, punish the barbarian Persians, represented by the Centaurs, for their efforts to conquer Hellas.[15] The pediments also have been read in other political ways, including the west as a warning against internal strife in Greece[16] and the east as an Olympian claim to control all of the Peloponnese.[17]

However, a thorough examination of the sculptures themselves and a consideration of their larger physical and social context lead to different conclusions. Rather than serving as a warning or negative paradigm to the athletic competitors, and others for that matter, about hubristic behavior and the dike administered by the gods, when read in their original context, the myths depicted by the sculptures originally offered positive

14. Olympia, Temple of Zeus, c. 470–456 B.C., Herakles v. Cretan bull metope. Photo: H. R. Goette.

15. Olympia, Temple of Zeus, cutaway drawing of cella. Reproduced with permission from H-V. Herrmann, *Olympia: Heiligtum und Wettkampfstätte* (Munich 1972) 131, Fig. 92.

models of heroism, arete, and glory expressly aimed at the Olympic competitors, who were urged to emulate these examples in various areas of their lives.[18] The chapter also will treat the larger social and physical context of Olympia because, as we will see, the ancient viewer's perception of the temple's images was largely shaped by the activities and other monuments at Olympia. These included its games for both males and females, its military dedications, and its use as a display place for deeds of glory that can exalt a man beyond his mortality to everlasting *kleos* (glory, fame).

Today's meager architectural remains of the temple of Zeus, constructed by Libon of Elis, according to Pausanias 5.10.3, are somewhat discouraging to the modern visitor, but the sculptures survive in very good condition and have received the intense scrutiny of dozens of scholars since their discovery in 1831 and 1875 (Figs. 4, 7, 10, 14, 16).[19] The sculptures are some of the best-known monuments of antiquity and are often discussed as exemplars of the Early Classical or Severe Style of sculpture, but stylistic issues will not be the focus here. Although the temple was of stuccoed limestone, its architectural sculptures were of Parian marble and were originally painted; traces of paint still can be seen clearly. Restorations of Pentelic marble were made to the corner figures of the west pediment sometime after the fifth century. The use of Parian marble is noteworthy; imported from the island of Paros in the middle of the Aegean Sea, the marble would have been enormously heavy and expensive to transport not only across the sea, but also across the Peloponnese to Olympia, an indication of just how important the sculptures and this project were.[20] Recent studies have demonstrated that the peculiar smoothness of many areas of the sculptures, particularly the hair of a number of pediment figures, is not a stylistic choice but is the result of erecting and leaving the sculptures in an unfinished state, perhaps because of a lack of funds concurrent with the need to finish the job, maybe for the Olympiad of 456.[21]

Let us consider the sculptures and their mythological themes more carefully, beginning with the labors of Herakles on the metopes (Figs. 13, 14, 16). Herakles' labors were performed either because of Hera's enmity or at the order of King Eurystheus of Argos. Homer, Hesiod, and other early authors mention various of these labors, as well as other adventures,

16. Olympia, Temple of Zeus, c. 470–456 B.C., Augean stables metope. Photo: H. R. Goette.

but they are not treated as a set in literature until the fifth century B.C. [22] From left to right on the west side, the hero sits, exhausted by his efforts after his struggle with the Nemean lion, tangles with the Hydra, presents the Stymphalian birds to Athena (Fig. 13), subdues the Cretan bull (Fig. 14), captures the Keryneian hind, and conquers an Amazon. On the east, left to right, we have the labor of the Erymanthian boar, the horses of Diomedes, Herakles fighting Geryon, Herakles holding up the world while Atlas retrieves the apples of the Hesperides, the hero fetching Kerberos from Hades, and Herakles cleaning the Augean stables under the direction of Athena (Fig. 16). Herakles begins as an unbearded youth and ages over the course of the twelve metopes, as indicated by the growth of his beard and the maturing of his physique and demeanor. Athena serves as Herakles' helpmate or companion in four of these compositions. The completion of these labors guaranteed

Herakles' immortality (though he did not die immediately afterward); he was apotheosized at the time of his death, and Herakles was the only mortal to be honored in this fashion. Herakles' adventures and labors had repeatedly appeared on earlier Greek vases and in Greek sculpture, such as the sixth-century B.C. Chest of Kypselos. The Chest is no longer extant but is known from the elaborate description of Pausanias 5.17–19 and from Dio Chrysostomus 11.45, who makes only a brief mention of this object as a wooden chest dedicated by Kypselos himself and visible in the opisthodomos of the Heraion, which, by this time, seems to have served as a storage place for earlier dedications.[23] Pausanias describes the chest as created of cedar, ivory, and gold, and as possessing five superimposed rows of mythological decoration, whose individual figures often are named by inscriptions. Scholars have reconstructed the Chest in a number of ways, primarily as rectangular or cylindrical in shape,[24] though the most recent reconstruction favors the latter.[25] According to Pausanias, the decoration included images of Herakles' combat with the Hydra, his retrieval of the apples from Atlas, the struggle with Geryon, and his fight against the Centaurs led by Pholos.

The metopes at Olympia, however, mark a watershed in the history of Greek art and myth: they present the first crystallization of the concept of twelve labors. Thereafter, most of these particular twelve adventures become canonical in cyclical visual representations of the labors, a change from earlier practice when any selection of the many adventures and labors of Herakles might be used as temple decoration (though we will see in Chapters 2 and 3 that variations and substitutions could be made to suit an individual site or monument). Herakles is an apt subject for the temple at Olympia: as noted above, he is sometimes credited with founding the Olympic Games as a thanks offering to Zeus for his help in Herakles' defeat of Augeus (Pind. *Ol.* 10.24). We are told that Herakles founded the games at the site of the Pelopion, which Herakles also founded (Paus. 5.13.2). As if this were not enough, Pausanias reports that Herakles established the central ash altar to Zeus at Olympia (Paus. 5.13.8) and also introduced the wild olive into Greece from the land of the Hyperboreans; these olive trees provide the victory crowns for the Olympic victors (Pind. *Ol.* 3.16ff.; Paus. 5.7.7). And, of course, Herakles is the son of Zeus, the god honored by the temple.

17. Olympia, Temple of Zeus, c. 470–456 B.C., west pediment, central figures. Photo: H. R. Goette.

The pediments, 26 m wide and 3.3 m high at center, also are innovative in several ways. The myth of the Centauromachy in the west pediment was easily recognizable to any Greek because of the Centaurs' distinctive half-human/half-equine bodies (Figs. 10, 11). Although the myth has a few variants, two major conflicts occur between human and Centaur opponents: the struggle at the Thessalian wedding of Perithoos, and Herakles' fight with Pholos and the Centaurs, who use stones and firebrands as weapons. Here, the presence of women under attack and Herakles' absence clearly indicates the wedding. A solitary stationary figure, now generally believed to be Apollo, the god of moderation and order, stands in the center of the pediment, his right arm outstretched, as if presiding over the fray (Fig. 17). Flanking him on each side is a youthful (beardless) Lapith fighter: Perithoos on one side, Theseus, an Athenian hero, on the other, arm poised overhead, lunging toward his Centaur opponent. Radiating out from this central group of three males are intertwined groups of energetic, struggling figures (Fig. 18): Centaurs attacking Lapith women, who resist their advances; Lapith men using daggers, perhaps an ax and sword, counterattacking Centaurs, who carry no weapons; and reclining figures in the corners. The identities of the corner figures are unknown, although they are sometimes labeled as nurses; because they are later replacements, we are unable to say anything about their original appearance. Theseus' and Perithoos' poses – lunging

18. Olympia, Temple of Zeus, c. 470–456 B.C., west pediment, struggling figures. Photo: H. R. Goette.

with arms poised overhead to strike – are noteworthy; they are borrowed from one of the figures belonging to the Athenian statue group of the Tyrannicides (Fig. 19), who were falsely credited with having overthrown Athens' tyranny in 510 (although they did contribute to its downfall), but the association stuck, and the poses of the commemorative statues of 477 were quickly borrowed by other artists, in the fifth century and later, to signify "heroism" when applied to any figure (see Chapter 3).[26]

19. Naples, Museo Nazionale G103–104, Roman copy of Tyrannicides group. c. 477 B.C.
Photo: Bartl, Deutsches Archäologisches Institut, Rom, Neg. D-DAI-Rom 1958.1789.

The Centauromachy on the temple at Olympia marks another
innovation: the first instance of the use of this myth in architectural
sculpture. Although the myth is already mentioned in the Homeric
poems and known from earlier vase paintings and armor, the earlier
objects do not make clear reference to the combat at the wedding; for
example, women are omitted from their depictions, the Centaurs fight
with branches or stones, and the objects often include the episode of
the invulnerable Lapith Kaineus, who is pounded into the earth by a
boulder wielded by two Centaurs (Fig. 20).[27] First-time viewers of the
Olympia pediment must have been stunned to have seen over-life-size

20. Florence, Museo Archeologico 4209 (François Vase), Attic black-figure volute krater, detail: Theseus on Delos, Centauromachy, c. 570 B.C. Photo: Soprintendenza Archeologica per la Toscana-Firenze.

equine figures struggling with humans, male and female, in twisted, tortured poses.[28] Sixth-century pedimental sculptures on temples or treasuries usually consisted of much smaller, often stiffly-posed figures: they tended to be hieratic figures shown frontally, such as the east pediment composition on the Temple of Apollo at Delphi of c. 510 (Fig. 22), or moving somewhat awkwardly in limited positions, such as the pediment depicting Herakles struggling with Apollo over the Delphic tripod, which appears on the Siphnian Treasury at Delphi of c. 530. Closer in date to the temple at Olympia are the marble pediments from the Temple of Aphaia on Aigina of c. 490–480 B.C., which portray battles in which the central figure of Athena participates (Fig. 21). The fighting figures move more freely than those on the temple at Delphi though there is

21. Aigina, Temple of Aphaia, c. 490–480 B.C., east pediment. Photo: H. R. Goette.

22. Delphi, Temple of Apollo, c. 510 B.C., east pediment reconstruction by A. F. Stewart, drawing by C. Smith.

still a static quality to their action, as if the figures were posing. What is more, the Aigina figures are about one-third life-size and therefore, would not have the same effect as the over-life-size figures at Olympia. Olympia itself had earlier pedimental sculpture on the Megarian Treasury of c. 510 B.C., which portrays the Gigantomachy, an energetic battle between gods and giants who try to overthrow them, a myth that will be discussed more fully in Chapter 2 and elsewhere in this text (Figs. 23, 24). The Megarian Treasury thus offers a compositional precedent for the active composition on the nearby temple of Zeus, but the latter's use of the Centauromachy is an important first in the history of Greek art, since this theme is taken up and recurs repeatedly in architectural sculpture, sometimes as variations of its first manifestation at Olympia (see Chapter 2).

At first glance, the Centauromachy on the west pediment appears to be a peculiar choice for this building since it is a Thessalian myth, seemingly disconnected from an Olympian context. Yet both heroes featured on the pediment have a pedigree that makes them suitable for this temple: Perithoos was the son of Zeus, according to *Iliad* 2.741, 14.317–318, and

21 (*continued*)

23. Olympia, Megarian Treasury, c. 510 B.C., pediment sculptures. Photo: H. R. Goette.

king of the Lapiths, while Theseus was great-grandson of Pelops and an Athenian hero (Paus. 5.10.9). The Centauromachy was also the subject of a monumental wall painting in the Theseion, a hero shrine for Theseus, in Athens, whose date is posited in the 470s B.C. (see Chapter 5). The painting no longer survives and is known only from a written description; scholars have sought to find a relationship between the wall painting and the Olympia west pediment, usually arguing that the former influenced the latter,[29] for example, in the use of the Tyrannicides as a model. This is possible but may be based, erroneously, on the notion that all artistic currents flow outward from Athens. In addition to the two heroes'

24. Olympia, Megarian Treasury, c. 510 B.C., pediment reconstruction by G. Treu. Reproduced with permission from H-V. Herrmann, *Olympia: Heiligtum und Wettkampfstätte* (Munich 1972) 102, Fig. 70.

25. Olympia, Temple of Zeus, c. 470–456 B.C., west pediment, Lapith Q. Photo: H. R. Goette.

ancestry, a genealogical link between the Thessalian Lapiths and Eleans makes this myth particularly apt for the temple.[30]

The sculptors at Olympia took pains to tailor their composition to local needs and concerns. One scholar has pointed out that the tangled poses of Centaurs wrestling with Lapith men echo actual wrestling holds that would have been familiar to the Olympian athletes who filed past the west façade of the temple of Zeus as they entered the Altis at the start of the games, and, as one scholar has noted, one Lapith has a distinctive cauliflower ear, a common injury in boxing and wrestling, which differs from the normal ears of the Lapith youths on the pediment (Fig. 25).[31] Such references invited the athletes to see themselves in the victorious Lapiths,[32] whose heroism is underscored by the Tyrannicide poses of Theseus and Perithoos as the Lapiths wrestle the Centaurs and successfully defend the Lapith women and their own honor from disgrace. Although Apollo appears elsewhere at Olympia, as attested by statues and altars (Paus. 5.15.4, 5.15.7), and Pausanias (5.7.10) credits Apollo with Olympian victories, Apollo is absent from all other written and visual accounts of the Centauromachy, so his commanding presence on the west pediment is all the more striking. His presence may well be a reference to the oracle he established at Olympia (Pind. *Ol.* 6.64–67).[33] Here, he exhorts the Lapiths to behave heroically by behaving athletically, emphasized by recognizable wrestling holds.

Furthermore, the Lapith women are unusually prominent here unlike many other, later depictions of the Centauromachy that show the Lapith males fighting the Centaurs but few, if any, women (the Parthenon south metopes discussed in Chapter 2 are exceptions). The presence of these women would have had special meaning to the ancient viewer because women played an important role at Olympia, both as spectators and as athletes. Pausanias (5.6.7, 6.20.9) relates that the Olympic athletic games were viewed not only by men but also by virgin women; the only married woman permitted was the priestess of Demeter Chamyne.[34] Ancient literary sources, such as Pindar, *Pythian* 9.97–100, suggest, and modern scholars speculate, that virgin women viewed the athletes as potential husbands and evaluated them accordingly.[35] This is not to say that such women were able to make their own selection of a spouse, a task that normally would be done by a woman's father; rather, I wish to suggest that women had the opportunity to look, appraise, and consider this issue.

What is more, girls also participated in athletic games at Olympia in the Heraia, which occurred every four years in connection with the male events. This footrace for adolescent girls was probably instituted by the early sixth century B.C. at the latest[36] and is described only by Pausanias (5.16.2–4). He relates that this footrace was founded by Hippodameia, that it took place every four years (a parallel to the male games founded by Pelops), and that the girls ran with one breast bare.[37] The race was followed by a cow sacrifice in honor of Hera, whose temple, as we have noted, was in the Altis. Sixteen married women supervised the competition and also wove a peplos in honor of Hera. Scholars interpret

26. Olympia, Temple of Zeus, c. 470–456 B.C., west pediment, female Lapith R. Photo: H. R. Goette.

the Heraia as a prenuptial rite of passage, designed to advance girls to marriageable status,[38] which was governed by Hera, and believe that Sparta, where females exercised and danced naked in initiation rites, may have been the inspiration for the partial female nudity in the Heraia, as also may have been the case for the male Olympic events.[39] Pausanias does not report who the spectators of this race were, but considering that unmarried females were among the spectators of the male events, we may posit a parallel event where men were among the crowd watching the female participants in the Heraia and that they, too, may have been shopping for a suitable mate.[40] The girls' partial nudity (Fig. 26) suggests not merely the athletically gifted Amazons, who were often portrayed in art with one breast bared,[41] but also the male Olympic athletes, who were fully nude when they competed. In other words, the Heraia may have included a token gesture of nudity as opposed to the full nudity of Spartan female athletes or Olympic male athletes. If husband appraisal really took place at Olympia, then the ancient female spectator would have understood Pelops as enviable husband material and would have identified with Hippodameia.[42] Male viewers would see Pelops as an exemplar of heroic/martial prowess, a leader among men.[43]

To return to the women in the Centauromachy of the west pediment: viewers of both sexes observing the unusual inclusion of women in this, the first large-scale sculptural rendering of the myth, could be reminded of the women at Olympia in the Heraia and as spectators at the male games, women who were elevated to marriageable status in the former and seeking husbands in the latter. Moreover, several of the Lapith women have one breast bared, a further reference to the competitors in the Heraia, who competed with one breast bared; here, however, the women are manhandled, and a Centaur aggressively grabs the breast of one woman, sometimes identified as Perithoos' wife (her name is Hippodameia or Deidameia). Although the Lapith women do not seek husbands, they are assaulted by the Centaurs at a wedding and defended by the heroic, athletic Lapiths, overseen by the god Apollo, who towers over all as the epitome of youthful beauty. The west pediment is thus directed at the male spectators, offering examples of courageous and heroic behavior, and perhaps also at the female spectators, maybe the participants in the Heraia, who were encouraged to maintain chaste behavior in the face of base lust.

The east pediment's still, tense composition contrasts strongly with its counterpart on the west (Figs. 7, 8). Were it not for Pausanias' identification of the east pediment's subject, the modern viewer might never know what is depicted. Pausanias names several figures, including those in the center, whom we can identify as follows: Pelops (G, the unbearded male) and Hippodameia (K) on one side of a centrally placed Zeus (H), Oinomaos (I, who is bearded) and his wife Sterope (F) on the other (Fig. 27). But Pausanias' use of the terms "right" and "left" in describing what he sees is ambiguous, and he also misidentifies the sex of one figure (O) with the result that the original placement of the central figures and some of the others is in doubt. Scholars have seized upon this uncertainty and spent the last century trying to fix the places of the five central figures, resulting in over seventy reconstructions to date.[44] The rendering of Zeus' neck muscles suggests that he turned his head toward his right, perhaps bestowing divine favor to the protagonist, presumably Pelops, on this side of him, while his thunderbolt, the symbol of his imposition

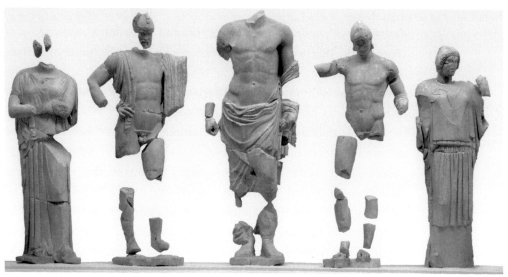

27. Olympia, Temple of Zeus, c. 470–456 B.C., east pediment, central figures F, I, H, G, K. Photo: H. R. Goette.

of justice, would have been held in his left hand, perhaps indicating that Oinomaos was placed on this side. But this is hypothetical, and an argument has also been made that Zeus' uneasy gesture, gripping his garment with his right hand, indicates that he looks at the object of his wrath.[45] As we shall see, the ambiguity as to who is to the left and right of Zeus has influenced scholars' understanding of the pediment, but fortunately, the precise placement of Pelops, Hippodameia, Zeus, Oinomaos, and his wife Sterope is not critical to our discussion. On each side of the central group is a chariot and seated or crouching figures. Pausanias (5.10.6–7) identifies two of these as charioteers and says that Oinomaos' charioteer sits in front of his horses, but it is uncertain which crouching figure should be placed in front of which set of horses. An old man on each side (L, N) is recognizable as a seer on the basis of his pose and appearance (Figs. 30, 31), and Pausanias reports that the corner figures (A, P), whose placement is certain, are personifications of local rivers.

As noted above, the divine favor version of the Pelops myth in which the hero defeats King Oinomaos with horses given to him by his former lover Poseidon has its earliest attestation in the victory ode of Pindar, *Olympian* 1, composed in 476 B.C. The cheating version in which Pelops bribed Oinomaos' charioteer is first known from the Athenian writer Pherekydes of c. 440 though the myth certainly may have existed prior to this date. The corrupt charioteer, usually named Myrtilos, subsequently threw himself, or was pushed, off a cliff and as he fell, he called down a curse on the house of Pelops, the famous curse of the house of Atreus, one of Pelops' descendants.

We have already noted that scholars usually accept the cheating version of the myth as operative on the east pediment. But it is unlikely and implausible that the patrons of the temple would have portrayed their hero as a cheat, and there is nothing in the material record either before the temple or on the east pediment itself to suggest that the cheating version was intended. Pausanias' description of the Kypselos Chest of c. 550 B.C., which was dedicated at Olympia, included the chariot race of Pelops among its array of mythological decoration, and Pausanias goes out of his way to tell us that Pelops' horses have wings and Oinomaos' do not (Paus. 5. 17.7),[46] suggesting that the divine favor version of the Pelops myth was influential on this depiction. The two extant vase paintings of Pelops preparing for, or involved in, the chariot race from the first half of the fifth century, that is, contemporary with the temple at Olympia, make no obvious reference to cheating or trickery, such as would be provided by a depiction of Myrtilos and Pelops alone together. Instead, the two Attic black-figure lekythoi of c. 500, one in Göttingen and another in Athens, refer to the winged horses given to Pelops by Poseidon (Figs. 28, 29). The Göttingen example depicts the competitors racing in chariots; Pelops' horses have wings, and Oinomaos holds two spears and has a shield.[47] On the Athens lekythos, Oinomaos sacrifices at an altar while Pelops (his identity is uncertain) mounts a chariot drawn by winged horses (note the armor piled nearby).[48] The two instances of Pelops' winged horses suggest the divine intervention version of the myth.

The composition of the east pediment of the temple of Zeus offers no indication of the cheating version either. Scholars have cited the expression of figure N, known as the Old Seer, as an indication of Pelops' cheating and the subsequent disaster for Oinomaos because the seer seems to gaze and gesture with concern at the chariot wheel before him or at omens above him (Fig. 30).[49] But, as noted above, two seers appear in the pediment (L, N), one on each side, and their facial expressions from what we can see are similar (Fig. 31). Furthermore, since the exact placement of Oinomaos and Pelops on either side of Zeus is unknown, we cannot be certain of which chariot belongs to Pelops and which to Oinomaos, and thus we do not know which chariot is next to the Old Seer.

28. Göttingen, Georg-August-Universität J22, Attic black-figure lekythos attributed to the Sappho Painter, Chariot race of Pelops and Oinomaos, c. 500–490 B.C. Photo by Stephan Eckardt and reproduced by permission of Norbert Eschbach.

Seers, in fact, are appropriate to the narrative, since they were well established in connection with the oracle at Olympia (e.g., Pind. *Ol.* 8.1–17; Xen. *Hell.* 3.2.21–22, 4.7.2; Strabo 8.3.30), so their presence here could be simply a local reference,[50] like the personifications of the Alpheios and Kladeos Rivers in the corners of the pediment (A, P),[51] or they could foresee the outcome of the race, Oinomaos' defeat.[52] The presence of at least one charioteer has also prompted some to interpret the pediment as referring to the cheating version of the myth, but since we do not know which figure is the charioteer, whose charioteer he is, or what he is doing, this seems a rash assumption. The absence of wings on any of the horses (D, M) might also provide hope for those who wish to see the cheating version here, since Pausanias tells us that Pelops' horses had wings on the Kypselos Chest, the two lekythoi show the same, and Pindar mentions winged horses. Unfortunately, most of the areas where we would expect to find wings, the front part of the horses' torsos, are lost and have been restored. Thus, nothing about the pediment's composition itself indicates that the cheating version was intended.

It also is implausible that the Eleans would have celebrated their hero and founder of the games, Pelops, with sculptures that depicted him as a cheat,[53] particularly since athletes took their oath of fair play in front of a nearby statue of Zeus (Paus. 5.24.9), whose image dominates the east pediment of his temple (H). Zanes, bronze statues of Zeus paid for with fines levied on cheaters, lined the entrance to the stadion

29. Athens, National Museum, Attic black-figure lekythos 595, Chariot race of Pelops and Oinomaos (CC968), c. 500–490 B.C. Photos: C. Haspels, Deutsches Archäologisches Institut, Athen, Neg. D-DAI-ATH-1969/1116, 1969/1117, 1969/1119.

(Paus. 5.21.2–3; Fig. 32).[54] Pausanias (5.21.4) piously reports that the inscriptions on the Zanes make it clear that the victory is to be won not by cheating but by strength and swiftness, and that the purpose of the Zanes is to warn against cheating, specifically bribery, apparently the most common offense. Last, had Pelops been regarded as a cheat

29 *(continued)*

at Olympia, the Achaians would hardly have claimed descent from him as they did on their prominent sculptural dedication of the late archaic period located just next to the temple of Zeus;[55] the inscription, according to Pausanias (5.25.10), read, "To Zeus, these images were dedicated by the Achaeans, *descendants of Pelops*, the godlike descendant of Tantalos."

That the pediment may have acquired this meaning for later viewers is entirely possible, because myths change over time and from region

30. Olympia, Temple of Zeus, c. 470–456 B.C., east pediment, Figure N.
Photo: H. R. Goette.

to region. Sophokles and Euripides both wrote plays in the later fifth
century B.C. about Oinomaos, presumably using the cheating variant as
befitting a tragedy, which may have been the inspiration for a number of
fourth-century Apulian vases on which Myrtilos, Oinomaos' charioteer,

31. Olympia, Temple of Zeus, c. 470–456 B.C., east pediment, Figure L. Photo: H. R. Goette.

32. Olympia, Zanes bases. Photo: H. R. Goette.

appears with Oinomaos, Pelops, and Hippodameia.[56] How did this version arise? To explain Pelops' absence from earth in *Olympian* 1.28–51,
Pindar recounts that "one of the envious neighbors," presumably jealous
of the favor that Pelops enjoyed with the god, concocted the story that
Pelops' father, Tantalos, boiled his son in a cauldron and served him to
the gods. Pindar has been accused in this instance and others of inventing
a new myth, but whether he is or is not in this instance is less important
than his emphasis on the envy bred by success and the trouble that goes
with it. This is a frequent theme in Pindar's epinicians as he cautions
the victorious athletes he glorifies to live prudently so as not to attract
the envy or ill feeling of others. Perhaps it was Elis' failure to follow this
prescription that led to the alternate reading of their hero, Pelops, that
is, Pelops as cheater, on the temple of Zeus at Olympia. In recounting the
Archidamian war, the background leading to the outbreak of the Peloponnesian War, Thukydides 1.27.2 relates that the Eleans backed Corinth
against the Corcyreans in 435 and were soundly punished by the Corcyreans for it. Along with this historical alliance between Elis and Corinth,
there is a mythological connection between the two cities: the race of
Pelops and Oinomaos terminated at the isthmus of Corinth. It may be
that Pherekydes' account of the cheating myth of c. 440 was designed to
discredit Pelops and Elis, a small slap at Elis because of Athens' alliance
with Corcyra in 433.

But this study is concerned with the original intention of the Eleans,
who commissioned the building; presumably the Olympian officials
whose approval was undoubtedly required; and the sculptors, who
designed and executed the work. So if the Eleans did not have the cheating version in mind in 470, what did viewers see when they looked at the
east pediment?

One of the most striking but least remarked upon aspects of Pelops
and Oinomaos is their armor (Fig. 27): they both wore helmets and held
spears (now gone), and Pelops also held a shield as evidenced by the
remains of a shield band on his left forearm and once wore a metal cuirass,
perhaps of bronze, as indicated by the holes for attachment on his shoul-
ders and above his pubic line.[57] Armor also appears on the two black-
figure lekythoi that portray the chariot race between the two antagonists
(Figs. 28, 29), and Pindar, *Olympian* 1.77, mentions Oinomaos' bronze
spear. Such hoplite weapons are peculiar equipment for a chariot race.

33. Olympia Museum, Bronze helmet from Olympia. Photo: H. R. Goette.

We can account for Oinomaos' armor with which he killed the unsuccessful suitors, according to some sources, and he is the son of the war god Ares, but the use of hoplite weapons for competitors in an athletic contest, a chariot race, would have resonated particularly with the viewer at Olympia, where hoplite armor was evident in abundance. Armor of all kinds from all places in Greece was dedicated at Olympia, a showcase for military trophies and thank offerings dedicated to Zeus beginning in the Geometric period and continuing through the fifth century (Fig. 33), and military victory monuments clustered around the eastern end of the Temple of Zeus. The offering of actual armor slackened in the second half of the fifth century, but there are still extraordinary military victory monuments in the late fifth century, such as the Nike of Paionios of 424. Some of the most famous examples of armor votives dedicated to Zeus include the spoils of the Persian Wars offered by the Athenians, such as a Persian helmet (Olympia B5100), and the helmet of the Athenian general Miltiades (Olympia Museum B2600). There are even examples of armor decorated with images of Herakles and Theseus, who also appear

34. Olympia Museum B1010. Photo: H. Argive shield band. Wagner, Deutsches Archäologisches Institut, Athen, Neg. D-DAI-ATH-Olympia 1568.

in the sculptures of the temple of Zeus, such as an Argive shield band from the first quarter of the sixth century found near the Stadion (III) at Olympia (Fig. 34): various myths are shown in the band's metope fields, including Theseus killing the Minotaur and Herakles killing the Nemean lion. Unlike the depiction on the Temple's metope, however, the hero here engages in combat with the lion, which was the more common way of depicting this myth at all times. Moreover, the temple of Zeus itself was funded from a military campaign, and its entablature was adorned with Spartan military trophies.

The military dedications at Olympia, the site of the Olympic games, suggest an association of military endeavor and athletic contest.[58] This idea finds concrete expression in the altar of Zeus Areios, Zeus the warlike, at Olympia, which Pausanias 5.14.6–7 cites as the location where Oinomaos sacrificed before his races against the suitors. The armed race or *hoplitodromos*, which was added to the roster of athletic events at Olympia in c. 520 to provide military training (Paus. 5.8.10),[59] also combines military and athletic agon. And we have noted the foundation of Panhellenic games in the sixth century B.C. in response to the development of hoplite warfare.[60] Olympia has a further connection to the military: its oracle, like that at Delphi, was consulted on military matters in the sixth and fifth centuries B.C. [61]

We learn from ancient writers of a strong and persistent association between athletics and warfare in Greek society.[62] Numerous authors attest that athletic competition was regarded as excellent preparation for warfare and was ideal for training young warriors to fight.[63] The second-century A.D. writer Plutarch describes the Spartan military practice of placing a Panhellenic athletic victor next to the Spartan king in battle (*Quaest. Conv.* 2.5.2; *Lyc.* 22.4), presumably not purely as an honor for the athlete but also as a benefit to the king; Panhellenic victors were sometimes chosen as military commanders (Hdt. 5.102, 8.47; Paus. 4.17.9), and the crown victor possessed talismanic force[64] and extraordinary powers. In addition, scholars point out that the conduct of actual hoplite warfare and athletics was much the same with rules, discipline, taunting,[65] and victory monuments. Indeed, athletic competition was regarded as a kind of warfare, an idea that receives confirmation at Olympia itself, where military and athletic victory monuments stood side by side in the Altis: the labors of the great athlete Herakles, a descendent of Pelops, ornamented the metopes of the temple of Zeus, and numerous altars within the Altis honored Herakles, including one dedicated to Herakles Parastates, Herakles the Defender, or Herakles the Right-Hand Man in the Flank (Paus. 5.14.7). We have also noted the appearance of Herakles (and the hero Theseus) on sixth-century armor dedicated at Olympia.

In an effort to explain the origin of the various Panhellenic games, some scholars point to funeral games in honor of heroes, such as those for the warrior Patroklos, and posit that Pelops' death provided the aition for the foundation of the Olympic games.[66] Pelops' tomb was said to be beneath the Pelopion at Olympia, and his ivory shoulder was an honored relic displayed in Elis (Paus. 5.13.4–6).[67] We do not think of Pelops as a conventional warrior, but he does wear armor on the east pediment, and the Greeks believed that the Achaians had to have possession of his bones – and Herakles' bows and arrows – in order to take Troy (Apollod. *Epit.* 5.10; Paus. 5.13.4). To be sure, athletic contest and battle are frequently combined in the Homeric poems;[68] in addition to the funeral games for Patroklos, we might also recall the contest of the bow between Odysseus and the suitors in the *Odyssey*, which results in deadly combat.[69] But we see this connection later, too: Pindar, *Isthmian* 1.51–53, declares that victors in war and athletics receive the same prize, praise from others,[70] and he lauds athletic victors in language usually reserved for the praise of warriors.[71] Finally and most tellingly, Pausanias 5.20.3 reports that the olive wreaths awarded to the Olympic victors were kept in the temple of Hera on a table together with images of, among others, a personification of Agon (Contest) and of Ares, the god of warfare and father of Oinomaos.[72] The victors displayed their crowns in the pronaos of the temple of Zeus (5.12.5).

Thus, the fifth-century viewer of the east pediment would have seen Pelops, hero of the Eleans, dressed in combat gear, ready to race against Oinomaos, the king of Pisa, who was also armed for battle. The temple was constructed from the spoils of Elis' military conquest of Pisa and it is plausible, as some have suggested, that Pelops and Oinomaos were understood as allusions to the recent military conquest of Pisa by Elis, the raison d'être for the temple. When the ancient viewer, more specifically the ancient athletic viewer, saw Pelops he saw the model of a heroic warrior/athlete, the founder of the Olympic games, the representative of Elis, and the conqueror of Oinomaos (Pisa).

This vision of military and athletic valor and arete is reinforced by the sexual associations of Olympia and its games. The Heraia and spectators at Olympia – women watching and perhaps assessing male athletes, and perhaps men watching girls at the Heraia – have already been discussed. But we should also consider the games and spectatorship in the context of the strongly homoerotic society that was classical Greece. In the divine favor version of the myth recounted by Pindar among others, Pelops received divine horses from his former lover, Poseidon. Yet another mythological pederastic couple is associated with Olympia: Zeus and Ganymede, represented by a terracotta sculptural group, probably an akroterion (Olympia Museum T2), of c. 470, the time of the inception of the temple, and by numerous images of the couple dedicated near the Pelopion (Paus. 5.24.5). Both pederastic pairs are mentioned in Pindar's *Olympian* 1 (lines 40–45), composed in 476 to celebrate Hieron of Sicily's victory in the chariot race at Olympia (N.B.: Hieron also dedicated a helmet at Olympia). Pindar describes Pelops' victory over Oinomaos in this poem. To explain Poseidon's intervention on behalf of Pelops, Pindar recounts Poseidon's love for the boy, which led to Poseidon's abduction of Pelops to Mt. Olympos, and the poet compares this to Zeus' love for Ganymede, who was also abducted by his divine lover. The mythological theme of pederasty had a real-life counterpart at Olympia, where the male, youthful competitors raced, boxed, wrestled, and so on in the nude before a largely male audience, who would enjoy this display of potential *eromenoi* (literally, the "beloved ones," that is, the younger partners in pederastic relationships), as evidenced by Pindar, frag. 123.10–12 and *Olympian* 9.94, where Pindar describes one victor: "what a shout as he walked amid the circle of onlookers, young and noble in achievement as in looks!"[73] The combination of athletics and pederasty is common enough in Greek cities; for example, there is ample evidence from Athens that the gymnasion was a chief locus of pederastic activity, and the Dorian cities, of which Olympia is one, included pederasty together with athletics as part of military training. When we consider the assemblage of themes thus far, athletics, the military, and pederasty, the myth of Pelops' armed chariot race with Oinomaos in which Pelops is aided by divine horses given to him by his erstwhile lover Poseidon would seem particularly apt for this temple to Zeus, lover of Ganymede and god of justice at Olympia, the place where nude young men competed before the eyes of an admiring male audience.

Further consideration of Hippodameia's role in the myth and her appearance on the temple helps to unpack more levels of meaning from the east pediment. Scholars now accept the figure plucking at her peplos as Hippodameia (K; Fig. 27);[74] this gesture belongs to the *anakalypteria*, the moment in the Greek wedding ceremony when a bride lifts her veil and reveals herself to her husband. As part of Greek art iconography, it is used to signal "bride" or "female sexual partner" or "modesty" and so it is appropriate in this context, since the aim of Pelops' armed chariot race was marriage with Hippodameia. Athletic contests between a male suitor and the father of the bride, or among only the male suitors, are a common feature in Greek myth. Penelope's father Ikarios, for example, held a footrace in which his daughter's suitors competed for her hand (Paus. 3.12.1–2, 3.13.6).[75] The mythological prenuptial race represented by the myth of Pelops has a real-life counterpart at Olympia with one dramatic difference:[76] the Heraia, the athletic event for girls at Olympia,[77] discussed above. Here, girls, not young men, race in a prenuptial event.

Rather than a negative exemplum cautioning against hubris, a mythological analogy for the defeat of the Persians by the Greeks, a defense of lawful marriage, or a general vision of dike imposed by the gods, the pediments of the temple of Zeus were intended as an inspiring exhortation to the Olympic athletes. To paraphrase the message: "Successful athletes, who behave like heroes, such as Pelops, Theseus, and Perithoos, will win honor, glory, and wives not by violence like the Centaurs but by athletic prowess and martial honor in both types of agones. Win, and win honorably, and all will be yours." Nike, not dike, seems more prominent in the minds of the Eleans, victors over Pisa, and patrons of this temple. This interest is reflected in the Nike akroterion that alights on the temple roof[78] and the Nike held in Zeus' hand within the cella.[79]

The metopes contribute to this program of heroic, athletic glory. Herakles' twelve labors occur in both Peloponnesian and distant locales,[80] choices suited to a Panhellenic sanctuary, the site of Panhellenic games, and visitors and votives from all over Greece (Fig. 13).[81] Herakles clearly provides an athletic model to the Olympic athlete; he was especially famous for his skills in running (Paus. 5.7.7), wrestling, and the pankration (Paus. 5.8.4).[82] Some of the metopes depict the hero in the manner of contemporary athletes,[83] including Herakles' cauliflower ear in the Nemean lion metope,[84] and the numerous metopes that depict him physically engaged with his opponent in activities that recall Olympian events, such as Herakles' wrestling with the Cretan bull and the Keryneian hind, or slaying the Hydra, whose ever-renewing heads, another popping up as soon as the first is dispatched, requires darting, quick movements recalling boxing skills or the like to cauterize their stumps.

Quite aside from the obvious athletic model that Herakles provides to the Olympic athlete, the hero also offers the promise of immortality to his most disciplined imitators, for it was the successful completion

35. Olympia Museum Λ 45. Statue base of Poulydamas, c. 330 B.C. Photo: H. R. Goette.

of Herakles' physically taxing labors that ensured his apotheosis to live among the gods after his death. Diodoros Siculus (12.9.6), for example, describes Milo of Croton, multiple Olympic victor, leading his city's military forces against Sybaris while wearing his Olympic crowns (how could they have been preserved so long?) and equipped with Herakles' lion skin and club. The pankratiast Poulydamas of Skotussa, who won at Olympia in 408, was honored by a statue: the extant base (Olympia Museum Λ 45) is carved in reliefs that show Poulydamas wrestling a lion on two faces; on the third, Poulydamas appears in the court of Darius II, where he lifts a man over his head as a demonstration of his strength (Paus. 6.5.7; Figs. 35–37).[85] Pausanias (6.5.4–6) describes the episode of Poulydamas defeating a lion without the aide of any weapons, which he did specifically to emulate Herakles' defeat of the Nemean lion. Not only is Poulydamas' conquest of the lion modeled on Herakles' Nemean lion labor, but so is the actual iconography on the base. The Nemean lion labor is depicted on the base in two sequential scenes: the actual fight, and Herakles resting after the completion of his triumph. Earlier depictions of Herakles wrestling the Nemean lion usually show the fight in progress, sometimes with the animal poised over the hero's shoulder, similarly to the way in which Poulydamas hoists the man before King Darius.[86] The image of Herakles resting after his labor is unusual, and by the fourth century, the scene of the Nemean lion labor is uncommon in Greek art altogether, but its appearance on the Poulydamas base is an echo of one of the sculpted metopes of the nearby Temple of Zeus, which depicts the hero after his conquest of the Nemean lion.[87] Thus the Poulydamas base, found in and probably displayed in the Echo Hall

36. Olympia Museum Λ 45. Statue base of Poulydamas, c. 330 B.C. Photo: H. R. Goette.

opposite the east side of the temple,[88] would have resonated with the temple's ornament as if to underscore the powerful analogy to Herakles, the son of Zeus.[89]

Of course, the mortal athletes did not strive for actual immortality; rather, they sought everlasting *kleos* (glory), and the Olympic victors got it. Undying fame was usually only available to military heroes, but victors at the Olympic games enjoyed a renown unmatched in the ancient Greek world. Viewed against this background, the visual and thematic connections between the athletes and the heroes depicted on the temple sculptures are even more comprehensible. The Olympic events were the most prestigious of the Panhellenic games (note Pind. *Ol.* 1.1–7), the

37. Olympia Museum Λ 45. Statue base of Poulydamas, c. 330 B.C. Photo: H. R. Goette.

victory most coveted, and had a profound effect on the rest of the victors' lives. Panhellenic victors, particularly at Olympia, commemorated their victories by erecting statues in the sanctuary, and while most statues themselves do not survive, the inscribed bases on which they once stood do; notable exceptions include the bronze Charioteer of Delphi of 484 or 476 B.C., erected for a victory in the Pythian Games, and the bronze head of the Olympic boxer Satyros of Elis of c. 330–320 B.C. by the sculptor Silanion. The significance of this honor cannot be overstated. The Altis was the central sacred space at Olympia where the temples to Hera and Zeus, the ash altar to Zeus, and the hero shrine to Pelops, the founder of the games, were located, and where athletic and military victors of the past memorialized their achievements. Among these monuments were images of Herakles and monuments that featured life-size or over-life-size bronze statues; some of these statues were of famous mythological heroes, such as those belonging to the Achaian dedication of c. 480 B.C., which, we know from Pausanias (5.25.8–10) and from the extant remains, depicted nine Achaian heroes drawing lots from Nestor's helmet to determine who would meet Hektor in single combat. When a new Olympic victor erected his statue in the Altis, he joined a company of previous victors and mythological heroes. Additional honors awarded to the athletic victors at Olympia included a public proclamation by herald, which mentioned both the victor and his home town, and banquets on the last day of the games, organized either by the Eleans (Paus. 5.15.12) or by the victors themselves (Andokides, *Against Alkibiades* 29). When they returned home, Panhellenic victors, especially Olympic victors, were given extraordinary honors, variously including free meals for life (*IG* I^3 131 of c. 430, an Athenian law), a front seat at the games or in the theater, public praise in the form of commissioned poems, and a public statue, often erected posthumously.[90] Both at Olympia and in the athletes' hometowns, praise and the metaphorical crowning of the athletic victor were reiterated and reenacted each time the inscription on the statue was read aloud, the usual mode of reading in ancient Greece.[91] Crown victors were also singled out to found colonies (e.g., Paus. 3.14.3). Pindar, *Olympian* 1.97–99 tells us: "And for the rest of his life, the victor enjoys a honey-sweet calm, so much as games can provide it."

Olympic victors were not only likened to heroes – some were actually heroized. Hero shrines and sacrifice were offered to victors after their deaths, and this was especially true in south Italy and Sicily. Such honors are also attested for others, including Theagenes of Thasos, Olympic victor of 480 and 476, who was reputed to have won 1,400 athletic victories (Dio. Chrys. 31.95–97; Paus. 6.11.5, who also recounts [6.11.2] that Herakles was Theagenes' father!).[92] Pausanias says that his bronze statue was erected in the Agora in Thasos, and that he received cult offerings befitting a god (6.11.8). A circular building (base diameter 0.61 m, total height of base 0.73 m) on Thasos has been identified as his heroon, and nearby was a circular base inscribed with cult formulae and Theogenes' list of victories.[93] Herodotos 5.47 records that the Olympic victor Philippos of Croton of c. 520 B.C. was honored by Egesta with a hero's shrine erected on his tomb, where he was worshipped after his death. Pausanias 6.11.8–9 recounts that many statues of Theagenes of Thasos, the Olympic victor mentioned above, were set up in numerous places, where they were worshipped and could heal the sick. Theagenes' statue was not unique in its ability to heal, and what is more, cities appeased other Olympic victors' statues or erected statues because the deceased victor was believed to have *caused* disease or famine, or withheld athletic victories from a given city. For example, Oibatos of Dyme, who won the Olympic stadion in 756, withheld victory from his city until they erected a statue to him at Olympia in 460 on the advice of the Delphic oracle.[94] Once victory statues became standard in the fifth century, cities began to erect statues to Olympic victors of the past, such as Poulydamas' statue mentioned above, which, although commemorating a victory of 408, was only created by Lysippos (Paus. 6.5) in c. 330 B.C. Such gestures were clearly politically motivated in some cases – scholars, for instance, have argued that the Poulydamas base is the product of a Thessalian attempt to create a tribal hero of the Olympic victor[95] – and attest to the power and prestige accorded to both the Olympic victor and his city. The victors in the stadion, in fact, gave their names to the calendar year. The losers, on the other hand, went home to public humiliation.[96]

The epinician odes of Pindar contribute to this picture of the honored Panhellenic victor. These lyric poems, commissioned for Panhellenic victors, praised the victor in both overt and oblique ways, always naming the victor's hometown, describing his family line, often in mythological allusions, and frequently likening the victor to great mythological heroes. Pindar's poems can be mined for the information they reveal

about cultural values: honor for the victor, his family, and his city; risk
that leads to glory; judicious leadership; the need to avoid envy; homoerotic admiration; wealth; piety for the gods and the need for their favor
to succeed; and good breeding – these themes are ubiquitous in his works
and these are the values of the aristocracy, who comprised most of the
Olympic and other Panhellenic victors throughout the archaic period
and through much of the fifth century B.C. (athletics became more and
more widespread among nonaristocrats as the fifth century wore on).[97]
The poems, therefore, enable us to grasp the perception of athletic victors
by their peers – what was admired, what was not. From *Olympian* 6.9–11,
for example, we have an emphasis on the necessity of risk for a success
to have any significance: "A deed done without danger, hand to hand
or aboard the hollow ships, lacks glory but men remember if someone
dares and wins."[98] Elsewhere, Pindar warns that athletic success and the
consequent praise can bring envy or hubris, which can disrupt the community and occlude the victor's achievement. For example, at the end of
his praises in *Olympian* 2, Pindar says, "But enough: upon praise comes
tedious excess, which does not keep to just limits but at the instigation of
greedy men is eager to prattle on and obscure noble men's good deeds."[99]
As evidence for this concern with the envy of others, it was decreed at
Olympia in the second half of the fifth century B.C. that only a three-time
Olympic victor could erect (or have erected for him) a statue at Olympia
(Pliny, *HN* 34.16), and it could not be over-life-size (Lucian, *Pro eikonibus*
11) – one can only imagine what had come before!

One might argue that this decree and Pindar's treatment of envy and
hubris would support interpretations of the temple sculptures as warn-
ings against hubristic behavior. But both Pindar's epinicians and the site
of Olympia itself were celebrations of glory and human achievement,
both on the battlefield and on the racetrack. And the cuttings on extant
statue bases of the fifth century were both life-size and over-life-size,
that is, heroic scale. If the temple were truly meant to speak to us about
hubris and dike, one would expect all hubris, all the time. Instead we have
a much more nuanced collection of themes including Herakles' labors;
the heroic actions of Perithoos and Theseus overseen by the prime example of youthful masculine (nude) beauty, Apollo; and the preparations
for the event that would lead Pelops to marriage, the founding of the
games, athletic glory, and eternal kleos. To be sure, hubris is present in

both the Centaurs' and Oinomaos' actions, but this is not all there is and, I believe, is not the dominant chord. To speak only of dike is to see only the gods and to miss the glory and arete of the heroes. As athletes gazed up at the sculptures on the temple of Zeus at Olympia, they would have seen heroic models for their own mortal agon. Yet Olympic victors would have achieved a glory that far outlasted their mortal bodies, one that was closer to Herakles' immortality. In *Pythian* 1.83–84, Pindar states that "hearing others extolled rouses secret hatred." But he also goes on to say, "nevertheless since envy is better than pity, do not pass over any noble things. . . . Do not be deceived . . . by shameful gains, for the posthumous acclaim of fame alone reveals the life of men who are dead and gone to both chroniclers and poets. . . . Success is the first of prizes. To be well spoken of is second. But he who finds them both and keeps them wins the highest crown."[100]

For the athlete entering the Altis for the first time or approaching the Stadion, the moment chosen for the sculptures of the east pediment mirrored his own experience. Pelops is shown just before his race with Oinomaos, which corresponds to the actual Olympic competitor's experience. At this moment, the image of Pelops offered a model of courage and inspiration to the Olympic competitor. Viewed after the actual athletic event – especially if the athlete had been victorious – Pelops' image – and those within the temple – affirmed the winner's heroic status. When the victor entered the Temple of Zeus to display his crown as the herald at Olympia announced his victory, the athlete walked under the images of Pelops, founder of the games, and Herakles, model athlete and son of Zeus. After c. 438–430 B.C., the colossal seated statue of Zeus carrying an image of Nike in his outstretched hand oversaw the ceremony (Fig. 15).

Discussion of the temple's cult statue has been postponed until now because it was executed and dedicated several decades after the rest of the building was completed. What stood in the temple in the interim is unknown, though it is difficult to believe that the temple possessed no cult image between the time of its completion in 456 and the dedication of the statue in the 430s. Some scholars have suggested that the Temple of Hera was once originally solely for the worship of Zeus, and then at a later stage, both deities were worshipped. According to this thinking, Zeus' original cult image stood in the fifth-century Temple of Zeus until its colossal statue was installed, and it was during this time that the Temple of Hera, as we know it, was given over solely to Hera.

In any case, the chryselephantine Zeus made by Pheidias is known to us today only from ancient written descriptions,[101] some Roman reliefs, a few images on ancient gems and Elean coins, and some bits of the terracotta molds used to cast glass inlays of drapery, either that of Zeus or of the Nike held in the god's right hand.[102] Zeus' throne and footstool were elaborately decorated in paint and relief, where Pheidias reiterated themes, myths, or figures from the temple's architectural sculptures – Theseus and Perithoos (we do not know what they are doing), Herakles wrestling the Nemean lion, Hippodameia and her mother, the Hesperides carrying apples, and Atlas carrying the world, the last two of which echo the metope that depicts Atlas holding the world while Herakles fetches the applies, and Herakles (and Theseus) fighting in an Amazonomachy. Numerous other mythological figures and narratives also appear, including, among others, Nikai (like those on the temple's roof); sphinxes ravishing the children of the Thebans; Apollo and Artemis slaying Niobe's children; Ajax's rape of Kassandra; Herakles freeing Prometheus; Achilles slaying Penthesilea; Graces (Charites) and Seasons (Horai), the daughters of Zeus; and finally, the birth of Aphrodite on the base of the throne. The last is one of several birth scenes that appear on cult statue bases in the mid-fifth century b.c.: the birth of Pandora on the Athena Parthenos base in the Parthenon (see Chapter 2), the birth of Erichthonios on the Hephaisteion base in the Hephaisteion (see Chapter 3), and the birth of Helen on the Nemesis base at Rhamnous. Its appearance seems odd since there is no immediate cult link between Aphrodite and Olympia, but we might consider the emphasis on marriage in the temple's two pediment sculptures, the dual cult of Zeus and Hera at the site, perhaps together in a single temple, the Heraia performed by girls about to be married, and the erotic element inherent in the male athletic games and their spectators. Against this background, Aphrodite's importance in instigating sexual desire that can lead to marriage (or its disruption as indicated by the Centaurs on the west pediment) might be a suitable explanation.

The cult statue and its ornate trappings formed a stupendous spectacle that must have been dazzling and overwhelming to the viewer, inviting close inspection and study, if possible. The conglomeration of themes recalls other, earlier dense mythological ensembles, such as the throne

sculpted by Bathykles at Amyklai near Sparta in c. 550 B.C., of which
fragments and a written description (Paus. 3.18.9–3.19.5) remain, and
the Kypselos Chest of c. 560 B.C., mentioned earlier, which included many
myths, seemingly disconnected from each other. In material and theme,
the temple's gold and ivory statue and throne equals the Chest, but
surpasses it because of its wondrous size and dramatic setting.

In this discussion, we have mentioned a number of earlier monuments
and buildings – the temple of Hera, the Megarian Treasury; shrines, and
altars – the Pelopion, the ash altar to Zeus, numerous altars to Herakles;
armor, military and athletic monuments; the Zanes; the Achaian Heroes
Monuments; and activities, such as the male and female athletic games
and the athletes' oath, that would have shaped a fifth-century viewer's
perception of the temple and its sculptures.

Yet the temple's sculptures and cult statue continued to exert a strong
influence on later visitors and patrons, whose subsequent monuments
resonate with and amplify the themes seen on the temple of Zeus. Most
immediately, one can see their profound effect on the Philippeion at
Olympia, begun by the Macedonian king Philip II in c. 338 B.C. and probably completed at the time of his death in 336 (Fig. 6). The placement
and interior statues of the structure enlarge upon the heroic themes
championed by the sculptures on the Temple of Zeus.[103] Like the many
altars erected in honor of Herakles and the Pelopion at Olympia, the
Philippeion offers a place for hero worship, in this case of a living ruler,
who was also an Olympic victor. This circular Ionic building with interior engaged Corinthian columns is partially extant and differs from
standard Classical temple design, having similarities instead to other
fourth-century circular structures, such as the Tholos at Epidauros and
that at Delphi, both buildings whose functions currently are unknown.
Its placement is significant; located along the northwestern side of the
Altis, it would have been among the first buildings seen by athletes and
others at Olympia after its construction in 338, and this prominent location was surely an intentional choice.

Pausanias 5.20.9–10 reports that the building contained chryselephantine statues of Philip II, Alexander the Great, Alexander's mother,
Olympias, and his grandparents, Amynthas and Eurydike, made by the
sculptor Leochares, whose name is well known to us from other ancient

literary sources. The use of costly chryselephantine statues should imme-diately catch our attention, for this material usually was reserved for images of deities,[104] such as the colossal Zeus in the nearby temple. If Pausanias' description is accurate – and some scholars are skeptical – there can be no doubt that Philip intended the viewer to make the con-nection between his and his family's images and those of the magnificent statue.[105] Although the statues themselves do not survive, their extant bases bear cuttings that indicate that the statues were life-size figures shown side by side on a semicircular base; one may have been seated but the others were standing. While their disposition is uncertain, the condi-tion of the end blocks and a brief mention in Pausanias (5.17.4) permit a tentative reconstruction with Olympias and Eurydike framing the three male figures in the middle.

In building the Philippeion, Philip's aim certainly was, as Pausa-nias claims, to thank Zeus for his favor in the Macedonian victory at Chaironeia in 338, thus it accords with the many military victory thank offerings, including the Temple of Zeus and the Spartan shield on its façade, in the Altis. In addition, the prominent structure's physical place-ment in the sanctuary along a main walkway into the Altis, and near altars, the hero shrine of Pelops, and other military and athletic dedications, and its chryselephantine images also implicitly placed the Macedonian ruler and his family in the realm of heroes, an illustrious line of military victors, and even the god Zeus. Alexander claimed descent from Her-akles, who is honored numerous times at Olympia, and Philip himself won an Olympic equestrian victory in 356 B.C. and did not hesitate to demand divine worship (Aelius Aristides 38.480; Clem. Al. *Protr.* 4.54.5) or to have his image depicted with those of the Olympian deities (Diod. 16.92.5),[106] as seen on silver coins with a victorious jockey on the obverse, together with an inscription ΦΙΛΙΠΠΟΥ and an image of Zeus' head on the reverse. Other coins issued by Philip, in fact, make the link between king and god even more explicit by depicting both with an anastole, and it is noteworthy that the depiction of Zeus on Macedonian coins only first occurs under Philip's rule.[107] Although the Philippeion has been likened to a heroon and even closely related to the Pelopion, there is no evidence that worship was ever offered at the Philippeion,[108] so such an idea must remain hypothetical.

38. New York, American Numismatic Society 1944.100.12983, Silver tetradrachm minted by Alexander, c. 330 B.C. Photo: Courtesy of the American Numismatic Society.

Yet both the siting of the building and its images betray Philip's intent to glorify and heroize himself, his son Alexander, and his family. The choice of chryselephantine statues was surely made to liken the Macedonians to the gods, and this supposition receives confirmation from coins minted both before and after Alexander's death, which pair Alexander on the obverse with the enthroned Pheidian Zeus on the reverse as if to equate the two (Figs. 38, 39). Placed where it is and filled with images of the ruler and his family, the Philippeion aggressively asserts Philip's claim to be numbered and honored among other gods and heroes worshipped at Olympia. These included Pelops, whose hero shrine (and presumably tomb) lay nearby, and the heroes depicted on the temple of Zeus a short walk beyond the Philippeion, as if physical proximity, together with illustrious accomplishments, could bestow the status of legendary heroes on mortal aspirants. This kind of thinking is, in fact, a continuation of what we have already observed at the Temple of Zeus, where mortal athletes could strive to achieve the luster of a Pelops by winning athletic victory and the accompanying kleos for themselves at Olympia.

In this chapter, we have seen that the main temple's architectural sculpture depicted myths that were closely linked to the site and can be fully

39. New York, American Numismatic Society 1944.100.12983, Silver tetradrachm minted by Alexander, c. 330 B.C. Photo: Courtesy of the American Numismatic Society.

understood only when one considers them in their context. The patrons and designers of the Temple of Zeus' sculptural program were thoughtful in their choice of themes, the composition of the sculptures, and how a contemporary viewer might have interpreted the images. Myths of local concern, such as the chariot race of Pelops and the Centauromachy, as well as myths with a more Panhellenic caste, such as the labors of Herakles, including some with local references, were recruited for decorating the temple. Elements of the sculptures' composition, as well as the themes themselves, exhibit a close connection with Olympia – its games, military victory monuments, and religious worship – and addressed male and female visitors, especially athletes, who were offered heroic models of comportment for their own activities at Olympia and elsewhere. Earlier monuments, such as the Chest of Kypselos, may have provoked a sense of competition and inspiration in the Elean patrons and Pheidias in the creation of the cult statue, which reiterates and contributes to the overall ensemble and the viewer's encounter with the sculptures. The temple and its decoration continued to exert a strong influence on later structures, erected not by cities but by monarchs, at Olympia, as is evident in the

Philippeion, where the analogy between mortal and hero or mortal and god is no longer allusive but literal.

The Centauromachy's first appearance as architectural sculpture at Olympia was soon repeated at site after site. Like the Gigantomachy, the Centauromachy had a broad appeal and was adaptable to regional concerns. Its Thessalian–Elean genealogical roots may have been the inspiration for its use at Olympia, and elements of the depiction were carefully shaped to be comprehensible and appealing there. Its next appearance in architectural sculpture – on the Parthenon on the Athenian Akropolis – indicates the myth's versatility and malleability; in this new context, the myth takes on new and different meanings.

CHAPTER TWO

THE ATHENIAN AKROPOLIS, FEMALE POWER, AND STATE RELIGION

This chapter moves us from a largely rural Panhellenic sanctuary to the heart of one of the great urban centers of the ancient Greek world, the Akropolis in Athens, *the* chief religious location of the city. The myths depicted on its main building, the Parthenon, form the core of this chapter, but because of the nature of the site and the interrelatedness and cross-references of its many myths and rituals, the discussion will be wide-ranging. This study offers the opportunity to observe the reuse of the Centauromachy in a different context, where this now familiar myth takes on new meanings for the ancient viewer when combined with other, different myths and considered against the background of the religious activities that occurred on the Akropolis, other monuments located on the site, and myths associated with the Akropolis. What also will be apparent is that, as was the case at Olympia and the myth of Pelops, for example, certain myths are chosen for the architectural decoration because of their close and particular association with the site.

So much has been written about the Parthenon and its location, the Akropolis of Athens, that it seems as if there must be little new to say.[1] It needs to be stated at the outset of this discussion that this chapter is not intended as an exhaustive treatment of the Parthenon, its surroundings, or the secondary scholarship on both, which have often been discussed in terms of their importance to the Athenian polis and their embodiment of Athenian political or philosophical ideas. Instead, I wish to focus on one facet of the Parthenon's images – the role of women in the myths depicted on the Parthenon and on other structures and monuments on the Akropolis – and argue that other, more subtle ideologies were also expressed by the buildings, their placement, and their decoration, which reveal fifth-century Athenian, particularly male, views regarding women, who feature prominently in the building's sculptural themes, and their place in the polis. Read against the backdrop of the larger physical context of the Akropolis, where female deities, female mythological figures, and actual women and girls were prominent participants in religious rites, the images of women in myths, some concerning the city's legendary past, yield new insights into the intentions of the Parthenon's patrons and designers, and into the meanings available to the contemporary viewer, male and female.

From a distance, the Akropolis sits in isolation above the modern city, a romantic nineteenth-century vision surrounded by the clamor, noise, and pollution of congested, sprawling Athens (Figs. 40, 41, 104). Its marble ruins, a symbol of Greece's glorious past, beckon to the tourist eager to engage with the ancient Greeks. Today's visitor to the Athenian Akropolis must pass blocks of shops, restaurants, offices, and dwellings, and clamber up numerous stairs to finally reach the path ringing the base of the Akropolis, which eventually brings the weary visitor to the Beule Gate, beyond which lies a long, steep staircase to the Propylaia, the entryway to the Akropolis proper (Figs. 40–42).

This sense of lofty isolation above the city's hustle and bustle below was the same for the ancient visitor, who also had to climb a steep slope to reach the sanctuary (and this is the norm for Greek sacred sites; Olympia is a notable exception). Today's visitor immediately encounters guards, trashcans, and thousands of tourists with their tour guides like so many parade marshals, marching their wards around the slippery plateau. It can be disconcerting, even disappointing, to be surrounded by the hub-bub, yet the grandeur of the monuments prevails. In the fifth century B.C., the personnel and paraphernalia of the tourist industry would have been absent, but the hordes of people and marshals corralling their groups would have been a familiar sight on festival days when the city assembled by tribes or in other groups led by marshals and processed to the sanctuary of their patron goddess, Athena. One of the most important such festivals was the Panathenaia, the annual festival in honor of Athena's birthday or in commemoration of the Gigantomachy,[2] when Athenians, both citizens and *metics* (resident aliens) paraded from beyond the Dipylon gate, through the gate and into the city walls, across the Athenian Agora,

40. Athens, Akropolis, aerial view. Photo: A. Loxias, Athens.

41. Athens, Akropolis, view from west. Photo: H. R. Goette.

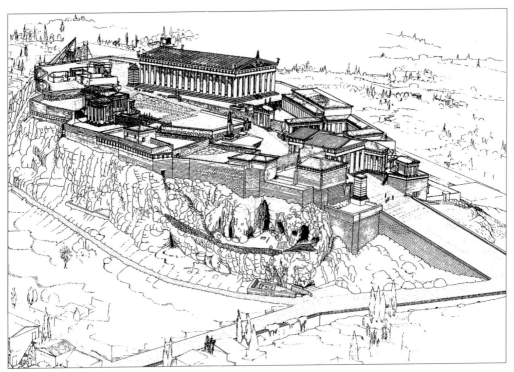

42. Athens, Akropolis, reconstruction, fifth century B.C. Drawing by M. Korres, reproduced with permission.

up the Akropolis, and to the altar and Temple of Athena on the summit in which the ancient olive wood *xoanon* (iconic statue) of Athena was housed (Fig. 104).[3] Sacrifices and invocations were made to the goddess, and every fourth year during a more elaborate version of this festival, the Greater Panathenaia, a new peplos was presented to the cult image, and athletic and musical contests took place.

The Panathenaia is but one possibility that has been suggested as the subject of the continuous Ionic frieze sculpted on the Parthenon, whose remains now dominate the Akropolis (Figs. 43–45). Inscribed building accounts enable us to date the Parthenon's construction to c. 447–432 B.C. and indicate that the building was funded by monies from the Delian League, an organization of cities originally created after the end of the Persian Wars in 479 as a defensive alliance against further Persian invasions. Led by the Athenians, League members contributed money and ships to this joint effort. In 454, these funds were moved from the island of Delos in the Aegean Sea to the Athenian Akropolis, a significant signal of Athens' hegemony over what, in truth, had become a maritime empire. The use of these funds for the construction of the Parthenon certainly

43. Athens, Akropolis, Parthenon, c. 447–432 B.C., view from northwest. Photo: H. R. Goette.

ran counter to their original purpose, but the members of the League were powerless to prevent it, and the building is justly regarded by scholars as emblematic of Athens' imperial might. As construction proceeded, so Plutarch tells us in his biography of Perikles (*Per.*12), there were grumbles of protest, and Athenians in the civic assembly objected that the city was being decked out like a whore. Perikles, the chief Athenian *strategos* ("general," an elected position) and instigator of this project, replied that he would be happy to underwrite the entire project so long as his name would be inscribed on the building after its completion. The Athenians, clearly recognizing the significance of the project and the implications of such a proposal, immediately backed down.

The Parthenon was not referred to by this name until the fourth century; prior to that time, building accounts designate it as *ho neos*, the temple, a generic term, but beginning in the fourth century, it was called the Parthenon or *hekatompedos*.[4] Both Parthenon and hekatompedos are terms used for *parts* of the building in fifth-century inscriptions, but not to refer to the whole (Figs. 43, 44).[5] The Parthenon's design, using a 4:9 ratio as the guiding principle, combined both Doric and Ionic elements in a seemingly rectangular structure of Pentelic marble, which, in reality, has no straight lines. An exterior Doric colonnade, 8 × 17, with the usual Doric frieze above surrounds the core of the building, which was adorned with an Ionic frieze running round the top of its exterior;[6] the continuous Ionic frieze apparently was not

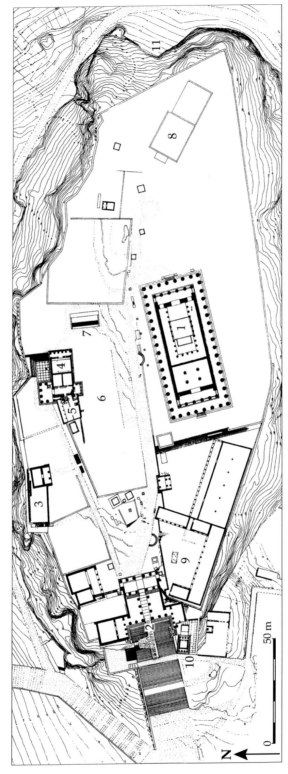

1. Parthenon - 2. Propylaia - 3. Building III - 4. Erechtheion - 5. Pandroseion - 6. Dörpfeld Foundations (Old Athena Temple) - 7. Altar of Athena - 8. Pandion - 9. Temple of Artemis Brauronia - 10. Temple of Athena Nike - 11. Shrine of Aglauros

44. Athens, Akropolis, plan, fifth century B.C. Reproduced and adapted with permission from W. Hoepfner, ed., *Kult und Kultbauten auf der Akropolis* (Berlin 1997) inside front cover.

45. Athens, Akropolis, Parthenon, c. 447–432 B.C., cross-section to show friezes. Drawing reproduced with permission from A. K. Orlandos, *He architektonike tou Parthenonos* 2 (Athens 1978) 335, fig. 229.

part of the original design but the result of a change in plan, as scholars have demonstrated (Figs. 44, 45).[7] Like so much else about the Parthenon, the inclusion of this Ionic feature in a Doric building is a first; other Ionic elements, such as Ionic columns, had appeared in earlier structures, and the Parthenon's opisthodomos possessed four Ionic columns,[8] but the inclusion of two friezes of different orders was new.

Pheidias designed the building's rich sculptural decoration and oversaw a small army of workmen, who fashioned sculpture for the structure's two pediments and carved ninety-two metopes and a 160-m-long frieze, all of painted Pentelic marble with some details, such as horses' reins, added in bronze. Sculpted metopes were not a common mainland feature, and the Parthenon's immediate predecessor, the Temple of Zeus at Olympia, had only 12 sculpted metopes. The Parthenon had 92. The explosion of 1687 and further losses over time, including Lord Elgin's removal of many pieces to London in 1801–1805, have left the sculptures on the Parthenon in fragmentary condition. Drawings of 1674 attributed to Jacques Carrey, together with the surviving sculptures, both on the building and in various museums, primarily the British Museum, enable us to reconstruct the sculptures' original appearance to a great extent.

Although the metopes would have been the first elements sculptured during the construction of the building, a visitor to the Akropolis in the latter part of the fifth century initially would have been struck by the larger pediments above, which measure 28.8 m wide and 3.4 m high at the center and contained over-life-size free-standing sculpture attached to the pediments' back walls and floors (plaster casts now substitute for the sculptures, which recently were removed to the Akropolis Museum). Pausanias (1.24.5) identifies the contest between Athena and Poseidon for the patronage of Athens in the building's west pediment, the side immediately facing the visitor to the Akropolis (Figs. 43, 46); this is the first extant depiction of the myth, which afterward appeared in other media. According to one tradition, Poseidon hurled down his trident, which produced a salt spring, but with Athena's gift of an olive tree to the city (olives were, and still are, of prime importance to Greek culture), she secured the victory. Another version of the myth holds that the two gods raced to the Akropolis in horse-drawn chariots to produce their gifts; whichever arrived and offered a gift first would win. In either case, a quarrel ensued, which was settled by a divine judgment or a jury of Athenians. Later writers (August. *De civ. D.* 18.9) recount that Athena won with the help of the Athenian women, who, together with the Athenian males, served as judges in the contest; the more numerous women outvoted the men in favor of Athena. Although our literary testimony for this is late, the story may have been known earlier and might explain the large number of women included in the west pediment.[9] In spite of the outcome of the contest, one should not overlook Poseidon's importance to Athens, particularly in the Persian Wars period and the years after, when naval power was the means by which Athens controlled its allies and conquered its enemies.[10] Athena and Poseidon appeared in V-formation in the pediment's center as they sprang away from the space between them (this motif recurs at Pergamon; see the Conclusion), which originally was filled by either the olive tree; Poseidon's trident; Zeus, who

A.

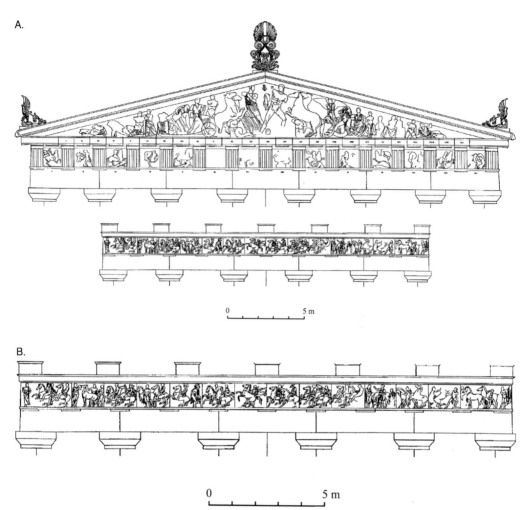

B.

46. Athens, Akropolis, Parthenon, c. 447–432 B.C., west pediment (A.) and Ionic frieze
(B.) reconstruction by E. Berger. Reproduced with permission from E. Berger, "Parthenon-
Studien: Zweiter Zwischenbericht." *AntK* 20 (1977) Falttafel III. B. Enlargement of Ionic
frieze.

adjudicated the dispute; Zeus' thunderbolt; or a combination of these.
Athena's and Poseidon's chariots, other deities, and legendary figures
of Athens' earliest history, such as King Kekrops and his daughters, and
King Pandion (Fig. 47), flank the central pair, witnesses to the contest
and representative of Athens' importance to the divine cosmos.

The awe-inspiring size and splendor of the west pediment sculpture was complemented by brilliantly colored metopes sculpted with
Athenian men defeating Amazons, the legendary race of warrior women,
in bravura two-figure compositions in the Doric frieze below.[11] The

47. Athens, Akropolis, Parthenon, c. 447–432 B.C., west pediment, Figures B–C. Photo:
G. Hellner, Deutsches Archäologisches Institut, Athen, Neg. D-DAI-ATH-1976/1610.

metopes survive in very poor condition, but again, drawings together
with the remains enable us to gather some idea of the originals (Fig. 48).
Numerous battles between Amazons and Greek males appear fighting
each other in Greek literature and in Greek vase painting, on sculpted
terracotta reliefs, and in relief decoration on bronze armor dedicated
in Delphi, Olympia, and elsewhere already in the seventh and sixth
centuries B.C.[12] Such images consist of both group battles and single

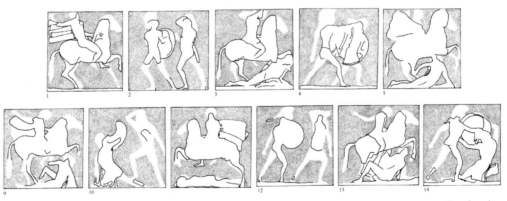

48. Athens, Akropolis, Parthenon, c. 447–432 B.C., west metopes, reconstruction drawing
by M. Cox. Reproduced with permission from J. Boardman, *The Parthenon and Its Sculptures*
(London 1985) 233.

one-on-one combats, such as those between Herakles and an Amazon, and Achilles and the Amazon Penthesilea, and one also sees Theseus abducting the Amazon Antiope.[13] Depictions of fights between Amazons and Greeks are attested on the Athenian Akropolis already c. 625–575 B.C. in vase paintings found there.[14] The explanation of these fractious encounters varies according to ancient author and time period. In the case of the group combats, ancient written sources proffer several causes for the friction between Amazons and Greeks: as one of his many labors, Herakles must capture the girdle of the Amazon queen, Hippolyta; Theseus sometimes accompanies Herakles and is often credited with abducting Antiope and bringing her back to Athens with him. This led to a second combat between Amazons and Herakles when the female warriors invaded the Athenian Akropolis to retrieve Antiope. Ancient authors also relate that Amazons fought on the side of the Trojans in the Trojan War. It seems logical to conclude that the Parthenon metopes, like the exterior decoration of the shield held by Athena Parthenos within the building (see below), evoked the Akropolis invasion.[15] The Amazons exerted a strange fascination on Greeks, particularly Athenians, of the fifth century. Viewed as living at the furthest distance from the Greeks, a remoteness that increased as the Greeks explored more and more of the world, the Amazons were imagined as coming together only once annually to mate with men but otherwise living without male society. Male children born of these unions were exposed; females were raised to emulate their adult counterparts: skilled in the use of weapons, hunting, and horsemanship, that is, like men. Encounters between Greek heroes and Amazons, of which there are several in myth (e.g., Achilles and Penthesilea), always result in the Amazons' defeat, either by death or sexual conquest.

Pausanias' identification (1.24.5) of the subject of the Parthenon's east pediment is critical, since the central figures were already gone by the time that Carrey made his drawings (the central figures were removed when the building was converted to a church in the sixth century A.D.), which, together with the extant sculpture, permit a reconstruction (Fig. 49). The birth of Athena was a well-known myth and commonly depicted on archaic and classical vases, yet the Parthenon is the first representation of this myth in architectural sculpture. According to the mythical tradition, Zeus had sex with Metis, a non-Olympian deity, who embodies cunning. Fearful of a prophecy that his child would overthrow him as

A.

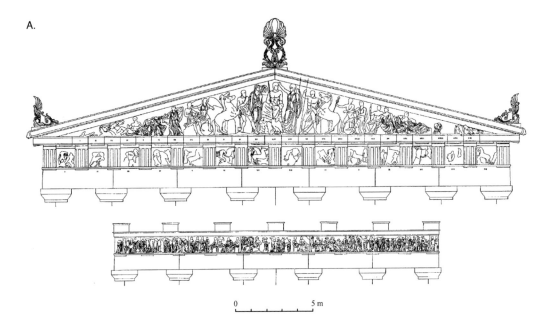

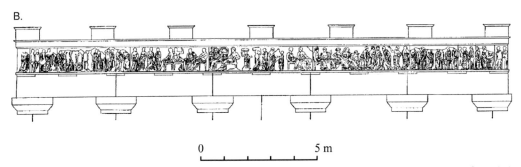

B.

49. Athens, Akropolis, Parthenon, c. 447–432 B.C., east pediment (A.) and Ionic frieze (B.) reconstruction by E. Berger. Reproduced with permission from E. Berger, "Parthenon-Studien: Zweiter Zwischenbericht." *AntK* 20 (1977) Falttafel II.

he himself had ousted his father, Kronos (who had likewise deposed his father Ouranos), Zeus swallowed Metis so that she could not bear their child. While indigestion might be the expected result, Zeus instead developed a headache, which Hephaistos, god of metalworking, cured by splitting open Zeus' head with an axe. Athena, fully grown and armed for battle, sprang out. Although Metis is logically the mother of Athena, as befits the goddess of wisdom and *techne*, the Greeks, particularly the Athenians, tended to refer to Athena as born from Zeus alone. Thus it is not surprising that Athena is so androgynous, and it is for this reason that a female deity is able to preside over Athens, a patriarchal city if

50. Athens, Akropolis, Parthenon, c. 447–432 B.C., east metopes, reconstruction drawing by M. Cox. Reproduced with permission from J. Boardman, *The Parthenon and Its Sculptures* (London 1985) 235.

ever there was one. To return to the east pediment: scholars have endeavored to determine the central figures' original placement based on the appearance of the myth in earlier and contemporary vase painting and have produced numerous reconstructions;[16] what can be determined with certainty is that the chief players in the myth, Zeus, Athena, and Hephaistos, appeared in the center of the pediment. Flanking the central figures again were horses or chariots or both, followed by deities who witnessed the event.

Thus, the two pediments present myths of immediate importance to the Athenians: the birth of Athena directly over the entrance to the Parthenon, and on the opposite side, her vying with Poseidon, god of the sea (and horses), for the patronage of Athens, an honor surely worth quarreling over. The former took place in the realm of the gods, a suitable choice for the entrance to the Parthenon, which leads to a statue of the goddess, while the contest of Athena and Poseidon, facing the entryway to the Akropolis and the city beyond it, was imagined as taking place on the Akropolis itself.

Immediately below the east pediment, two- and three-figure combats of the Gigantomachy and figures driving horse-drawn chariots filled the east metopes, which are badly damaged; again, earlier drawings help to fill out the picture (Fig. 50). The fight between the Olympian deities and the race of the Giants, who tried to overthrow them, was a common theme in art and literature long before the time of the Parthenon; it is already attested in Hesiod's *Theogony* of the late eighth century B.C., where the poet alludes to the critical role of Herakles (951–952) expounded by later writers – the gods could not win without his aid.[17] This theme was frequently used for architectural sculpture in the sixth century B.C.

51. Delphi, Temple of Apollo, c. 515–510 B.C., west pediment, reconstruction by
A. F. Stewart, drawing by C. Smith.

in many places, such as on the north frieze surrounding the Siphnian
Treasury at Delphi c. 530–525 B.C., on the west pediment of the Temple
of Apollo at Delphi of c. 515–510 B.C. (Fig. 51), and on the east pediment
of the Megarian Treasury at Olympia of c. 510 B.C. discussed in Chapter 1 (Figs. 23, 24). Some of the earliest depictions of the myth appear
on numerous Attic vase paintings of the mid-sixth century onward that
were found on the Athenian Akropolis.[18] Athena also was critical to the
effort, and therefore it is not surprising that this myth is manifested elsewhere on the Akropolis: the west pediment of the Old Temple of Athena
constructed c. 510 B.C. displayed a Gigantomachy in three-dimensional
Parian marble figures, including Athena attacking a giant (Fig. 52), and
the peplos presented to the ancient xoanon of Athena housed in this
temple and later in the Erechtheion always had the Gigantomachy woven
into its fabric.[19] Again, we can remark on the suitability of a theme for
its location in the placement of the Gigantomachy over the entrance to

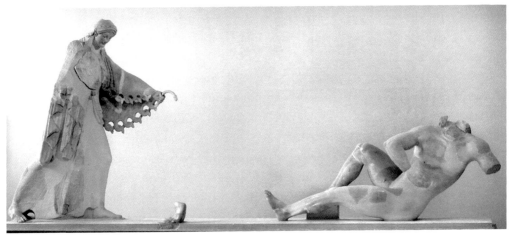

52. Athens, Akropolis, Old Temple of Athena, c. 510 B.C., pediment sculptures.
Photo: H. R. Goette.

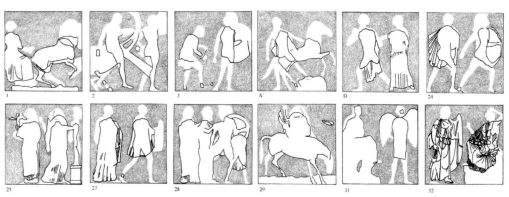

53. Athens, Akropolis, Parthenon, c. 447–432 B.C., north metopes, reconstruction drawing by M. Cox. Reproduced by permission from J. Boardman, *The Parthenon and Its Sculptures* (London 1985) 234.

the building that honored Athena, particularly if the Panathenaia celebrated the Gigantomachy as some scholars have suggested. Thus, the east sculptures of the Parthenon belong to the realm of the gods and their achievements, while the west sculptures – the contest for Athens, the fight between Athenians and Amazons – laud Athens and its heroic achievements.

The Parthenon's north metopes also are badly damaged but enough is visible to permit identification of the theme: the fall of Troy, the direct result of the evil brought to mankind by the beauty of Helen (Fig. 53). While the Trojan War itself forms the subject of the *Iliad*, the actual fall of Troy – depicted in a series of somewhat standardized episodes – is first attested in literature of the seventh to sixth centuries B.C.,[20] and appears in Greek art already in the seventh century B.C. The first depictions found on the Athenian Akropolis date from the end of the sixth century B.C., and wall paintings of this theme by Polygnotos appeared in the Stoa Poikile in the Athenian Agora and in the Lesche of the Knidians at Delphi, both of c. 475–460 B.C. (the paintings are lost but we know of them from Paus. 1.15.2, 10.25.1; see Chapter 3, Fig. 77).[21] Various episodes of the Fall of Troy were earlier juxtaposed on single objects, such as the seventh-century B.C. terracotta relief pithos from Mykonos, which provides the earliest extant representation of the Ilioupersis (Fall of Troy). Various individual confrontations are placed in metope-like panels on the body, and a delightful depiction of Greek soldiers within the wooden horse adorns the neck (Fig. 54). The Parthenon metopes, however, mark the first appearance of various episodes of this myth combined together in architectural sculpture. Like the other Parthenon metopes, those on

54. Mykonos, Museum 2240, Cycladic clay relief pithos. Photograph: E.-M. Czakó, Deutsches Archäologisches Institut, Athen, Neg. D-DAI-ATH-Mykonos 69.

the north consist of two- or three-figure compositions, which include Menelaos approaching Helen, in front of whom stands Aphrodite with a small Eros on her shoulder (N24–25);[22] Helen seeking refuge at the Palladion of Athena (N24–25); perhaps Aineias fleeing the city with his father Anchises or Aphrodite, Thetis, and Neoptolemos (N28);[23] scenes that might be an embarkation from a ship (N2).[24] There are also warriors (N3)[25] and various encounters of women and men (ND – perhaps Polyxena or less likely, Aithra; N27 – maybe Kreousa or Polyxena).[26] Here we see both the conquest itself and the effects of war on the city.

By virtue of their position, the remaining south metopes are in the best condition of any of the metopes on the building (Figs. 55–58). To view

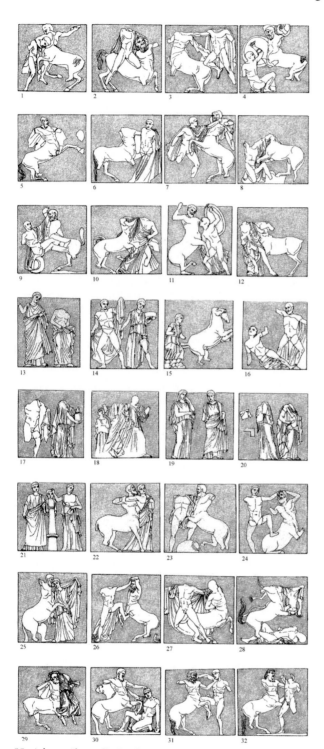

55. Athens, Akropolis, Parthenon, c. 447–432 B.C., south metopes, reconstruction drawing
by M. Cox. Reproduced by permission from J. Boardman, *The Parthenon and Its Sculptures*
(London 1985) 236–237.

56. Athens, Akropolis Museum, Parthenon, c. 447–432 B.C., south metope 12.
Photo: H. R. Goette.

the south metopes in situ requires one to stand close to the southern edge
of the Akropolis and experience the least capacious viewing space of any
aspect of the Parthenon, and to be furthest from the main processional
way between the Parthenon and the Old Temple of Athena or the later
Erechtheion. Consequently, the metopes were not so damaged by vandal-
ism in the post-antique period as they were by the 1687 explosion, which
shattered the central metopes, remains of which still come to light on
the Akropolis. The extant metopes clearly show Centaurs battling Lapith
Greek men or attacking Lapith Greek women at what can only be the
Thessalian wedding, a theme we already encountered at the earlier Temple of Zeus at Olympia discussed in Chapter 1. Like the Lapith women
at Olympia, several of those on the Parthenon's south metopes have one
breast bared (South 12, 22, 29; Figs. 56, 57), in this case not because
of a cultic connection; sculptors of the Parthenon metopes may have
worked on the Olympia sculptures and therefore would have been familiar with this iconographic motif from this earlier well-known temple

57. London, British Museum, Parthenon, c. 447–432 B.C., south metope 29.
Photo: H. R. Goette.

(South 12 seems to be a quotation with small changes from Figs. H-I on
the Olympian west pediment; cf. Figs. 10, 11 and 56), and it is also possible
that the painting of this theme of the 470s in the Theseion, known
only from Pausanias (1.17.3), exerted some influence (the relationship
between the Theseion painting and the Centauromachy was discussed
in Chapter 1). The Lapiths struggle with athletic-looking Centaurs, who
vary in age and elsewhere fight with, and occasionally vanquish, their
largely nude male Lapith opponents (e.g., S28, Fig. 58), and one Centaur
looks as if he is trying to mount a Lapith woman on South 25. Unlike
their Olympia counterparts, the Centaurs on the Parthenon occasionally use vessels, branches, or clubs as weapons, while the Lapiths wield
armor.

The eight missing central metopes, surviving only in the Carrey drawings, have vexed scholars for over a century; details in the drawings are

58. London, British Museum, Parthenon, c. 447–432 B.C., south metope 28. Photo: H. R. Goette.

not beyond dispute but can guide the placement of various fragments as they are found on the Akropolis (Fig. 55). The drawings indicate that Centaurs were absent from South metopes 13–21. Instead, the following appear: a woman and partially clad man stand near each other on 13; a man, nude save for a mantle behind him, moves away from a woman holding a circular container on 14; a charioteer guides a horse-driven chariot in South 15; a male falls at the feet of another in South 16; a female displays an object to a male in South 17; two females move away from a statue in South 18; two females stand quietly in South 19 and seemingly move apart in South 20; and two females, one partially undraped, flank a statue in South 21.[27] Some compositions, e.g., South 15 and 16, seem to stretch over two metopes, separated by an intervening triglyph. Scholars have proposed numerous identifications for the central metopes, including another aspect of the wedding at which the framing Centauromachy took place,[28] scenes from the early history of Athens, images referring to the various cults of Athens, the myth of Daidalos and Ikaros for South 15 and 16 (and Daidalos is a descendent of Erechtheus),[29] and the myth of Ixion, the ancestor of the Centaurs.[30] Regardless of what theme is restored in the lost metopes, one can say with certainty that the action of the Centauromachy flanking the central metopes is broken, and another theme – whether part of the same story or not – intervenes. In keeping with the thematic tendencies of the west pediment and metopes of the Parthenon and other structures and images on the Akropolis, which emphasize the foundation and legendary past of the city (see more on this below), it is plausible that the intermediate metopes referred to the early history of Athens or to the cults of Athena, as indicated by the statues. Wesenberg, however, has made a suggestion that would explain the strange break in the narrative in the south metopes: that the central metopes, which do not depict Centaurs, were originally destined for use above the east pronaos and opisthodomos, and when the architectural plan of the building changed to use a continuous Ionic frieze rather than Doric metopes and triglyphs in these locations, the already prepared metopes were shifted to the exterior south side, where they form the central metopes today.[31] Korres, however, demonstrated that the measurements of the structure could not accommodate the metopes here, so as attractive as Wesenberg's idea is, it must be discarded.[32]

The pervasiveness of the Centauromachy in fifth- and fourth-century art, particularly architectural relief sculpture, where it is often combined with the Amazonomachy, as is the case here on two adjacent sides of the Parthenon, permits us to consider the varying meanings and uses of a single myth in different contexts. Like the Temple of Zeus at Olympia, which also uses the Centauromachy as part of its decoration, the Parthenon addresses both a local and a wider audience. But because the Akropolis is not a Panhellenic site for athletic events but the chief religious sanctuary of a powerful maritime hegemon in the mid-fifth century B.C., the range of targeted viewers, the means to address them, and the intended messages are different. Moreover, the south metopes are much less conspicuous to the Akropolis visitor than was the enormous depiction of the Centauromachy on the west pediment of the Temple of Zeus that greeted every visitor to the Altis at Olympia; while the latter focuses on the struggle with heroic Lapiths fighting fiercely and urged on, or inspired by, Apollo, the Parthenon's Centauromachy, presented in discrete, nearly square vignettes, allows for the possibility that the Lapiths can be worsted by their opponents as, for example, in South 28. While Olympia's Lapith fighters addressed the Olympia visitors, particularly the Olympic athletes, who were urged to behave valiantly like the Lapiths, who struggle in actual wrestling holds, the Parthenon's Centauromachy spoke first to Athenians – not necessarily athletic competitors – and then to the wider world, although the Lapiths' poses – wrestling holds and knee blocks – give an athletic impression. Neither Apollo nor any other god is anywhere to be seen in the Parthenon version save for the small statues of deities that appear in the mysterious metopes that interrupt the struggle. References to the legendary past may exist in both instances: the Olympia version may boldly proclaim the genealogical links between the temple's patrons, the Eleans, and the legendary heroic Lapiths, and while it is possible that the Parthenon's South metopes 13–21 may refer to the city's legendary past, we know that the Thessalian Centauromachy prominently featured the Athenian hero Theseus among its protagonists, who, by the time of the Parthenon's construction, was firmly embraced by the Athenian democracy as their civic hero.

In light of this, one would expect to see Theseus in the Centauromachy, perhaps also elsewhere on the Parthenon and definitely on the Athenian Akropolis. In the Centauromachy at Olympia, scholars plausibly identify Theseus and Perithoos as the two Lapiths flanking Apollo, both in the pose of the Tyrannicide Harmodios. Yet Theseus is not immediately recognizable in the surviving Parthenon south metopes or the Carrey drawings. In fact, in spite of the fact that Theseus was emblematic of the fifth-century Athenian democracy, particularly in the first half of the century, he is nearly absent from the Akropolis to judge from the surviving remains and literary accounts (although he appears on sixth-century Attic vases found on the Akropolis[33]). Considering the prevalence of images and shrines devoted to Athens' early legendary kings and families on the fifth-century Akropolis (in addition to the figures in the Parthenon sculptures, there are the Pandrosion, the shrine to Pandion, and the Erechtheion, for example; Figs. 40, 42, 44), his omission is

59. Athens, Akropolis Museum, Parthenon, c. 447–432 B.C., west frieze VIII.15, horseman. Photo: H. R. Goette.

particularly surprising. Scholars have attempted to identify Theseus in some of the more visually prominent figures on the Parthenon sculptures: for example, the Lapith on metope S27 or S32 and the figure restraining a rearing horse on the west frieze (VIII.15; Fig. 59),[34] but in no case is his identity made certain through attribute or context.

As for sculpture standing on the Akropolis, Pausanias mentions three sculptural groups including Theseus, and sculptural fragments recovered from the Akropolis may depict Theseus and an opponent. Pausanias cites the groups of Theseus fighting the Minotaur (1.24.1), which, to judge from Pausanias' account, was located between the Erechtheion and the Parthenon; Theseus retrieving the objects left for him by king Aigeus, his father, from under a rock (1.27.8); and Theseus sacrificing the Marathonian bull to Athena on the Akropolis, a dedication by Marathon, perhaps made just after the Battle of Marathon in c. 490.[35] A marble Minotaur and Theseus in the National Museum, Athens (1664, 1664a), may be Roman copies of the original Minotaur group.[36] Theseus has been identified in another fragmentary marble male torso of c. 510 B.C. with a second figure's hand on the back of his left shoulder (Akropolis Museum 145); the opponent is recognized in a partially extant bearded face with a hand at its throat (Akropolis Museum 370). Based on the positioning of the right arm of the extant torso, and the bearded opponent, scholars identify the two figures as Theseus fighting Prokrustes.[37] Apart from the figure's (Akropolis Museum 145) slight build and the lack of hair along his back, both of which simply signify youthfulness, there is nothing to clinch the identification as Theseus.[38]

After the return of Theseus' bones to Athens in the 470s, a political gesture orchestrated by Kimon as a demonstration of piety, worship of the hero may have centered on the Theseion, where the bones were installed.[39] If the Theseion originated only in the 470s and not earlier (Pseudo-Aristotle, *Ath.Pol.* 15.4., dates it to the Peisistratid period), it is curious that the hero is largely absent from the Akropolis prior to this time, as well. By contrast, Herakles, a hero often paired with Theseus on monuments from c. 490 onward, makes numerous appearances in architectural sculpture on the sixth-century Akropolis, though he, like Theseus, is not prominent on the Akropolis in the fifth century (some have identified him as a protagonist in various of the east metopes, but the metopes are so fragmentary and difficult to read that this seems an impossible task[40]). The fifth-century Akropolis seems to diminish emphasis on individual heroes, except those legendary kings, such as Kekrops, who had already been venerated for centuries, and instead, focuses more on the goddess Athena and on glorifying Athenian achievements. Yet both Herakles and Theseus, particularly the latter, are prominent in the nearby fifth-century Agora, as we shall see.

Let us return to the Parthenon metopes and consider their mythological themes in the context of the Akropolis. What did the patrons have in mind when they selected these themes? The usual interpretation of the struggles depicted on the Parthenon metopes sees them, particularly the Amazonomachy on the west, as visual metaphors for recent historical events: the repulse and defeat of the Persians by the Greeks, led by Athens, thus their allegorical meaning is that of civilization defeating the forces of barbarism or chaos.[41] This point of view has been so often repeated that it is usually presented as established fact although it is, in truth, hypothesis.[42] The fact that the Centaurs are actually related to the Lapiths, however, makes such a parallel questionable, as does the fact that several Centaurs, such as Chiron, were portrayed elsewhere as benevolent, helpful, or beneficial figures. Apparently, some Centaurs could be brutes, but others were quite civilized. It is true that the repulse of the Amazons figures in *epitaphioi logoi* as one of the great deeds of the Athenians and is numbered among others, such as the repulse of the Persians, in fourth-century texts, such as Lysias 2.4–47 and Demosthenes 60.8–10, but the Amazons inspired an ambivalent attitude in the ancient Greeks, particularly fifth-century Athenians. While they posed a threatening alternative to traditional male society, some mythical Amazons were integrated into Athenian life (Antiope and/or Hippolyte were abducted and taken to Athens), and Paus. 1.2.1 and Plut. *Thes.* 27.4–5 describe monuments and memorials dedicated to Amazons in Athens. In actuality, we know that other easterners, such as Skythians, came to Athens in the sixth century B.C., where they served as mercenaries; some Skythians or Persians were depicted in monuments on the Akropolis, where they are shown as riders.[43] Their inclusion in the polis bespeaks a more subtle relationship between Athenians and easterners than is usually allowed by the paradigm of a strict dichotomy between Greek and foreign, which is posited by modern scholars.[44] In the case of the Ilioupersis, the parallel with the Persian Wars – a barbarian eastern people defeated by the civilized Greeks – does not hold up under scrutiny. The myth of a sacked city certainly would have resonated with fifth-century Athenians, whose own city had been sacked by the Persians not so long before in c. 480 B.C., and this episode echoes the Amazon attack on the Athenian Akropolis depicted in the west metopes of the Parthenon. But for the Ilioupersis-as-Persian-War parallel to work, we must imagine that the Athenians either envisaged themselves as the hapless Trojans, who ultimately are defeated, or as the victorious Achaians, whose savage conquest of Troy was carefully recorded on the metopes. This less than complimentary view of the Greek sack of Troy also occurs in near-contemporary vase painting, such as the images on the Vivenzio hydria of c. 480 by the Kleophrades Painter, which portrays scenes of the brutalities of the Achaians in the sack of Troy (Fig. 60): the rape of Kassandra in Athena's sanctuary and Neoptolemos' pitiless attack on old Priam.[45] Neither vision – defeated Trojans or hubristic victors – would have been

60. Naples, Museo Nazionale 81669 (2422), Attic red-figure hydria attributed to the Kleophrades Painter (Vivenzio Hydria), Ilioupersis. Photo: Soprintendenza per i Beni Archeologici delle province di Napoli e Caserta.

palatable to contemporary Athenian viewers as an image of themselves. If an analogy is intended with recent historical events, then it must operate at a generalized level: the invasion of a city – Athens, perhaps – by outsiders, or victory against a long-time Eastern enemy.

However, another possibility emerges if we consider the role of Helen, the instigation for the Trojan War. Like the Amazons on the adjacent west metopes, Helen is a woman who undermines and destroys men, not by her ferocious fighting ability like the Amazons, but by her extraordinary beauty and sexual allure. Her sexuality is her most potent weapon, and the unbridled desire it inspires brings men to their ruin. The Amazons depicted on the west metopes present an inverse analogy: their hypermasculinity is what leads them to create havoc among men. They possess erotic appeal (why else would Theseus and Herakles have abducted Amazons? consider also Achilles and Penthesilea), but the suppression of their nature and the extremity of their masculine conduct make them repellant to the Greek male imagination. These two visions of female sexuality and its dangers when left unregulated thematically unite the two sets of metopes most immediately visible to the viewer to the Akropolis. The metopes on the north and south sides, however, both concern marriage – one corrupted, another disrupted; the former caused by a flighty, unfaithful wife, the latter indicated by Lapith women (and men) chastely defending their honor. And the eastern metopes of the Gigantomachy, given over entirely to the realm of the gods and the fantastic giants, represent the triumph of the gods, effected by the key participation of Athena, the androgynous daughter of Zeus, and the symbol of Athens, whose sexuality is suppressed or at least secondary to her masculine characteristics: Athena embodies both male and female, warrior and *kourotrophos*, and both are necessary for the survival of the city.

A consideration of the Parthenon's other sculptural decoration adds to this picture. Scholars have written more about the Parthenon frieze than about any other work of ancient Greek art or architecture.[46] It has elicited wonder, fascination, romantic reverie, and angry scholarly and political exchanges and provided a touchstone to be emulated and resisted by Western artists from the Renaissance on. The Ionic frieze ran over the pronaos and opisthodomos columns and circled the cella (Fig. 45).[47] It was sculpted in relief and painted for the entirety of its c. 160 m, of which about 30.5 m have been lost. The paint and attachments in bronze aided visibility; because of its awkward positioning – behind the external Doric frieze, beneath the roof, and some 12.2 m off the ground – it would have been seen to best advantage only at some distance outside the building. Standing directly beneath it, one would have to crane one's neck, and even then, only a small portion could be seen between the columns at any one time.

The overriding cause of so much scholarly activity has been the subject of the frieze, which is not known with any certainty. The frieze presents a procession, which begins at the southwest corner of the building, where figures on the south frieze turn their backs to the west frieze figures and move down the south side toward the east of the building. Those on the west frieze move north, then turn and file down the north side and around the corner to the east. Horses mounted by riders are the

61. London, British Museum, Parthenon, c. 447–432 B.C., north frieze XL.109–111, horsemen. Photo: H. R. Goette.

dominant theme of the west side, and the western halves of the northern and southern friezes (Figs. 59, 61), and apobatai – armed men leaping on and off of moving chariots – also appear (Fig. 62). About halfway along, the procession yields to figures on foot, who carry offerings, including hydriai, musical instruments, and phialai, or lead sacrificial animals (Figs. 63, 64). The two lines of figures converge on the east frieze, where numerous standing men (East 17–23, 43–46), some bearded (therefore older), some not (therefore younger), who represent the ten eponymous heroes of Athens, archons, marshals, or magistrates (Fig. 65),[48] framed by women bringing offerings (mirrored in the later Erechtheion caryatids; see Fig. 71)[49] flank larger Olympian deities, whose attributes or position in relationship to each other make them the only clearly identifiable figures in the entire frieze (Fig. 66). The deities in turn frame the central scene of the east frieze placed immediately above the doorway to the

62. Athens, Akropolis Museum, Parthenon, c. 447–432 B.C., north frieze XXIII.63–65, apobatai. Photo: H. R. Goette.

building: two adolescent girls carry objects on their heads and approach an adult female, while an adult male and a child fold or unfold a piece of cloth (Fig. 66).

A religious procession is occurring but just what kind, when, and where are hotly debated. The earliest interpretation and one that is still prevalent is that the frieze represents that Panathenaic procession that took place as part of the Panathenaic festival, and specifically one of the Greater Panathenaias, held every four years, in which a new peplos was delivered to the statue of Athena. If the frieze depicts the Panathenaic procession, it compresses space and time and shows all activities as occurring

63. Athens, Akropolis Museum, Parthenon, c. 447–432 B.C., north frieze VI.16–19, hydriaphoroi. Photo: H. R. Goette.

simultaneously,[50] or perhaps in three segments – the preliminaries in the Agora, the actual procession, and the aftermath with the folding of the old peplos (though whether it is this action or the unfolding of the new is uncertain).[51] But this seemingly simple explanation is complicated by the fact that the frieze omits many of the key elements attested for the Panathenaic procession, such as hoplites and a wooden ship to whose mast the peplos was attached as a sail, but includes others, such as the renowned horsemen, who are undocumented in our ancient written sources for the festival. The Olympian deities turn their back on the ceremony and face the procession. Moreover, if the frieze depicts everyday Athenians, it would be revolutionary in the history of Greek art: the first architectural sculpture to depict quotidian mortals instead of gods or identifiable heroes. Finally, the xoanon that received the new peplos

64. London, British Museum, Parthenon, c. 447–432 B.C., south frieze XLIV.133–136, sacrificial animals. Photo: H. R. Goette.

was not housed in the Parthenon but elsewhere on the north side of the Akropolis, which would make this ceremony a peculiar choice for the Parthenon frieze.

Yet there are answers to some of these objections. Our sources for the components of the procession are centuries later than the date of the building, which may explain the absence or presence of various elements, since the festival may have changed over time; even if the written sources accurately describe the procession, the sculptors may have selected only certain portions or included other components, such as the cavalry, to refer to contemporary developments: the Athenian cavalry had recently been reorganized and greatly enlarged, for example.[52] And the appearance of mere mortals in a space usually reserved for gods and heroes may be unheralded, yet such an innovation was commensurate with others in the Parthenon and of Periklean Athens, more generally speaking.

65. London, British Museum, Parthenon, c. 447–432 B.C., east frieze IV.20–23, eponymous heroes. Photo: H. R. Goette.

Many scholars accept the view that the frieze depicts the Panathenaic procession, but rather than a generic, timeless Panathenaia, some recognize a specific Panathenaia:[53] the first Panathenaia with legendary, not contemporary, Athenians;[54] or a contemporary Panathenaia.[55] More recently, a suggestion has been made that the east frieze depicts a mythological scene, the sacrifice of the daughters of King Erechtheus at the

66. London, British Museum, Parthenon, c. 447–432 B.C., east frieze V.29–37, peplos scene flanked by gods. Photo: H. R. Goette.

time of the Athenian war with Eleusis.[56] While the east frieze may indeed
refer to the mythological realm, this specific proposal rests on several
untenable assumptions that quickly dissolve upon closer inspection.[57]
Most compelling, however, is the recent proposal by B. Wesenberg to
view the frieze as representing not one Athenian festival but several: the
Arrhephoria, as indicated by the cloth-handling scene in the center of the
east frieze (this festival is discussed in greater detail below), the Greater
Panathenaia, demonstrated by the peplos delivery and the apobates, and
possibly the Greater Dionysia, at which bronze hydriai, such as those
carried on the north frieze, were delivered to the city as tribute from
allies. Thus, the frieze celebrates the religious life of the city generally,
as well as Athens' military hegemony.[58] Such a reading has the advantage of taking account of all of the surviving evidence without forcing
pieces to fit or speculating about what does not survive. Furthermore,
as Wesenberg and Pollitt point out, the themes emphasized in this interpretation are precisely those themes celebrated in the Periklean funeral
oration recounted in Thukydides 2.35.1–46.2, delivered in c. 430, one
year after the outbreak of the Peloponnesian War and a short time after
the completion of the Parthenon itself.[59]

The richly decorated statue of Athena Parthenos in the cella of
the Parthenon reiterates several of the Parthenon sculptures' exterior
themes. Crafted over a wooden core, this 12.2-m-high chryselephantine statue was a creation of Pheidias himself in c. 438.[60] Although the
colossal statue does not survive, its appearance is known from literary descriptions (Pliny, *HN* 36.18–19; Paus. 1.24.7) and is preserved by
later reproductions in various media, such as vase paintings, statuettes,
reliefs, coins, and gems, which permit reconstructions (Figs. 67, 68). The
standing figure of Athena wore a peplos of 40 talents of beaten gold,
which provided Athens with a treasury – portions of it could be removed
in times of need (Thuk. 2.13.5) – and held a 1.83-m-high Nike in her
outstretched right hand. Her skin and the gorgoneion on her aegis were
of ivory. Her helmet was elaborately decorated, as were her sandals, the
sides of which were sculpted in relief with the Centauromachy, a thematic correspondence with the south metopes on the exterior of the
building. A shield leaning by her side was ornamented with the Amazonomachy in sculpted relief on the exterior, recalling the west metopes
(and here on the shield, the attack on the Akropolis is made explicit by

67. Athens, National Museum 1633, Varvakeion Athena. Photo: H. R. Goette.

the fortifications depicted), and a painted Gigantomachy adorned the interior, a corollary to the theme of the east metopes. A gold serpent coiled at the goddess' feet, probably originally at her right side, but then moved to her left inside the shield at some later point, perhaps as early as the mid-fourth century B.C.[61] The colossal statue stood upon a base (8.064 m wide × 4.10 m deep) that was adorned with painted marble figures depicting the birth of Pandora attached to a dark Eleusinian limestone background.

68. Athena Parthenos statue in the Parthenon, c. 438 B.C. Reconstruction reproduced by permission from A. K. Orlandos, *He architektonike tou Parthenonos* 3 (Athens 1978) 355, fig. 236.

The resonant themes on the Athena Parthenos statue take on added value when considered together with the myth portrayed on the base. Hesiod (c. 720 B.C.) offers the first extant written accounts of the birth of Pandora in his *Theogony* 570–591 and *Works and Days* 57–105. As part of Prometheus' punishment for stealing fire from the gods and trying to deceive Zeus, Zeus ordered the creation of the first woman, a mixture of earth and water fashioned by Hephaistos and adorned by Athena and other deities, including Aphrodite, who gave her beauty and desirability, and Hermes, who added a deceitful nature and the character of a bitch. Thus, Pandora is a καλὸν κακόν or beautiful evil. She was given a jar and warned not to open it, but in typical female fashion – so the Greeks imagined – she was unable to control her curiosity and consequently released all evil into the world; only hope remained within the jar. Zeus announced that her husband, Epimetheus (i.e., mankind) would be unable to live without her (i.e., woman), yet living with her would bring nothing but misery.

While the birth of Pandora seems to break the pattern of the Athena Parthenos' sculptural adornment echoing themes from the metopes – one would expect to find the Ilioupersis of the north metopes – the myth is, in fact, a thematic cousin of the Ilioupersis. The destruction of Troy was ultimately attributable to a kalon kakon, a beautiful evil, in this case, Helen. Pandora is a suitable choice to stand beneath the feet of the virgin goddess, since Pandora was handcrafted by Hephaistos and adorned by Athena, the deities of techne.[62] Beyond that, the use of the Pandora myth in this prominent location also may underscore the ability of the capricious gods both to shower mortals with blessings and also to inflict punishment and pain, a theme repeatedly taken up by fifth-century tragedians, particularly Euripides, whose works were first produced in the second half of the fifth century B.C., that is, contemporary with the Parthenon and after.[63] It is noteworthy that both in the Temple of Zeus at Olympia and here, the cult statues designed by Pheidias include the birth of a significant mythological figure on the base – Aphrodite at Olympia, and Pandora in the Parthenon (see Chapter 1). We will return to this issue in Chapter 3.

In sum, the Parthenon's various sculptures depict myths concerning the history of Athena and her patronage of the city, myths of Greeks – especially Athenians – and gods fighting various rebellious forces, and the creation of the first woman. The birth of Pandora accords not only with the Ilioupersis but also with the other themes in the highly visible metopes, which refer to female agency in a number of ways. On the west metopes and the exterior of the Athena Parthenos shield, Amazons try and fail to invade the citadel of Athens, the heart of the patriarchal city, and threaten its male populace. Possessed of weapons and the skill with which to use them, these powerful and independent females occupy a world unregulated by men and offer an example of women run amok, who are, in the Classical Athenian view, justifiably conquered and broken, either by death or marriage. Directly above the metopes, however, in the divine realm of the west pediment, the androgynous female deity Athena triumphs over her male antagonist, Poseidon.[64] By contrast, the east metopes on the opposite side of the Parthenon reveal a divine order challenged by uncivilized Giants, who are soundly defeated by the Olympian gods, including Athena, who, like the Amazons, is androgynous but whose extraordinary status is justified by her divinity and paternity. The south metopes offer the example of Lapith women, who virtuously struggle to maintain their chastity against the unwelcome and uncouth advances of the barbarian Centaurs at a wedding celebration. Protected by the Lapith men, who rush to their rescue, these women embody female vulnerability and modesty, and their plight permits the Lapith men to demonstrate heroic action and courage. The Ilioupersis on the north metopes presents the destruction and chaos wrought by the power of a beautiful and seductive woman, who is worthy of both contempt and fear because her sexual potency can literally lure men to their deaths.

Greek literature is equivocal in its judgment of Helen, sometimes heaping scorn upon her and elsewhere treating her sympathetically, and in some instances, she condemns herself.[65] She willingly accompanies Paris to Troy in some accounts, particularly early ones, and resists in others, especially those from the fifth century on. Euripides, apparently following the lead of the sixth-century poet Stesichoros, describes how an *eidolon* or image of Helen was substituted for her – that she did not actually go to Troy, but that her double did. Such an account, while seemingly redeeming Helen, emphasizes her illusory quality. Helen offers a negative paradigm – a recurrent motif in Greek literature – for wifely and feminine conduct. Pandora is both the source and summary of these female characters. Women were necessary to the survival of the city – without them, there would be no new citizens, soldiers, or workers – yet to judge from literature, legal documents, speeches, and visual evidence, the perception of them was tinged with anxiety: women's seemingly irrational, emotional nature, curiosity, and sexuality had to be kept in check (by their male superiors) or they could and surely would bring disaster to their families and community.

Another contemporary event may have spurred an interest in women and marriage on this prominent state-funded building. In 451/0 the

Athenians approved a new law to restrict Athenian citizenship to those males whose parents were both Athenian citizens; prior to this time, the law had been more liberal, and allowed citizenship to those with only one Athenian citizen parent. Andrew Stewart points out that in the mid-fifth century, Athens was threatened with an overabundance of metic women, who threatened to shut out Athenian women from marriage opportunities with a limited number of available Athenian citizens.[66] It may be that the Parthenon's sculptures – particularly the metopes (the Amazons suit this vision of foreign women) and also Athena's and Pandora's births – reflect this state concern with legitimate citizenship and the family, the role of Athenian women, and the significance and benefits of Athenian marriage.

We can see reverberations and variations on these themes concerning women, marriage, and motherhood in mythological images and religious practices elsewhere on the Athenian Akropolis. A tangible example of the dual view of the feminine described above is the mythological figure of Prokne, who appears on the Athenian Akropolis in sculpted form, a dedication by the renowned sculptor Alkamenes (Fig. 69).[67] According to myth, Prokne, the daughter of the legendary Athenian king Pandion, was married to King Tereus of Thrace as part of a peace settlement between Athens and Thrace. Her sister, Philomela, came to visit her in Thrace, where her brother-in-law, Tereus, raped her and subsequently cut out her tongue so that she could not reveal what had taken place. But Philomela resourcefully managed to find a means to communicate her plight: she wove the tale into a garment, which she displayed to her sister. Prokne took vengeance on her husband by butchering their child Itys and serving the child as dinner to his father. When Tereus realized what had transpired, he pursued Prokne and Philomela, and some of them or all three (the literary sources vary on this point) were transformed into birds.

The sculptural group by Alkamenes of c. 430–410 B.C. portrays the still, standing figure of Prokne, her left hand held to her chin, contemplating her imminent action: the murder of her son, Itys, who squirms in his mother's skirts. Although Prokne's right lower arm and hand are absent, one can see the path of the lowered right arm and its proximity to Itys' head and make a plausible case for reconstructing her holding a knife to or near her son's throat. Although the Prokne group was not found in situ, Pausanias' account suggests that the group's original placement

69. Athens, Akropolis Museum 1358, Prokne and Itys. Photo: H. R. Goette.

was along the north flank of the Parthenon, close to the third column
from the east, that is, almost directly across from the Altar of Athena. Like
the sacrificial animals slaughtered for the goddess, Itys apparently was
a sacrificial victim, since the murder is often recounted as taking place
during Bacchic rites, and the boy once wore a festal crown in metal on
his head, as indicated by attachment holes. The visual placement of the
group invited the visitor to the Akropolis to compare the actual killing

of animals and the imaginary killing of Itys. While one might regard Prokne solely as a monstrous mother, a figure of childish nightmares, a contemporary Athenian is likely to have had a very different, more mixed reaction. Prokne protects her family's honor by taking vengeance on an outsider, who has wrought havoc by his barbaric acts of sexual aggression and violence. Moreover, in the time after the institution of the more restrictive citizenship law, Prokne's and Itys' fates may also demonstrate the dangers inherent in marrying a foreigner – dangers not only to the individual but to the entire royal family. While the vehicle of Prokne's vengeance is her son, a seemingly grotesque choice, the act of sacrificing her own child to protect the honor of her household would have been familiar to a contemporary Athenian, particularly Athenian mothers, who relinquished their own sons by the thousands as sacrifices in the Peloponnesian War (431–404 B.C.) against the Spartans and their allies. Read in this way, the dedication on the Akropolis may actually have offered an image of consolation or comfort to Athenians, especially mothers, as they filed past it on festival days, such as the Panathenaia. Prokne's moment of contemplation inspires the same kind of response in the viewer: she weighs her personal loss against the greater need of the state and inspires others to do the same, even though it involves a terrible act of sacrifice.

Scholars often point to stylistic similarities between Prokne and the nearby Erechtheion caryatids, yet they share more than a visual correspondence (Figs. 70, 71). Like Prokne, the caryatids refer to Athens' early history: they stand above the grave of King Kekrops and hold their phialai like so many women on fifth-century Attic white-ground lekythoi, a vase type commonly associated with the funerary realm because of their decoration and findspots (Fig. 72). The caryatids here are young Athenian women, rendered permanently in stone, dutifully making offerings at the grave of one of the earliest kings.[68] While it has been long acknowledged that the unique layout of the asymmetrical Erechtheion is closely tied to the necessity to honor traditionally venerated cult sites, its sculpted caryatids also evidence an association with the legendary Athenian past and later fifth-century Athenian efforts to honor it. Indeed, origins – such as the births of Athena and Pandora – and the past history of Athens are themes that recur on the Akropolis in the second half of the fifth century (and we might recall Perikles' citizenship legislation in 451/0 that refined

70. Athens, Akropolis, View of Erechtheion, west side. Photo: H. R. Goette.

71. Athens, Akropolis, Erechtheion, south porch. Photo: H. R. Goette.

72. Basel, Antikenmuseum und Sammlung Ludwig Kä 402, Attic white-ground lekythos attributed to the Bonsanquet Painter Man and woman at grave. Photo: H. R. Goette.

Athenian citizenship), as Athenians both enjoyed their dominant stature and struggled to maintain it. The absence of Theseus from the Akropolis, discussed above, seems all the more peculiar in this light.

In the Prokne myth, Philomela's chosen medium of communication, weaving, is an apt one, since no activity more clearly signified the adult, feminine, domestic realm, and this, too, has a place on the Akropolis. The location posited for the Prokne and Itys group is close to that of a naiskos and altar identified with Athena Ergane, the goddess of techne,[69] who is particularly associated with weaving and craftsmen. This shrine is located in the northern pteroma of the Parthenon, an ancient site that existed on this spot in earlier incarnations of the building, which would put the date of her cult on the Akropolis back to at least the second half of the sixth century B.C.[70] Written texts document her cult on the Akropolis from the end of the fifth century onward, and offerings of terracotta relief plaques were made to her by woolworkers in the late archaic period.[71] If the Prokne group was indeed located in proximity to the cult site of this manifestation of Athena, we might consider that the sculptural dedication was made to Athena in her guise as Ergane.

This emblematic activity of the domesticated female, weaving, was closely associated with the Athenian Akropolis in religion and myth in other ways, as well, particularly with regard to Athena. The peplos woven for the xoanon of Athena has already been mentioned;[72] its weaving took place on the Akropolis and was begun nine months before the Panathenaia at the Chalkeia, a festival celebrated by bronzeworkers in honor of Hephaistos and Athena Ergane (see Chapter 3), when the loom on which the peplos would be woven was erected and work was initiated by the Ergastinai (adult females who supervise the weaving) assisted by the Arrhephoroi, two or four young aristocratic girls chosen from a list submitted to the archon basileus. Funded by wealthy Athenian citizens as a liturgy, the Arrhephoroi lived and worked on the Akropolis, perhaps in Building III (Figs. 40, 42, 44),[73] during their period of service, which concluded at the annual festival of the Arrhephoria. This nocturnal rite began at the Akropolis, where the Arrhephoroi received objects unknown to them (*ta hiera*) in a basket, which they carried on their heads as they descended the Akropolis and proceeded to or beyond a sanctuary of Aphrodite. There, they deposited these baskets and received others, which they also carried on their heads, retracing their steps back to the Akropolis. Once they arrived, they deposited the new baskets and then were dismissed (Paus. 1.27.3).

Although the interpretation of this festival is highly controversial (Pausanias' account and a few brief mentions in other authors constitute the only ancient evidence), the Arrhephoria clearly seems to re-create, in ritual terms, the mythical-historical past, specifically the legend concerning the daughters of Kekrops and the origin of the Athenians, which is set on the Akropolis.[74] Unlike most other poleis in Greece, which were settled by invading groups of people who displaced others, the Athenians regarded themselves as *autochthonous*, sprung from the earth, so that their claim to the land of Athens was, in their view, uncontested and indisputable, and myth justified this view: Hephaistos, god of metalworking, pursued Athena, the virgin patron goddess of Athens, wishing to have sex with her. As he caught up with her, he became so excited that he ejaculated on her leg. Fittingly, Athena, whose characteristic realms also include arts and woolworking, wiped the semen off her leg with a wad of wool, which she then threw on the ground, embodied by the earth goddess Gaia or Ge. Nine months later, Ge emerged from the earth and delivered a child, Erichthonios, to Athena, who, in turn, deposited him into a box or chest for safekeeping. She entrusted the box to the three daughters of the first king of Athens, Kekrops, with the caveat that they not open the box. Like Pandora, who could not exert self-control but yielded to feminine curiosity, at least two of the daughters opened the box and were frightened by Erichthonios, who, according to some traditions of the myth, possessed serpentine legs. The girls were so alarmed that they threw themselves off the Akropolis and fell to their deaths (e.g., Eur. *Ion* 20–24, 267–274).

Scholars view the Arrhephoria as a cultic reenactment of the role of Kekrops' daughters in this myth – the girls are entrusted with baskets and forbidden to peer into them. The rite is also regarded as a coming-of-age ritual, designed to mark the end of childhood when the Arrhephoroi leave the realm of Athena to enter the shrine of Aphrodite; their weaving has prepared them for female adulthood with its social responsibilities of marriage and childbearing, both essential to the integrity of the polis.[75] The Arrhephoroi left a physical trace on the Akropolis: two inscriptions attest to statues of former Arrhephoroi dedicated to Athena and Pandrosos,[76] and some scholars recognize the two adolescent girls carrying objects on their heads in the center of the Parthenon east frieze as Arrhephoroi bearing their baskets with unknown objects upon their heads, and therefore interpret the scene as the delivery of the newly woven peplos to a female priest while the old peplos is removed and folded by the man and child (Fig. 66).[77]

A closer look at the myth of Erichthonios' birth uncovers even more about Greek attitudes toward females, divine and mortal, and about Athenian self-representation. The myth is intriguing not only because of the autochthonous origin of Erichthonios, who went on to become king and found one of the most illustrious lines in Athenian history, but also because of the emphasis placed on Athena and Hephaistos, the two deities associated with arts and crafts or techne (including weaving), who are parents (indirectly in the case of Athena) of this chthonic figure, founder of the Athenians. In other words, techne is embedded in the Athenian character. Athena naturally resists the challenge to her virginity (and thus shows greater fortitude than the weak mortal daughters of Kekrops), yet she is a pivotal figure in the myth – necessary for the birth of Erichthonios and also serving as kourotrophos or nurse after his birth (cf. Hom. *Il.* 2.547–548), a position she hastily relinquishes. Moreover, the daughters of Kekrops, whose names vary but who most often are known as Herse, Pandrosos, and Aglauros, reveal Greek perceptions about female curiosity, obedience, self-discipline, and hysteria. According to this view, most females, such as Pandora or Helen, are apparently incapable of exerting self-control, cannot moderate natural desire, and easily lose their heads. Yet the sole obedient daughter, Pandrosos, was revered by the Athenians and worshipped in a shrine (Paus. 1.27.3) eventually housed in the Erechtheion (Fig. 70); strangely enough, Aglauros, one of the disobedient daughters, was also worshipped, but on the east slope of the Akropolis rather than on its pinnacle.[78]

In addition to the now lost statues, known only from their inscriptions, of Arrhephoroi, other images of these religious participants may have stood on the Akropolis. Some scholars have recognized the famed archaic korai, some 54–75 three-dimensional marble statues of maidens, which were dedicated to the goddess on the Akropolis, as Arrhephoroi. Their inscriptions on bases belonging to some of them name Athena as the recipient but the dedicated korai did not necessarily represent the donors, who, to judge from those inscribed bases that can be firmly attached to korai, were often male (Fig. 73).[79] There is no indication of which aspect of Athena is appealed to by these offerings (in addition to Athena in her guise as Ergane, Parthenos, and Polias, Athena is worshiped in other manifestations on the fifth-century Akropolis),[80] and in many instances, it is not clear whether they depict the goddess herself or her worshippers.[81] Many of the korai once held objects, such as fruit and birds, presumably offerings, in their outstretched right hands, suggesting that the figures depict worshippers, or the extended hand could be receiving offerings and thus deities.[82]

While we do not know if women ever dedicated marble korai in the archaic period, girls, wives, and mothers feature elsewhere in myth and religious cult on the Akropolis in the fifth century. Women – sometimes

73. Athens, Akropolis Museum 680, kore. Photo: H. R. Goette.

quite humble women, such as washer-women or bread merchants – made offerings, such as basins and pillars, and bronze objects, including statuettes of Athena and a small shield, to Athena – sometimes specifically Athena Polias and Artemis Brauronia (see below) – on the fifth- and early-fourth-century Akropolis (many of these dedications have no specified recipient, and Athena and Artemis are not the only possibilities on the Akropolis, of course). These offerings were made both inside temples

74. Athens, Akropolis Museum, Parthenon, east frieze I.4–6, phialai bearers.
Photo: H. R. Goette.

and elsewhere, and temple inventories – not just those of the Parthenon but also of other temples, including the Erechtheion – record objects of terracotta and expensive silver phialai, as well as gold jewelry and gold wreaths, and ivory objects, dedicated by women on the Akropolis after c. 450.[83] Of the ten silver phialai inventoried in the Erechtheion treasury, eight were dedicated by women;[84] this is especially intriguing when one recalls the Erechtheion caryatids, who carry phialai in honor of Kekrops (Fig. 71), and the women phialai bearers on the Parthenon frieze (Fig. 74). In this coincidence, art seems to imitate life, and the actual votive objects are amplified by their specific associations with these two buildings.

In addition to making dedications, Athenian aristocratic parthenoi were basket carriers (*kanephoroi*) in the Panathenaia,[85] and also took part

75. Brauron Museum, krateriskoi. Photo: H. R. Goette.

in the Arkteia, a festival in honor of Artemis Brauronia, who was worshipped at her own sanctuary on the Akropolis beginning at least as
early as the sixth century B.C.[86] Based on Aristophanes' *Lysistrata* 642–
647, which enumerates the various stages of a girl's life, scholars interpret the Arkteia, like the Arrhephoria performed by slightly older girls, as
an initiation for young girls, who were exalted to a socially mature state
that readied them for marriage. Aristophanes indicates that girls wore
saffron robes and were *arktoi* or bears at Brauron. Combined with other
tantalizing mentions in ancient literature, together with images on black-
figure and a few red-figure krateriskoi, distinctive vessels used only in the
Arkteia and found almost exclusively in sanctuaries dedicated to Artemis
Brauronia (Fig. 75),[87] we deduce that girls danced, ran footraces, and at
some point shed saffron-colored robes, perhaps imitating bears' pelts,
during the Arkteia. While the major cult activity took place at nearby
Brauron, versions of this ritual seem to have occurred on the Athenian
Akropolis and elsewhere in Attika. The analogy of young girls to bears
may be puzzling at first but finds an explanation in the aition of the cult:
legend held that a young girl teased a bear, who lived in the sanctuary
of Artemis, and the bear harmed or killed the girl. In revenge, the girl's
brothers killed the bear, which was sacred to the goddess. The goddess
sent a plague as punishment, so in appeasement a girl was offered for
sacrifice, or Attic girls had "to play the bear," that is, the origin of the
Arkteia. When maiden sacrifice is specified, either Iphigeneia was sacrificed at Brauron (rather than at Aulis as told in other traditions) or the
girl was not killed at all but a bear (or goat or deer) was substituted in her
place (e.g., schol. *ad* Ar. *Lys.* 645). In sum, the ancient evidence suggests

that performing the Arkteia marked a critical stage in the maturation of a girl. Almost certainly it was the case that not all girls participated in the Arkteia, which seems to have occurred only once every four years (again recalling the Heraia); rather, a limited number of aristocratic girls seemed to have undergone this privileged rite.[88]

The footraces of the Arkteia recall those of the Heraia discussed in Chapter 1. While the latter were performed in honor of Hera, goddess of marriage, the former took place for Artemis, the goddess of hunting and wild animals, as well as the guardian of children. Artemis' dual nature – she both kills and protects animals – extends to children and adolescents: she had the power to bring death to a woman in childbirth – such a victim was said to have died by the arrows of Artemis – yet she also was entrusted with the oversight of children and adolescents, particularly girls, who were regarded as wild animals in need of taming, which came with marriage. Thus while Hera's domain is marriage, Artemis' is childhood, adolescence, and the transition to adulthood. Girls made prenuptial offerings of toys to Artemis Limnatis at Sparta (*Anth. Pal.* 6.280), the Hippocratic corpus furnishes evidence of adolescent girls making offerings to the same goddess after menarche,[89] and fourth-century B.C. inventories record offerings of clothing and occasionally objects of bronze, gold, and silver made by women on the Athenian Akropolis to Artemis Brauronia.[90]

The occurrence of two rituals, the Arrhephoria and Arkteia, with their emphasis on marriage and sexual readiness, on the Akropolis, sacred to the virgin Athena, is striking and emphasize the intense interest in, and official social control of, the female fertility so critical for the maintenance of the city and its population. The festivals celebrate the early origins and autochthony of the city, the importance of Athena and mortal females in the city's earliest myths, and Athena's critical role and the importance of the Akropolis in the tutelage and maturation of young parthenoi. The perception of the female in fifth-century Athens, at least as revealed through myth, religion, and art on the Parthenon and the Akropolis, seems far more complex and multidimensional than recent scholarship has led us to believe. Rather than a consistently one-sided negative view of the female, images and rites repeatedly emphasize the importance of females, female sexuality, and marriage to the city – as girls, wives, and mothers. To be sure, proper female conduct is circumscribed and prescribed by myths, such as the defeat of the bellicose Amazons by Greek men (the only acceptable militant androgynous female is the goddess Athena, who, of course, possesses divine status, protects the Akropolis from the Amazon invasion, and aids the Olympian deities against a Giant insurrection),[91] the calamities brought about by the insidious Helen and the vixen Pandora, and the chaste Lapith women who resist the Centaurs' aggression. Female sexuality is necessary for the persistence of the polis, but the pleasures of female sexuality can also be dangerous and undo men. One might recall that the women of Aristophanes' *Lysistrata* seize control of the Athenian Akropolis and maintain a sex strike when they wish to get the attention of Athenian men. Control of female sexuality, measuring it in stages, apportioning it through recognized marriage customs, and guarding female sexuality and marriage (and masculine pride) from violation are scarcely unique to the ancient Athenians. But our study has demonstrated the Athenian preoccupation with this matter was expressed in extraordinarily prominent visual depictions of myth and reflected in religious rites performed in the heart of this strong patriarchy.

As discussed in this chapter, the sculptural themes of the Parthenon are part of a complex network of associations and meanings formed by the monuments on the Akropolis and the activities that occurred on this site: the free-standing sculpture of Prokne, the korai, Arrhephoroi, the caryatids supporting the south porch of the Erechtheion, the Panathenaia, Arkteia, and Arrhephoria. The myths depicted on the building are tailored to their site, whether they are the Centauromachy or the birth of Athena, and we have seen that the myths address different audiences, particularly citizens, and reveal Athenian ideology about citizenship and the role of women in society, among other things.

While Athenians honored Athena and other deities during festival days on the Akropolis, their day-to-day existence repeatedly brought them to the Agora, the ancient city's commercial, governmental, and civic center. All of these aspects naturally were closely bound up with civic religion and civic spectacle, which placed emphasis on the city itself – its achievements both recent and past. It was in the Agora that another temple was constructed – begun before the Parthenon – that specifically addressed the male populace of Athens.

CHAPTER THREE

MAKING HEROES IN THE ATHENIAN
AGORA

The preceding two chapters have examined the question of myth and architectural sculpture in a Panhellenic sanctuary and on the central temple of a chief urban sanctuary. The current chapter focuses on the use of myth on a major temple in a civic, commercial, and religious space, the Hephaisteion in the Athenian Agora. The Centauromachy makes yet another appearance here, where it is combined with other themes, including the labors of Herakles, familiar from the Temple of Zeus at Olympia, to create new meanings for a different audience. The ideas transmitted by the Hephaisteion's sculptures are redoubled in the context of the Agora, where numerous other monuments contribute to the civic messages addressed to the Athenian citizen body.

The earliest public buildings that we can identify in the Classical Agora north of the Akropolis date from the late sixth century, and by the early fifth century (Fig. 76), this area seems to have largely eclipsed in importance the Archaic Agora, which was located to the east of the Akropolis (see map, Fig. 104). The Classical Agora (henceforth, "Agora") served as the chief commercial and governmental center of Athens; here was the marketplace, the setting for the law courts, the mint, the prison, and other administrative buildings; the central meeting and conversing place; and the gathering place for those celebrating religious festivals, such as the Panathenaia and the Eleusinian Mysteries. In the classical period, the Agora was graced with a number of buildings and monuments whose ornament is expressive of the relation between the city, its gods, and its heroes, including several religious shrines, particularly to heroes, and

76. View of Agora from Akropolis. Photo: H. R. Goette.

one major temple, the Hephaisteion (Figs. 77, 78). On any given day, the fifth-century B.C. Athenian Agora was peopled with Athenian adult males attending the democratic assembly; worshipers making offerings at shrines and altars; merchants hawking their wares to a mixed populace of freeborn and slaves, both male and female; young aristocratic men talking and walking with their philosopher mentors; civic officials hurrying to and fro, conveying documents and information to the Council House, the Assembly, and the Archives; bronzeworkers forging metal for armor, utensils, and votive dedications; and citizens consulting the latest tribal news on the "bulletin board" of the Eponymous Heroes Monument. On special festival days, this same space was filled with crowds cheering young male athletes competing in athletic games in honor of the patron goddess Athena, processions of hundreds of the city's men and women bringing offerings and animal sacrifices to the Akropolis, or would-be initiates gathering to make the 14-km walk to Eleusis to be inducted into the Mysteries of Demeter and Persephone. Religious, civic, mercantile, and athletic activities overlap in the Agora, operating under the guiding hand of democratic laws and civic ideology. How did

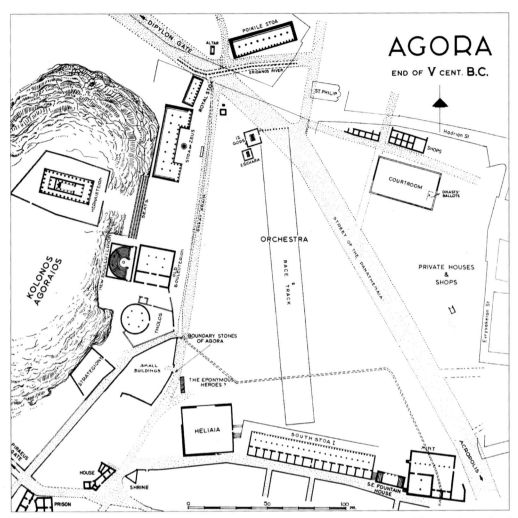

77. Athens, Agora, plan at the end of the fifth century B.C. Reproduced by permission of the American School of Classical Studies: Agora Excavations.

fifth-century Athenians perceive the numerous state-sponsored monuments that peppered the Agora around them, such as the paintings in the Painted Stoa of Greeks fighting Amazons or the Battle of Marathon in which the Greeks defeated Persian invaders? More critical for this study is the issue of how the mixed populace understood the sculptures of heroic deeds and battles that decorated the Hephaisteion, a temple to Hephaistos and Athena, which was begun between c. 460 and 449 B.C. and dominated the Agora, and how surrounding monuments, such as the sculpture of the Tyrant-Slayers of c. 477 B.C. (Fig. 19), influenced a

78. Athens, Agora, Hephaisteion, east façade. Photo: author.

contemporary viewer's understanding of the Hephaisteion's decoration. What meaning did the designers of the sculptures intend to convey, and to whom were these messages addressed? How do surrounding buildings and activities contribute to the viewer's experience of the temple? As was the case with the Parthenon and the Akropolis more generally, the Hephaisteion's sculptural decoration treated Athens' legendary past and also took up the theme of heroic behavior. In the Agora, however, the featured heroes are Theseus, legendary king of Athens and favorite of the fifth-century democracy, and Herakles, Panhellenic hero of unsurpassed strength. When viewed in the context of the rest of the structures and monuments in the west side of the Agora, and the festivals and activities that took place in the Agora, the temple's sculptures offered models of heroic behavior to Athenian citizens, particularly young men, who spent much of their lives in this central civic space.

The Doric peripteros on the Kolonos Agoraios in Athens is now generally agreed to be the Hephaisteion, mentioned by Pausanias (1.14.6) in his traversal of the classical Agora.[1] The Hephaisteion is the best-preserved ancient Greek temple, certainly due, at least in part, to its conversion to a church in c. 450 A.D. (Figs. 78, 79). It stands amid ancient foundries and metalworkers' shops and is thus an appropriate structure in which

79. Athens, Agora, Hephaisteion, south side. Photo: H. R. Goette.

to worship Hephaistos, the god of metalworking. The 6 × 13 structure was constructed of marble except for its lowest step, which is of poros, and is usually thought to have been begun just before the inception of the Parthenon, which would place the Hephaisteion then in the 450s or 449, or perhaps as early as 460 B.C.[2] Like the Parthenon, the building possesses architectural refinements but also has a special architectural and sculptural focus on the east end, the entry side, of the temple.

The structure was decorated with marble sculpture,[3] whose differing styles indicate that work on the building stretched over several decades, starting and stopping as manpower and funds were diverted elsewhere – to other building projects in Attika and Athens, such as those on the Akropolis, or to funding for the Peloponnesian War. The oldest-looking sculpted elements, the metopes, indicate a date perhaps before those of the Parthenon, so possibly in the 450s or early 440s.[4] Nine of Herakles' labors fill the ten metopes on the east façade of the building (Figs. 80, 81) – the Nemean lion, the Hydra, the Keryneian Hind, the Erymanthian

80. Athens, Agora, Hephaisteion, east metopes. Photo: H. R. Goette.

81. Athens, Agora, Hephaisteion, east metopes reconstruction drawing by M. Cox. Reproduced with permission from J. Boardman, *Greek Sculpture: The Classical Period* (London 1985) 151, fig. 111.

boar, the horses of Diomedes, fetching Kerberos, his combat with an Amazon, his fight against Geryon, whose narrative stretches over two metopes (an arrangement seen earlier on the Athenian Treasury at Delphi constructed after the Battle of Marathon in 490 B.C.[5]), and Herakles and the apples (perhaps with Athena?).[6] The labors chosen, such as the combat against an Amazon and Herakles' encounter with Athena, may have been selected with an eye to claiming this Panhellenic hero as Athenian (or at least Attic)[7] – we have already discussed the Amazonomachy's connections with Athens in Chapter 2 – and we can observe here the absence of certain episodes used at the Temple of Zeus at Olympia: the Augean Stables and the Stymphalian birds, which we noted in Chapter 1, made particular reference to the Peloponnese (Figs. 13, 16). Instead, here at the Hephaisteion, the Geryon episode occupies two spaces, and the appearance with Athena seems to be the presentation of the apples of the Hesperides to the goddess; the exclusion of Atlas, who was included

82. Athens, Agora, Hephaisteion, north metopes. Photo: H. R. Goette.

at Olympia, may have been intended to focus the viewer's attention solely on the hero and goddess.

Eight labors of Theseus adorn the last metopes on the northeastern and southeastern flanks (Figs. 82, 83) – the episodes of the Krommyon

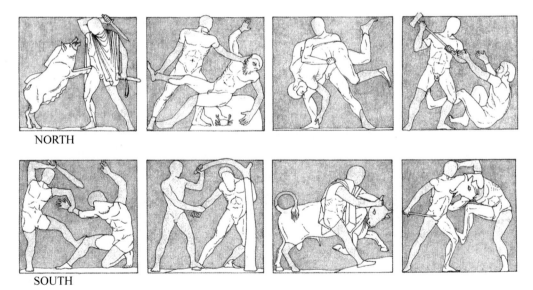

NORTH

SOUTH

83. Athens, Agora, Hephaisteion, north and south metopes reconstruction drawing by M. Cox. Reproduced with permission from J. Boardman, *Greek Sculpture: The Classical Period* (London 1985) 151, fig. 111.

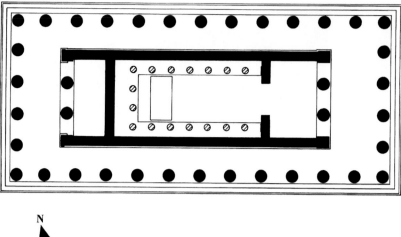

N

0   10   20 m

84. Athens, Agora, Hephaisteion, plan. Drawing by H. R. Goette after Travlos, *Athens* 263.

sow, Skiron, Kerkyon and Prokrustes (?) on the north, and the struggle with Periphetes(?), Sinis, the Marathonian bull, and the Minotaur on the south[8] – thus the metopes of Theseus "frame" those of Herakles, who was the model for Theseus' adventures (Fig. 84). The Theseus episodes chosen document the hero's adventures fighting brigands and savage beasts, step by step, on his travels from Troizen to Athens, where he claimed his place as son of King Aigeus, and then to Crete, whence, after defeating the Minotaur, he returned to Athens and took up the kingship of the city. Theseus appears in Greek literature by the eighth century B.C. – the Homeric poems (*Iliad* 1.265) include Theseus in Perithoos' fight against the Centaurs (and we have seen this in visual form already at Olympia; see Chapter 1) – and his cycle of adventures from Troizen to Athens are first attested in Bacchylides 18 from the fifth century and are a new development in vase painting in the fifth century.[9] Sixth-century Attic vase painting, such as the François Vase of c. 570 (Fig. 20),[10] includes Theseus, and he and Herakles are paired elsewhere on other earlier Athenian monuments, such as the sculpted metopes on the Athenian Treasury at Delphi built after 490 (Figs. 85–90). It is worth looking at the Athenian Treasury more closely because there are enough similarities with the Hephaisteion to suggest that the earlier building had some influence on, or connection with, the later. Here at Delphi,

85. Delphi, Athenian Treasury, east façade Photo: H. R. Goette.

Theseus and Herakles appear together in architectural sculpture for the
first time. The Doric structure (6.57 × 9.65 m), a single room and porch
designed to hold offerings made by the Athenians, faced the Sacred Way,
and its thirty metopes, six on the short ends, nine on the long ends,
were decorated with scenes of the adventures of the Athenian hero Theseus and the labors of Herakles, like the later Hephaisteion. Although
the ordering of the metopes is not certain, most scholars place Theseus'
adventures on the most easily visible east and south and the labors of
Herakles on the north and west (Figs. 85, 86, 109);[11] this accords with
the growing importance of Theseus to the Athenians in the early fifth
century. Among the Theseus adventures are most of those that appear
on the later Hephaisteion – Sinis, Periphetes, Prokrustes, Kerkyon, the
Marathonian bull, the Minotaur (Figs. 87, 88) – and the same is true for
the labors of Herakles (Figs. 89, 90) – both buildings use the Nemean
lion, the horses of Diomedes, the Keryneian hind (Fig. 91), and the fight

86. Delphi, Athenian Treasury, south and west sides. Photo: H. R. Goette.

with Geryon, which stretches over two metopes in both locations. While Theseus raises a hand in greeting to Athena on a metope of the Athenian Treasury (Fig. 88), it is Herakles who appears with the goddess on the temple in Athens, where he delivers the apples to her, perhaps in an effort to show Athens' claim on this Panhellenic hero (Fig. 92). Theseus' place is already secured and reiterated on the Hephaisteion and, as we shall see, in and on surrounding structures in the Agora, whereas on the Athenian Treasury in this Panhellenic, that is, international, venue, the Athenians emphasize their local hero and political symbol. The metopes of both the Athenian Treasury and the Hephaisteion also employ the Amazonomachy, but while we see only a single metope, Herakles defeating an

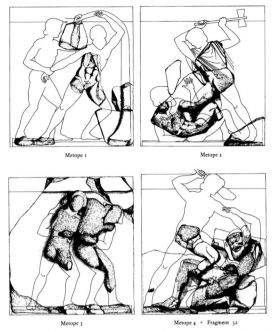

Metope 1   Metope 2

Metope 3   Metope 4 + Fragment 32

87. Delphi, Athenian Treasury, Theseus metopes. Drawing reproduced by permission from K. Hoffelner, "Die Metopen des Athener-Schatzhauses: ein neuer Rekonstruktionsversuch." *AM* 103 (1988) Abb. 1–8.

Metope 5   Metope 6

Metope 7   Metope 8

88. Delphi, Athenian Treasury, Theseus metopes. Drawing reproduced by permission from K. Hoffelner, "Die Metopen des Athener-Schatzhauses: ein neuer Rekonstruktionsversuch." *AM* 103 (1988) Abb. 1–8.

119

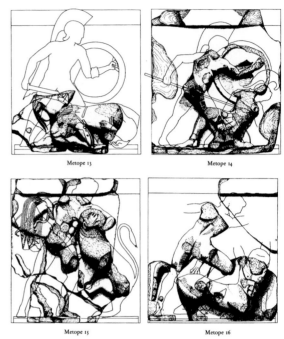

Metope 13 Metope 14

Metope 15 Metope 16

89. Delphi, Athenian Treasury, Herakles metopes. Drawing reproduced by permission from K. Hoffelner, "Die Metopen des Athener-Schatzhauses: ein neuer Rekonstruktionsversuch." *AM* 103 (1988) Abb. 13–16, 25–28.

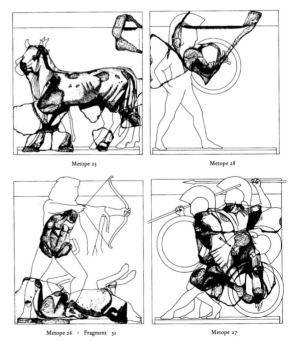

Metope 25 Metope 28

Metope 26 + Fragment 31 Metope 27

90. Delphi, Athenian Treasury, Herakles metopes. Drawing reproduced by permission from K. Hoffelner, "Die Metopen des Athener-Schatzhauses: ein neuer Rekonstruktionsversuch." *AM* 103 (1988) Abb. 13–16, 25–28.

91. Delphi Museum, Athenian Treasury, metope of Herakles and Keryneian hind. Photo: H. R. Goette.

Amazon, on the Hephaisteion (Figs. 80, 81), at least six metopes on the Athenian Treasury are devoted to this theme, which involves both Theseus and Herakles as protagonists against their female foes. For those scholars who identify Amazons with Persians, this sculptural choice and the fact that the extant side akroteria are of Amazons on horseback are clear celebrations of the Athenian role in the victory over the Persians at Marathon.[12]

The identical format of the metopes on the Hephaisteion, Parian marble, 0.63-m-high, two-figure compositions, invites viewers to compare these two heroes, who together represent the Greek ideal, the joining of

92. Athens, Agora, Hephaisteion, east metope, Herakles and Athena.
Photo: H. R. Goette.

brains, in the form of Theseus, and brawn, represented by the athletic
Herakles. As we shall see, these two heroes, particularly Theseus, offer
heroic models not only to the general spectator but also to a specific
group of viewers.

The two friezes (0.85 m high) were carved in situ and have been dated
on the basis of stylistic comparison to the 430s,[13] or perhaps as late as
c. 420.[14] The west frieze (8 m long) depicts the Centauromachy, a myth
used earlier at the Temple of Zeus at Olympia and in the contempora-
neous Parthenon (Figs. 93–95). Unlike these other treatments, however,
the Hephaisteion's Centauromachy is presented in a continuous frieze,
women are entirely absent, and the center of the composition focuses not
on a god, as was the case at Olympia, but on the figure of a Lapith, whom
most scholars identify as Theseus, posed as the Tyrannicide Harmodios
(Fig. 95). In addition, one compositional element of the Centauromachy,

93. Athens, Agora, Hephaisteion, west frieze. Photo: H. R. Goette.

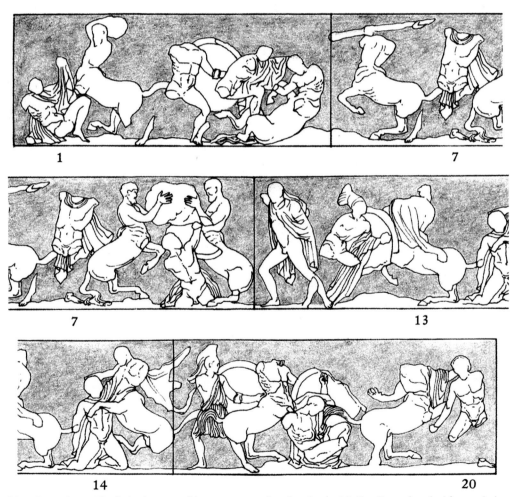

94. Athens, Agora, Hephaisteion, west frieze reconstruction drawing by M. Cox. Reproduced with permission from J. Boardman, *Greek Sculpture: The Classical Period* (London 1985) 153, fig. 113.

95. Athens, Agora, Hephaisteion, west frieze, Theseus, Kaineus, and Centaurs. Photo: H. R. Goette.

the Kaineus episode, is included here in the center; the Lapith Kaineus, invulnerable to conventional weapons, is flanked, and pounded into the ground, by Centaurs wielding boulders or tree limbs. This episode occurs on earlier and contemporary vase painting and bronze reliefs,[15] but is notably absent from the two Classical temples discussed in earlier chapters, where the inclusion of women emphasizes the disrupted wedding of Perithoos and the attack on the female guests. While one can say that the east frieze (11.40 m long) is devoted to a battle observed and framed by the Olympian gods (a general composition that recalls the Parthenon east frieze), the identities of the battle and most of its participants, some of whom wield boulders as weapons, remain uncertain (Figs. 96–98); we will return to this issue somewhat later. Scholars, however, often interpret the dramatically poised central figure, again in the pose of a Tyrannicide, this time Aristogeiton, as Theseus (Fig. 98).

The pediments also were adorned once with sculpture, as evidenced by cuttings in the pediments, but no sculptural fragments have been

96. Athens, Agora, Hephaisteion, east frieze composed from casts in the British Museum, London; the Skulpturenhalle, Basel; and the Abgußsammlung, Bonn, plus two additions from the original slabs. Photos and montage: H. R. Goette.

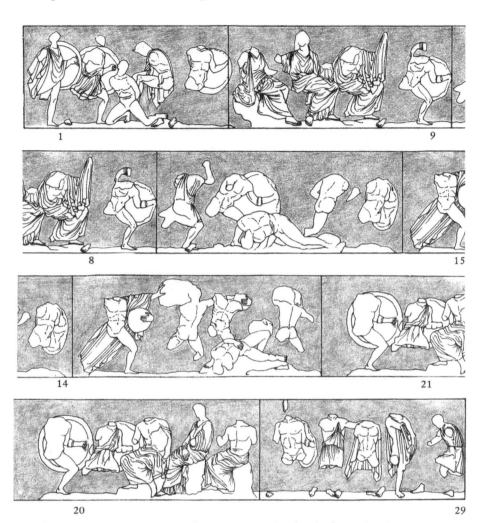

97. Athens, Agora, Hephaisteion, east frieze, reconstruction drawing by M. Cox. Reproduced with permission from J. Boardman, *Greek Sculpture: The Classical Period* (London 1985) 152, fig. 112.

attributed to the building with certainty, and we have no written evidence as to their subjects. Based on the evidence of other temples, both past and contemporary, it seems reasonable to suppose that Hephaistos and possibly also Athena appeared in at least the east pediment, and possibly

96 *(continued)*

98. Athens, Agora, Hephaisteion, east frieze, central figure. Photograph: G. Hellner, Deutsches Archäologisches Institut, Athen, Neg. D-DAI-ATH 1974/743.

in both; cuttings in the center of the east pediment indicate a seated figure, who is Zeus according to some reconstructions,[16] but a seated Hephaistos would be a suitable way of rendering the lame god. Perhaps the god appeared on a winged cart, as he does on two Attic red-figure cup tondi of the end of the sixth century B.C.,[17] or seated with Athena standing before him (and presumably others behind him and behind Athena), as he does on several fifth-century Attic vases (Fig. 99),[18] where the composition forms an ideal triangle (so suitable for the center of a pediment) in which the two deities are featured.

Fortunately, we know more about the temple's cult statues thanks to inscribed building accounts (*IG* I^3 472) of c. 421–416/415, which provide

99. Berlin, Staatliche Museen F2294, fragmentary Attic red-figure cup tondo attributed to the Foundry Painter, tondo. Photo: H. R. Goette.

information about the cult statues of Athena and Hephaistos and their installation, thus giving us a lower date for the completion of the entire sculptural adornment of the structure. This date is also confirmed by architectural details, specifically letter forms on the ceiling coffers, each of which was carved for its particular location.[19] Ancient authors mention a statue of Hephaistos by the sculptor Alkamenes (Cic. *Nat. D.* 1.83; Val. Max. 8.11, est. 3), whose Prokne and Itys was discussed in Chapter 2. On the basis of these passages, scholars surmise that Alkamenes was responsible for the images of Hephaistos and Athena that stood in the Hephaisteion's cella. Speculation about the appearance of the two bronze statues is based on reflections perceived in reliefs and free-standing Roman copies.[20] It is generally agreed that the two over-life-size standing figures formed a closed composition and that Hephaistos wore workman's clothing, an exomis and pilos, and held a hammer while an anvil stood before him (Fig. 100).[21] The myth of the birth of Erichthonios

100. Athens, Agora, Hephaisteion, reconstruction of cult statues by S. Papaspyridi-Karusu reproduced by permission from S. Papaspyridi-Karusu, "Alkamenes und das Hephaisteion." *AM* 69–70 (1954–1955) 83 Abb. 3.

seems to have been alluded to, either explicitly on the base for the cult statues or implicitly by the presence of the baby in Athena's arms.[22] This myth, which concerns the roles of Athena and Hephaistos as progenitors of the autochthonous Athenians (cf. Aisch. *Eum.* 13), emphasizes the importance of the two deities of techne in the production of Athenians (of course, Athena has numerous spheres of importance to the Athenians) and the Athenians' claim to their city.[23] Combined with the heroic deeds in the metopes and the friezes, the Hephaisteion presents a sequence of myths about the autochthonous Athenians and the early history of the city and offers heroic models for its citizens in the deeds of Theseus and Herakles, representatives of brains and brawn, respectively.

101. Athens, Agora, view from Hephaisteion to east. Photo: author.

The placement and concentration of sculpture on the Hephaisteion's east façade are oriented toward the Agora, and the choice of subjects and their disposition were made with an eye to the spectator passing from the Agora below to the temple (Figs. 101, 102). We have already noted the compositional arrangement and subjects of the temple's metopes.

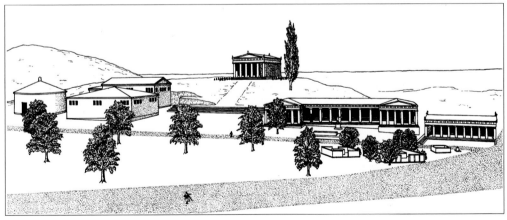

102. Athens, Agora, reconstruction of west side by W. Dinsmoor. Reproduced by permission of the American School of Classical Studies: Agora Excavations.

Together with the east frieze, which bridges the pteroma to meet the entablature at just the point where the lateral metopes of Theseus begin, they form a rectangular "box" on the east front (Fig. 84). Scholars have repeatedly commented on the symmetry of the individual sculptured elements, such as the framing of central scenes in the two friezes by symmetrical compositional devices moving out from the center, or the fact that at least one of the friezes, together with Theseus' eight metopes, yield nine adventures for this hero, a match to the nine labors of Herakles depicted in the east metopes.[24] Some scholars have also pointed out the correspondence between the individual scenes of the two sets of labors, offering Theseus as Athenian hero and Herakles as Peloponnesian hero.[25] In so conventional a design, then, the asymmetrical placement of sculpture and its clustering on the east of the Hephaisteion are remarkable and can be explained by the patron's and/or designer's intention to direct the viewer's attention to the east of the temple and to the sculptures.[26]

Why is the building decorated as it is and with an emphasis on the east side? What did the patrons intend, and what meanings were available to contemporary viewers? Scholars have repeatedly noted the abundance of Theseus imagery on this temple to Hephaistos. Theseus appears in half of the metopes, he has been identified as the figure posed as the Tyrannicide Harmodios in the fight between Centaurs and Lapiths on the west frieze, and some have even identified him as the Aristogeiton Tyrannicide on the east frieze.[27] However, the Theseus imagery on the Hephaisteion is explicable when one considers Theseus' close connections with the Athenian democracy and the city's legendary past, his role as model ephebe, Hephaistos' and Athena's roles in producing those citizens, and the Hephaisteion's integration into the visual landscape of the west side of the Agora, where stood the greatest concentration of buildings concerned with the institutions of the democracy;[28] by the later fifth century B.C., these included the Tholos, where the prytaneis of the Boule met and dined, the Old Bouleuterion (recently redesignated as the Old Metroon),[29] the Stoa of Zeus Eleutherios, and the Royal Stoa (Figs. 76, 77, 102).[30] And the Eponymous Heroes Monument, which honored the eponymous heroes of the tribes of Athens, may have been erected at the southwest corner of the Agora by the time of Aristophanes' *Peace* (1183–1184), produced in 421.

The Hephaisteion was part of a carefully planned complex of structures and framed by civic buildings. By the time of the Hephaisteion's construction or just thereafter, four long rows of soft poros slabs, forming benches at least 25 m and perhaps more than 37 m long (the so-called *synedrion* of later sources), were installed on the lower portion of the Kolonos Agoraios (Fig. 102).[31] The parallel placement of temple and benches, and the benches' central alignment with the temple's east façade, suggest an effort to coordinate the construction of the temple and benches or vice versa (Fig. 102).[32] These benches, which have been nominated as seating for the law court in c. 422 B.C.[33] or as the location of the original Bouleuterion (where the Boule or Council met),[34] were intended for a limited number of spectators (200–400), who could observe events in the Agora.[35] Indeed, when viewed from below, the temple and the benches before it are nearly centered within this larger complex of governmental buildings, a vista that was intentional and made possible by leaving the area in the Agora in front of the benches entirely open except, perhaps, for a low fence to demarcate this seating as a distinct location within the greater public space.[36] These physical adjustments indicate an effort to integrate the temple into the larger setting of the Agora and to encourage pedestrians to pass from one space to the other. Thus, participants in the city's democracy, that is, Athenian males, citizens, would seem to be the targeted audience for the Hephaisteion's sculptures, which projected virtues appropriate to the civic elite and their next generation.

Theseus' special association with the Athenian democracy is well established and does not need rehearsal here.[37] His defeat of unscrupulous brigands and savage beasts are analogues for democracy's defeat of its challengers.[38] The quotation of the Tyrannicide poses for both Theseus (Fig. 95) and the east frieze figure (Fig. 98), whomever it may be, as well as Theseus in his combat with the Minotaur (Fig. 103), certainly was intended not merely to heroize these fighters but to call to mind the Tyrannicides group (Fig. 19) nearby in the Agora (Timaios in the fourth century A.D. places them in the Orchestra; see Fig. 77)[39] and to imbue the figures, particularly Theseus, with pro-democratic and anti-tyrannical meaning:[40] in the Centauromachy,[41] Theseus nobly fights the irascible Centaurs, the embodiment of man's brutality (the Centaurs are, after all, partially human).

103. Athens, Agora, Hephaisteion, south metope: Theseus and Minotaur.
Photo: H. R. Goette.

As scholars have pointed out, Theseus served as an exemplary image
of service to the city and, however anachronistically, to the democracy.
The metopes highlight his (and Herakles') physical prowess. All but one
of the metopes – Herakles and Athena – emphasize physical conquest
of enemies, and we would expect this of Herakles (Fig. 92). But Theseus
was known for his intelligence and his ability to conquer his opponents
with his wits, as Ralf von den Hoff points out, who also has observed
that vase paintings of Theseus defeating the Minotaur and other opponents from c. 460–450 onward usually omit the fight itself and depict
the hero as triumphant.[42] Theseus is portrayed as both warrior and
citizen on contemporary vases and serves as a role model to Athenian
ephebes.[43] The physical aspect of the two heroes, particularly Theseus,
on the Hephaisteion, a public structure, may have been designed to appeal
to Athenian citizens in the making, who wished to recognize themselves
in Theseus.[44] Further evidence of Theseus as athletic exemplar and model

for young Athenian citizens is the athletic games, attested by victor lists, that composed part of the festivities of the annual Theseia first instituted in c. 475.[45] While the victor lists date to the second century B.C., it is possible that they reflect the character, at least to some extent, of the fifth-century incarnation of the festival,[46] especially since athletic games are eminently suited to this young ephebic hero. One might object that athletic games were also part of the Panathenaia, which honors Athena, who is not a role model for ephebes, but in fact, the Panathenaic games *were* meant to encourage, reward, and exhibit the best that Athens had to offer. Many Theseia events resembled Panathenaic ones, and the tribal Theseia contests were open only to Athenians – *paides* of various ages, *epheboi*, *neaniskoi*, and *andres*.[47]

The choice of this exemplary Athenian hero for the Hephaisteion may be even less surprising, since Hephaistos himself played a central role in Athenian legend and was instrumental in producing new citizens, both in myth and ritual. With his lame foot, Hephaistos is the only one of the gods to be physically imperfect, an irony considering that he is married to Aphrodite, the irresistible goddess of sexual love, according to *Odyssey* 8.266–366.[48] His deformity elicits scorn and contempt from the other gods but his ability to shape and craft elemental materials – metals, fire – into utilitarian items, sometimes wondrous products of techne, such as Achilles' replacement armor, or the bed in which he traps his adulterous wife and her lover Ares, or a throne that ensnares his mother Hera, can earn their respect. The god's cults are rare in Classical Greece, and he has a special place in myth and cult primarily in Athens (though he was said to have special associations with the island of Lemnos and is honored in a few other areas[49]), where he is venerated for his technical gifts – the technai that Athenians hold so dear. As discussed in Chapter 2, Hephaistos was regarded as father of Erichthonios, the autochthonous Athenian king, whose "mother" was Athena, another deity of techne; as already noted, this myth was alluded to in the Hephaisteion. Ancient literary sources sometimes indicate Hephaistos' special familial relationship to the Athenians; for example, Aischylos' *Eumenides* 13 refers to Athenians as the "children of Hephaistos," and this tutelary role with regard to Athenian citizens is borne out in ritual.[50] For example, participants in the Apaturia, where young men were enrolled in their phratries as citizens (and thereafter were eligible to participate in the democratic

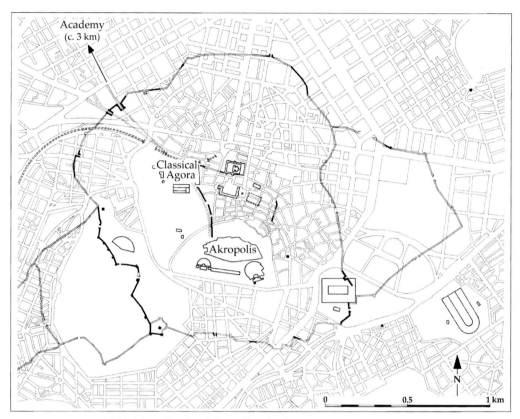

104. Map of ancient Athens. Drawing by H. R. Goette.

assembly and government offices), sang a hymn while holding torches and made offerings to Hephaistos.[51] We do not know where these ceremonies took place, but the Hephaisteion was central to other religious events. The Hephaisteia, celebrated by all the populace, is attested by *IG* I[3] 82 of 421/20 (the time of the Peace of Nikias), which indicates a reorganization of the cult of Hephaistos, so this was done just as the cult statues in the peripteros on the Kolonos Agoraios were begun, suggesting a growing importance of Hephaistos' cult. Dithyrambic choruses, a *lampadedromia* or torch race on foot, a procession, and an offering of cattle were made at the Hephaisteia,[52] from which three cattle would provide meat for metics (among whom were many craftsmen).[53] Some have argued that the torch race, a tribal race, run by ephebes was initiated by lighting the torches at or in the Hephaisteion,[54] though more recently, scholars have argued that the torch race began at the altar of Hephaistos in the Academy (Fig. 104),[55] so presumably the torches were lit there

105. Athens, Agora, Stoa Basileus. Reconstruction by W. Dinsmoor. Reproduced by permission of the American School of Classical Studies: Agora Excavations.

then brought to the Hephaisteion.[56] Thus, the Hephaisteion's imagery, concerned as it is with Theseus, model ephebe, together with Herakles, both physical exemplars of heroic, athletic behavior, would seem particularly apt for this structure, dedicated to a god who was pivotal in the registration of new Athenian citizens.

The sculptural themes, especially Theseus, on the Hephaisteion find resonances on monuments in the Agora below, and any viewer passing through the Agora, particularly along the west side, will have had the opportunity to see Theseus repeatedly invoked in sculpted and painted form. Depending on when the temple was constructed and how much of it and its decoration were designed at the time of the building's inception, we can talk about the Hephaisteion's imagery being influenced by earlier structures in this portion of the Agora and about the Hephaisteion's imagery shaping that of subsequent buildings. Following the (tentatively) established chronology, the Hephaisteion was begun before the Parthenon, and its metopes were in place by the 440s or so. By this time, both the Stoa Basileios and the Stoa Poikile were standing, and both were decorated with Theseus imagery. According to Pausanias (1.3.1), Theseus appears as a terracotta akroterion crowning the Stoa Basileios of perhaps 460,[57] where the hero throws Skiron into the sea (Fig. 105) – the building itself was used, among other things, as the seat of the Archon Basileus and for displaying the laws.[58] Theseus also fights the Amazons and emerges on the plain of Marathon, where Greeks fight Persians, in the paintings in the Stoa Poikile (Paus. 1.15.2–3) of c. 475–460 B.C.;[59]

Athena and Herakles are also present in the Marathon painting, as they are on the later Hephaisteion in one of the Herakles metopes. In addition to housing paintings, the Stoa Poikile served as a display place for military trophies, as a meeting place for philosophers and their pupils, as a public space for fishmongers, beggars, and performers, as the gathering place for those wishing to be initiated into the Eleusinian Mysteries, and as a space for legal proceedings. In the Stoa of Zeus Eleutherios of c. 430–420 B.C.,[60] closer to the temple, were paintings of Theseus, Democracy, and the Demos (Paus. 1.3.2–3). This structure housed not only the cult dedicated to Zeus, but also shields of Athenians who died protecting the city. Thus, Theseus, whose image recurs in this series of public buildings (but who, strangely, is nearly absent from the Akropolis though a few free-standing statues remain[61]) instrumental to the democracy and physically close to the Hephaisteion, is athlete, upholder or even instigator of the democracy[62] (numerous ancient authors mention that slaves and others took refuge at the Theseion[63]), and warrior: and we know that at least on one occasion, Athenian soldiers rallied and spent the night in his shrine (Thuk. 6.61.2; Andok. *De mysteriis* 45), suggesting the special importance he had for the military, whose role was to protect the city. [64]

Moreover, athletic and military events took place in the Agora, which invited comparison with heroic deeds of a Theseus or Herakles displayed on the temple nearby. Archaeological evidence suggests that the running events of the Panathenaia may have been held in the middle of the Agora during the second half of the fifth century B.C.;[65] runners dashed past the Tyrannicides group, and the spectators on the benches of the Kolonos Agoraios could watch from afar (Fig. 77, 102). These athletes serve as visual embodiments of the athletic prowess illustrated in the metopes of the nearby Hephaisteion. Admittedly, the metopes show images of wrestling and combat, but the importance may have been that the heroes were athletic, not the particular "sports" that they practiced. Military maneuvers performed in the Agora are attested for the fourth century B.C. and may have been performed earlier during the fifth century.[66]

To sum up thus far, viewers passing from the west side of the Agora to the temple or vice versa would be able to observe an ensemble of structures and visual décor that repeatedly invoked a limited menu of heroic deeds, both of the distant and recent past. The heroic figures on the Hephaisteion appealed to the citizens and ephebes, men of action – warriors, athletes, participants in, and defenders of, the city's democracy – whose "production" was overseen by Hephaistos and Athena. Additionally, these two deities of techne also were of significance to those involved in manual production. Viewers at the other end of the social spectrum, *banausoi* or *technitai*, were in close physical proximity to the Hephaisteion, which sits near bronze foundries, suitable to the god. Andokides (*De mysteriis* 40) mentions a bronze foundry below the temple, and evidence for bronze-casting, including clay molds for large bronze statues, was found southwest of the temple.[67] Harpokration (*Kolonetas*) of the second century A.D. remarks that hired men were called *kolonetai* because of their proximity to the Kolonos near the Agora, where the Hephaisteion is located. Craftsmen, then, also were among daily spectators of the Hephaisteion, and the temple and the gods worshipped there – who were rendered in bronze as befitting these deities[68] – would have had special appeal to them;[69] some scholars, in fact, have suggested that the impulse to build this temple came from craftsmen, whose initiative was supported by Ephialtes, followed by Perikles.[70] The place where the Athenian Chalkeia festival was celebrated by bronzeworkers in honor of Hephaistos and Athena Ergane is not known, though somewhere in the proximity of this temple to the bronzeworking god amid the bronze foundries around the Kolonos Agoraios would seem logical.[71] Sophokles frag. 844, which is often interpreted in connection with the Chalkeia, mentions "people who work with their hands" making offerings of *liknoi* to Athena Ergane and placing them "by the anvil with heavy hammer" (translation H. Lloyd-Jones, Loeb edition), suggestive perhaps of the cult statue of Hephaistos in the Hephaisteion (Fig. 100).[72] This postulation is given some validity when one recalls that the Chalkeia connects Hephaistos and Athena, in her guise as Polias, in another way: it was at the Chalkeia that the loom was erected for weaving the peplos ferried to Athena's statue on the Akropolis nine months later in the Panathenaic procession (see Chapter 2).[73] Thus, these two deities are fundamentally linked to the city's sense of identity and history – both distant and contemporary – and it is likely that the Hephaisteion in the Agora, which honors

Hephaistos and Athena Hephaistia,[74] played an important role in festivals honoring these gods of techne.

Thus, the temple's sculptures target male citizens, aristocrats and craftsmen alike.[75] Considering the integral role played by Hephaistos and Athena in the forging of new citizens, the inclusion of Erichthonios in the cult statue group, and the postulated date, c. 460–450, of the Hephaisteion's initial construction, it is worth considering whether the new citizenship law of c. 451/0 B.C. (see Chapter 2) provided some impetus for the building and its decoration.[76] If so, the temple would visually underscore the importance of legitimate citizenship to the city's well-being and sense of itself. But another political event may be even more relevant: the Ephialtic reforms of 462 B.C., which shifted power from the aristocratic Areopagos Council, which met on the Areopagos, to the assembly and the law courts, which met in the Agora, thus yielding more power to the citizen body at large, who, in turn, had the duty to execute these powers responsibly.[77] The sculptural themes of the Hephaisteion as outlined here are well suited to this development.

In light of the schema presented here, let us return to the Hephaisteion's east frieze (Figs. 96–98). Scholarly speculation on the frieze's subject has ranged widely: among the most common proposals are a battle between Greeks and Trojans on the Skamander River, as described in the *Iliad*, in which the central Aristogeiton-like figure is identified as Hephaistos intervening on behalf of Achilles (although we have noted that this same figure is designated as Theseus by others),[78] Theseus battling Pallas and sons, signified by the rock-throwing opponents (viewed as Giants), who try to overthrow their cousin, the king of Athens,[79] or a Gigantomachy.[80] Trojans require the central figure to be Hephaistos, for whom no such active, energetic iconography is attested, particularly in the fifth century B.C., and while the god does appear on the frieze, most scholars recognize him seated among the deities (Figs. 97 no. 24, 106). While the battle of Theseus and the Pallantids is appealing to those who wish(ed) to recognize the structure as the Theseion, that identification has been discarded by virtually all scholars, and what's more, the few (questionable) iconographical parallels do not strongly resemble the scene depicted on the Hephaisteion's east frieze.[81] As for the suggestion of the Gigantomachy: Giants are implausible because they should be fighting the gods, who here are seated on a rocky landscape watching the fray.

106. Athens, Agora, Hephaisteion, east frieze, Hephaistos. Photograph: G. Hellner, Deutsches Archäologisches Institut, Athen, Neg. D-DAI-ATH 1974/763.

One of the most striking things about the east frieze is the boulders wielded by the rightward-advancing adversaries, who battle against armor-clad males, who wear either chlamydes or exomides. The exomis is an interesting choice; while it is commonly worn by soldiers, it is also associated with slaves, laborers, and craftsmen, and particularly with the god Hephaistos, who is honored by this temple and whose cult statue may have worn the exomis.[82] Perhaps the protagonists are meant to be identified as followers of the god in some way, both as the heroic soldiers wearing the chlamydes, familiar from sculpture and vase painting, and as the more rustic figures wearing the exomis, associated with workers and

with the god himself. Buschor saw the boulders as evidence of an earthquake easily restrained by the god Hephaistos, portrayed in the center of
the frieze.[83] But as already noted, this figure cannot be Hephaistos. The
boulders, however, are intriguing, particularly when one considers that
the gods sit on rocks, and boulders figure prominently on the opposite
west frieze, where they are wielded by Centaurs. Some primordial battle
witnessed by the gods and fought with boulders against the more sophis-
ticated weapons of the victors would seem suitable. Perhaps we might
find a solution in an early battle of Athens, which would be a suitable
theme for a temple so intimately bound up with issues of autochthony
and the creation of Athenian citizens.

Plato (*Kritias* 112a–c) relates that early Athenians, living some 9,000
years earlier than he (c. 429–347 B.C.), created an enclosure around the
shrine of Athena and Hephaistos, like a garden enclosure round a house
(οἷον μιᾶς οἰκίας κῆπον ἑνὶ περιβόλῳ προσπεριβεβλημένοι), near where
the soldiers of Athens lived. We do not know if Plato was referring to
the Hephaisteion on the Kolonos Agoraios or to another (now unidentified) shrine in honor of the two deities, but he says that the shrine is
on the Akropolis, which in this legendary time stretched from the Pnyx
to Lykavittos; according to Plato, erosion created the valley between.[84]
Craftsmen lived under the slopes of this Akropolis, and its top was
occupied by the military, who dwelt round the temple of Athena and
Hephaistos. The domestic analogy – garden-like enclosure round a
house – is compelling not only because some scholars have suggested
that the plantings around the Hephaisteion from the Hellenistic period,
which may have existed earlier, might form this enclosure,[85] but also
when one thinks of the literary image of the temple, the Hephaisteion, as
house; the occupants of the temple, Athena and Hephaistos, as progenitors of Erichthonios, a legendary autochthonous Athenian king; and the
"family tableau" within the temple/house formed by the cult statues and
the reference to the myth of Erichthonios, perhaps on the base.[86] Plato
describes the two deities as siblings, born of Zeus, who share a common
nature – their love of wisdom and artistry – and hold one portion of land,
Athens, as their common territory. And Plato also assigns them a tutelary
role with regard to the city: the two divinities taught order (τὴν τάξιν)
of the polis to the autochthonous race of Athenians, which stems from
the two deities (*Kritias* 109c–d).

Plato recounts all this in the course of describing the greatest of early battles, the Athenian defeat of the inhabitants of imperialist Atlantis, which was shortly thereafter destroyed by earthquake (*Ti.* 24e–25d). I think that the east frieze of the temple of Hephaistos and Athena may portray this mythic battle,[87] observed by the gods and fought by opponents wielding large boulders against others wearing chlamydes and exomides, a garment commonly associated with workmen and the god Hephaistos himself. Unfortunately, there is no iconographic parallel to which we could compare the east frieze for confirmation, which, it is important to note, is also true of the fight of Theseus against the Pallantids, the conventional reading of the frieze. No other ancient author recounts the Atlantis myth, which has suggested to some scholars that Plato invented the myth.[88] If this is so, then the suggestion made here must be discarded because of Plato's fourth-century B.C. date. But it is worth noting that there is visual evidence for myths that have no written corollary (Exekias' Attic black-figure amphora of Ajax and Achilles gaming, for which there is no correspondence in ancient literature, immediately comes to mind[89]), and while it may be unusual to have only one written survival of a myth, this does not automatically mean that the single source was its inventor, that is, that it did not exist in some earlier form now lost to us. In any case, the evidence from the temple itself and Plato's association of the temple, the city's soldiers, Athena, and Hephaistos in the course of recounting the battle of Atlantis against Athens are highly suggestive.

In the west frieze, Centaurs flanking Kaineus hammer the Lapith into the earth with boulders, a curious inversion of the birth of Erichthonios from the earth, which was depicted within the temple. This juxtaposition points up the contrast between the unruly Centaurs, who use base raw materials as weapons, and the techne of the gods Hephaistos and Athena, who together forge a marvel, a civilized being sprung from the earth, the first Athenian, and consequently all his Athenian descendants.

If the Hephaisteion's east frieze does portray the Athenian victory over Atlantis, it is plausible that the central figure could be intended as Theseus, although he is not named as a fighter in Plato's account of this battle. The temple's imagery then would share a thematic focus on the exemplary deeds of Theseus, the champion of the Athenian democracy and model ephebe, together with Herakles, the great Panhellenic hero, and the Athenian victory over the greatest of its early opponents. Read in their physical and social context, such a conglomeration of myths is especially suited to this temple to Hephaistos and Athena, the mythological forbearers of the Athenians and chief deities of techne, whose production includes new citizens, who participated in the civic workings of Athens in the nearby buildings in the Agora.

Like the sculptures on the Temple of Zeus at Olympia that refer to local events and history, those on the Hephaisteion also are closely linked to Athenian history, politics, and the immediate environs. Theseus, the Athenian hero par excellence, is emphasized on the temple's north and south metopes, and also in the Centauromachy of the west frieze. But whereas the Centauromachy at Olympia is notable for its many "firsts" – the first use of this myth in architectural sculpture; its prominence and scale; the inclusion of women, who play such a prominent role at Olympia as both spectators and participants in the Heraia; the quotation of athletic poses from Olympic sports – the Hephaisteion's version of the Centauromachy – in this case, not the Thessalian wedding – is its opposite in every respect: it is much smaller, in a less prominent location – corresponding to the placement of the Herakles metopes at Olympia – and it excludes women. It does, however, directly quote the pose of the Tyrannicide Harmodios, which was easily visible in bronze in the Agora below, and in this sense, the two renditions of the myth share the characteristic of visually relating to their immediate physical context. But Perithoos and Theseus at Olympia also adopt Harmodios' pose. Why? It is likely that the Tyrannicides sculptural group in the Agora was influential on the poses of the two protagonists in the Olympia Centauromachy, but one does not have to assume a purely one-way stream of influence from Athens to Olympia, which some scholars have done in suggesting that the painting of the Centauromachy in the Theseion was the direct inspiration for the Olympia pediment. Instead, while the Tyrannicides poses may have been borrowed from Athens, it seems likely that the Panhellenic Olympia composition was the prototype for many subsequent Centauromachies, including the Parthenon metopes, where women are included. What is curious is that, save for the Tyrannicide pose, the Hephaisteion's Centauromachy is remarkably old-fashioned in composition, eschewing the complex intertwining compositions used at Olympia, omitting Apollo (another local Olympian reference), and instead including the

Kaineus episode, a first for sculpture, but possessing a lengthy history in the Attic vase painting tradition.

Herakles, athletic exemplar and son of Zeus, occupies the Olympian temple's twelve metopes but also the ten metopes of the east façade – the dominant façade – of the Hephaisteion. Athenian efforts to claim Herakles as their own, to assimilate him into the Attic orbit, already are evident at the Athenian Treasury at Delphi (Figs. 85–91),[90] which, like the later Hephaisteion, places its most prominent sculptures in the optimal vantage point for the intended viewer. Surely Herakles' prominence at the Battle of Marathon in c. 490 also contributed to his emphatic presence on the Treasury, which was erected just after this Greek victory. Although Herakles was widely worshipped in Attika already by the sixth century B.C.,[91] his special prominence on the Hephaisteion in the Agora may also be connected with the victory at Marathon, where athletic games were held in his honor already by the early fifth century,[92] and the Athenians' claimed preeminence in that outcome; we have already noted his presence in the Stoa Poikile painting of that theme.

It is impossible to determine the east frieze's battle subject with any certainty, but Plato's description of the location of the temple to Athena and Hephaistos sounds remarkably similar to the Hephaisteion, and a depiction of the battle between Athens and the inhabitants of Atlantis would certainly be in keeping with other elements of the Hephaisteion, such as its cult statues, that refer to the early, legendary history of the city.

CHAPTER FOUR

MYTH AND RELIGION AT DELPHI

Earlier chapters of this text dealt with temples in Olympia and Athens. Chapter 4 examines one of the other great sanctuaries and athletic loci of the ancient world: Delphi (Fig. 107), famous throughout the Mediterranean world for its oracle. Unlike the other sculpture discussed thus far, the sculpture of the fourth-century B.C. Temple of Apollo at Delphi did not present mythological narratives to the many visitors to Delphi but instead depicted hieratic images of Apollo, Dionysos, and their respective followers. This curious departure from the usual practice requires some explanation, which lies in the political and religious nature of Delphi, both in the fourth century and in the past. Delphi's oracle and its political clout set this sanctuary apart from Olympia and Athens, and the monuments erected at Delphi reflect this.

The Greeks viewed Delphi as the center of the world, the omphalos, and it is scarcely surprising that they did so considering its spectacular mountainous beauty. The Panhellenic site of Delphi was famed for its musical contests, its athletic games, the Pythian games, held every four years after 586 B.C. to commemorate Apollo's slaying of the Python, and especially its oracle,[1] the mouthpiece of the god Apollo, to whom the large sanctuary is dedicated (a second, smaller sanctuary is sacred to Athena Pronaia). At Delphi, Apollo was regarded as healer and purifier and was worshipped in the main temple from at least the late seventh century B.C. (Figs. 108, 109). This emphasis on the oracle rather than the Pythian games distinguishes Delphi from Olympia, which also had an

107. Delphi, aerial view. Photo: A. Loxias, Athens.

oracle, but where the main focus was always on the celebrated athletic events. Politics played a big role at both sites, but the special potency of the oracle inspired Panhellenic political struggles and displays of an extraordinary kind. Delphi received numerous offerings from cities and rulers, both Greek and foreign, such as Kroisos of Lydia. Beginning in the sixth century B.C., Greek poleis erected and aggressively used structures and sculptural monuments to make claims and counterclaims against each other. Olympia had a row of treasuries, which may have striven for prominence in their basically parallel placement on the largely even Kronos Hill (Figs. 3, 5, 6); at Delphi, poleis jockeyed for position along the switchbacks and sharply rising terrain of the Sacred Way leading

108. Delphi, Temple of Apollo from northwest. Photo: H. R. Goette.

to the Temple of Apollo, one of the most intriguing of ancient temples (Figs. 107, 108, 109). Not only does it have a lengthy and complex
archaeological history, but unlike most other Greek temples, it also has
a mythological pedigree that describes past incarnations of the temple's
structure in what we would term unconventional materials: laurel, feathers and wax, and bronze.[2]

The remains that we see today mark the sixth temple on the site if
we take the testimony of ancient authors at face value and count three
more fantastic predecessors, and it is the third archaeologically attested
structure. Epigraphical documents and literary evidence clearly place the
extant temple in the third quarter of the fourth century B.C. While details
of the temple's plan are disputed, its general layout is clear, and the fragmentary pedimental sculptures have been found and reconstructed with
a fair degree of certainty (Figs. 108–113). The pediments are remarkable
in two respects: the combination of their subjects is radically new in
Greek sculpture, yet these later-fourth-century pediments of the temple
of Apollo possess strikingly old-fashioned compositions. Why does the

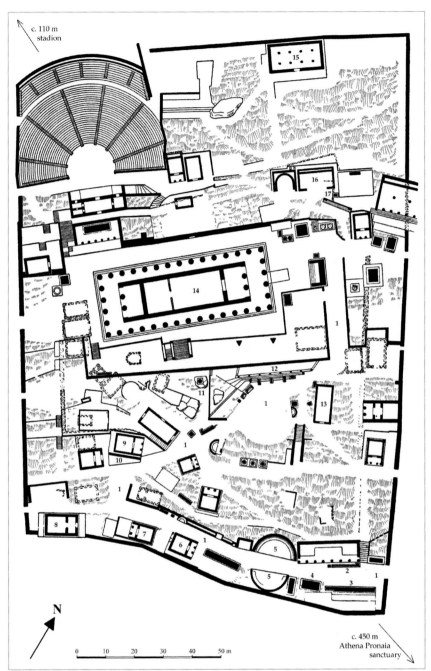

1. Sacred Way - 2. Base of the Arcadians - 3. Posited position of Base I of Marathon - 4. Argive Offering - 5. Argive Dedication of Rulers and Epigones - 6. Sikyonian Treasury - 7. Siphnian Treasury - 8. Theban Treasury - 9. Athenian Treasury - 10. Base II of Marathon - 11. Naxian Sphinx - 12. Portico of the Athenians - 13. Corinthian Treasury - 14. Temple of Apollo - 15. Lesche of the Knidians - 16. Daochos Monument - 17. Akanthos Column

109. Delphi, Sanctuary of Apollo, plan. Reproduced and adapted from P. de la Coste-Messelière and G. de Miré, *Delphes* (Paris 1943) 317.

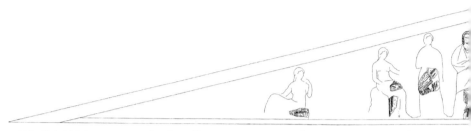

110. Delphi Museum, Temple of Apollo, c. 330 B.C., east pediment, reconstruction by F. Croissant. Drawing: École Française d'Athènes.

sculpture look as it does, and what does the choice of subjects signify? Who selected the themes, what did the patrons have in mind, and what meanings were available to contemporary viewers? How do earlier monuments influence the siting, design, thematic significance, and reception of the temple? This chapter will address these questions. A close examination of the sculptures and their historical circumstances reveals that the sculptures' compositions and subjects were driven by contemporary politics and the desire to stress an old, well-established, and special relationship between Athens and Delphi – the worship of Dionysos on

111. Delphi, Temple of Apollo, c. 330 B.C., east pediment. Photo: H. R. Goette.

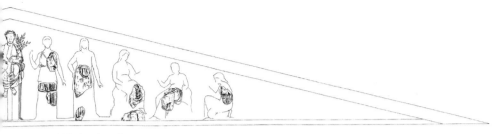

110 *(continued)*

Mt. Parnassos at Delphi by Thyiades from Athens and Delphi, and the
shared worship of Apollo and Dionysos at Delphi.[3] This Athenian-led
effort was designed to underscore Athenian leadership in the Greek world
and their dominance at Delphi, a visual and political battleground in the
face of the contemporary and very real Macedonian threat. The temple's
ornament was one play in a tit for tat power and public relations struggle
between Athens on the one hand, and its rivals and enemies on the other,
which is clearly traceable in the contemporary military and religious
dedications surrounding the temple. An even broader view reveals that
the fourth-century temple is but one in a line of Athenian monuments,
stretching back to the sixth century, that endeavor to assert Athenian
power at Delphi and within the Amiphictyonic League, the collective
body of Greek poleis that governed the sanctuary of Delphi and its vast
territorial and financial holdings.

Inscribed building accounts and literary sources attest that the fourth-
century temple replaced a late sixth-century B.C. predecessor after an
earthquake in 373/2 followed by a landslide.[4] The reconstruction was
undertaken by the Amphictyonic League, which raised funds by taxa-
tion and gifts from numerous of its member cities; additional funds
came from Phocis, which had to pay reparations for their actions in the
Third Sacred War (356–346 B.C.), which had interrupted the construction
of the temple. The accounts indicate that the lion-head spouts for the
gutter were in place in 340/339, which provides a terminus ante quem
for the date when the pediments' compositions had to be approved by
the *naopai*,[5] the overseers of the temple's construction, and also a terminus post quem for the exterior metopes. The architectural structure,
the frame, was finished in 334/3, and the pedimental sculpture finally
completed in 327/6.[6]

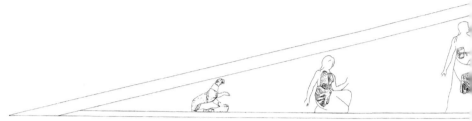

112. Delphi Museum, Temple of Apollo, c. 330 B.C., west pediment, reconstruction by F. Croissant. Drawing: École Française d'Athènes.

Measuring 21.64 × 58.18 m at the lowest step, the 6 × 15 temple incorporated part of the foundations of its late sixth-century predecessor and was constructed of limestone, conglomerate, stuccoed tufa, and marble. Metopes once were placed over the pronaos and opisthodomos, six per side, as was the case of the earlier temple of Zeus at Olympia. The two pediments, each approximately 18.5 m long and 2.3 m high, were decorated with Pentelic marble sculpture.[7] Pausanias (10.19.4) describes

113. Delphi, Temple of Apollo, c. 330 B.C., west pediment. Photo: H. R. Goette.

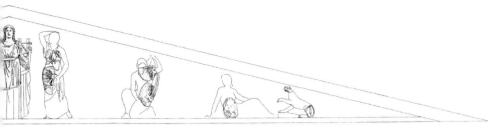

112 *(continued)*

the subjects: Artemis, Leto, Apollo, and the Muses, and Dionysos and the Thyiades, and names two Athenians as the sculptors (Praxias and Androsthenes). Approximately 147 fragments have been recovered and attributed to the pediments,[8] and 18 of the approximately 26 figures that once filled the two pediments have been identified.[9] The reconstruction of the two compositions has been controversial, but the most recent attempt is by the French scholar Francis Croissant, published in 2003.[10] All of the fragments cannot be accounted for, but what Croissant conjectures is the following: in the east, Apollo sits on a tripod and is flanked by two standing females, surely his sister, Artemis, and his mother, Leto, while additional women, presumably the Muses, stand or sit on rocks (Figs. 110, 111). Nearly all figures, particularly the central figures, are frontal and still. On the west, Dionysos, wearing a mitra and originally carrying a kithara in his left arm,[11] stands at center,[12] and his female worshippers, the Thyiades, identified by the animal skins they wear, stand, flanking him.[13] A few kneeling Thyiades and one reclining Thyiad fill out the pediments to the corners, where panthers raise one paw toward the center of the composition (Figs. 112, 113). While this reconstruction may not be without controversy, the argument presented here does not depend on the fine details of the reconstruction.

These quiet, static, largely frontal compositions are striking for their time. Contemporary pedimental sculpture elsewhere in Greece features energetic battle scenes, as at the Temple of Asklepios at Epidauros of c. 380, where the sack of Troy and the Amazonomachy are depicted with kinetically active and dramatically posed figures (Figs. 114, 115).[14] Likewise, the few remaining heads from the Temple of Athena Alea at Tegea of c. 345, closer in date to our temple, betray energy and drama in the sharp turns of their heads and the deep-set

114. Epidauros, Temple of Asklepios, c. 380 B.C., west pediment, Amazonomachy. Photo: H. R. Goette.

eyes beneath furrowed brows (Figs. 116, 117). By contrast, the Delphic pediments look stiff, old-fashioned, and conservative. Croissant is one of the few scholars who comment on the Delphi pediments' compositions, but goes no further than observing that they are not actual narratives but emblematic epiphanies of the two deities.[15] This, too, is unusual: unlike all the other structures examined in this text thus far, the sculpture adorning the main temple of this key sanctuary in the Greek world does not depict mythological *narratives* in which some event or action takes place, and this fact also distinguishes the temple

115. Epidauros, Temple of Asklepios, c. 380 B.C., east pediment, Ilioupersis, Priam. Photo: H. R. Goette.

114 *(continued)*

from many of the other, earlier structures at Delphi. These included archaic buildings whose sculptural decoration anticipates or resonates with that of the archaic Temple of Apollo and with each other, e.g., the Siphnian Treasury frieze of c. 530–525 B.C., decorated with the Gigantomachy, the theme of the west pediment of the sixth-century Temple of Apollo at Delphi; the Athenian Treasury of c. 490 B.C. with sculpted metopes showing deeds of Theseus and Herakles (Figs. 85–91), who features in the Gigantomachy on the Siphnian Treasury and the Temple of Apollo and on the Siphnian Treasury's east pediment, which portrayed the struggle between Herakles and Apollo over the Delphic tripod. In these structures, myth refers to Apollo's claims to the oracular shrine, to Athenian prowess, to the stunning victory of the gods over

116. Tegea, Temple of Athena Alea, east pediment. Photo: H. R. Goette.

117. Tegea, Temple of Athena Alea, c. 345 B.C., west pediment. Photo: H. R. Goette.

118. St. Petersburg, Hermitage Museum St. 1807, Attic red-figure kalyx krater, Apollo and Dionysos. Photo: The State Hermitage Museum, St. Petersburg.

the giants, all mythological combats or struggles; as we have seen, this is a leitmotif of Greek temple decoration. The fourth-century temple of Apollo, however, eschews these time-honored compositions in favor of largely static, divine epiphanies.

Remarkably, however, the combination of subjects is utterly *new* in monumental sculpture. It is true that Dionysos shared worship with Apollo at Delphi, and this had been the case for decades, as attested by fifth- and fourth-century vase painting,[16] such as an Attic red-figure kalyx krater of the early fourth century B.C. attributed to the Kadmos Painter, which depicts the two deities shaking hands above the omphalos at Delphi (Fig. 118).[17] And there are more such vase paintings of the late fifth and fourth centuries B.C.[18] The association of the two deities also is attested in fifth-century literature: the only verse to survive of Euripides'

Lykymnios refers to Bacchos, friend of laurel, who is saluted as "Paian Apollo of the melodious lyre,"[19] and Bacchylides composed a dithyramb (16) for performance at Delphi. Numerous passages of fifth-century drama specifically place Dionysos and Dionysiac rites *at Delphi*: for example, the Pythia's prayer at Aischylos' *Eumenides* 22–26 mentions Bromios, who reigns at the Corycian cave; Aristophanes' *Clouds* 603–606 has Dionysos dance with bacchantes at night on Mt. Parnassos at Delphi; the chorus in Sophokles' *Antigone* 1146–1152 addresses Dionysos and speaks of the Thyiades, who dance frenetically and celebrate all night at the Corycian cave;[20] and Euripides associates Dionysos with Mt. Parnassos on four occasions.[21]

Scholars also have noted that the sculpted Dionysos adopts the characteristic attributes of Apollo – the mitra and high-girt chiton, a kithara – as if Dionysos were likened to, or assimilated with, Apollo,[22] who is shown seated on the symbol of his oracle, the tripod (Figs. 111, 119).[23] Their female followers, the Muses with Apollo and the Thyiades with Dionysos, are distinctive in their dress (the Thyiades, for example, wear animal skins, Fig. 120) and demeanor (the Muses sit on rocks),[24] suggesting that these are, in fact, two distinct deities, yet the similarity in their appearance and bearing is striking.

Dionysos had not previously been prominent in the sanctuary's visual decoration;[25] in fact, Dionysos had *never* before featured as the central and starring figure of a pedimental composition anywhere in Greece known to us.[26] For an ancient Greek visitor to the sanctuary, the choice must have seemed extraordinary. What can explain the pediments' strange combination of innovative subject with old-fashioned composition?

Scholars traditionally argue that the similar appearance of Apollo and Dionysos reflects a new religious development in which Dionysos was assimilated to Apollo, or explain the presence of Dionysos here as a result of contemporary religious concerns or the popularity of the theater.[27] For example, Strauss Clay posits a connection between the temple's combination of Dionysos and Apollo, and the contemporary growth of theater as distinct from religion, and argues that the gods' similar appearance expresses the Delphic authorities' anxiety that Dionysos' popularity might overshadow that of Apollo.[28] Croissant suggests the integration of

119. Delphi Museum 1344+2380, Temple of Apollo, c. 330 B.C., west pediment, Dionysos.
Photo: Ph. Collet, École Française d'Athènes.

the Athenian Dionysos type to Delphic Apollonian religion in the fourth
century and stresses the importance of theater and Dionysos to fourth-
century Athens. In his view, the Delphic fourth-century pediments are
in keeping with Lykourgos' local religious politics.[29] While the growing
influence of theater and Dionysos in the fourth century may be a partial
explanation, I wish to argue that the primary motivation lies in contemporary Panhellenic politics: an Athenian effort to stress their special

120. Delphi Museum 21272, Temple of Apollo, c. 330 B.C., west pediment, Thyiad. Photo: H. R. Goette.

relationship with Delphi through a well-known and long-established religious connection as part of a campaign to assert Athenian dominance at Delphi and in the Greek world in light of the imminent threat from Macedonia, which was clear to the Athenians after 343.[30]

121. Delphi, Temple of Apollo, c. 510 B.C. east pediment. Photo: H. R. Goette.

Delphi's many monuments, both individual and governmentally sanc-
tioned, largely attest to military victories and fealty to Apollo, whose favor
was sought and often received for political and military endeavors, and
this is especially true from the late sixth century B.C. on. One such example of this is the immediate predecessor of the fourth-century temple of
Apollo, the late sixth-century temple, which was constructed c. 515–510
to replace *its* predecessor, which had burned in 548/7 (Figs. 21, 51, 121,
122).[31] The 6 × 15 Doric limestone structure was adorned with sculpted
pediments, 19.34 m long and 2.29 m high at the center. The reconstructed
fragments indicate that the west had an energetic Gigantomachy in limestone, akin to those on the Megarian Treasury at Olympia (Figs. 23, 24)
and in one of the pediments of the Old Temple of Athena on the Athenian
Akropolis of c. 510 (Fig. 52):[32] gods moving outward from the center,
combating giants who fall into the corners, where a snake and lion attack

122. Delphi, Temple of Apollo, c. 510 B.C. west pediment. Photo: H. R. Goette.

them, while Zeus and another deity stand in a frontal chariot in the center, overseeing the fray (one might think of the later west pediment of the Temple of Zeus at Olympia, where Apollo exhorted the Lapiths to defeat the Centaurs, Figs. 10 and 11). The east pediment had a static composition of Apollo and perhaps his sister Artemis standing in a frontal quadriga, and attendant figures flanking them – three females on one side, three males on the other – with animal combats – a lion attacking a stag, a lion attacking a bull – in the corners. The east pediment figures were all of Parian marble, a special commission of the Alkmaionid family of Athens, as Herodotos tells us (5.62; *FGrH* 328 F115), who sought – and received – the favor of the Delphic oracle, which advised the Spartans to aid the Alkmaionidai, exiled under the tyranny in Athens. Sparta obliged and, together with the Alkmaionidai, drove out the tyrant Hippias from Athens in 510. Philochoros (*FGrH* 328 F115) indicates that the Alkmaionidai rebuilt the burnt temple as a gesture of gratitude to Apollo after they defeated the Peisistratids.

While it may not be so surprising that the east pediment of the Alkmaionid temple is the same subject – an epiphany of Apollo – as that on the subsequent fourth-century temple, it is remarkable for our purposes that the fourth-century east pediment – and also the west pediment with Dionysos – echo the old-fashioned stiffness of their illustrious sixth-century predecessor, and I think that this is no coincidence. The sixth-century temple was constructed with Athenian patronage and, to judge from the workmanship, by Athenian craftsmen,[33] and its west pediment has a composition similiar to, and with the same theme as, a contemporary temple in Athens. Athenians played a prominent role in the construction of the fourth-century structure: the sculptors were Athenians, many of the builders and specialized craftsmen of the temple itself were Athenians,[34] and the sculptures are made of Pentelic marble, which comes from Mt. Penteli just outside ancient Athens, now a suburb of the modern city (the entire Parthenon is constructed of Pentelic marble). Athens was the only city to have a permanent voice in the Amphictyony,[35] and in that capacity, made special efforts to secure funding for the rebuilding of the temple, as attested by their honorific decree of 368 in which the Athenians – not the Amphictyony – thank Dionysius I of Syracuse for his donation to the temple fund.[36] In other words, the compositions on the fourth-century building were carefully chosen to echo the east pediment of the sixth-century temple to emphasize Athens' long-term association with the central temple of this sanctuary.[37]

Did the Athenians have a controlling voice in the choice of pedimental themes, as well? The Delphic naopai, which included representatives from Athens, surely would have had to approve any thematic choices, and it is entirely plausible that Athens was able to determine choices through money and political maneuvering, especially in light of their involvement with the past history of the temple and their status as a strong power until 338, just after the time when the pedimental designs had to have been finalized.[38]

The Thyiades' worship on Mt. Parnassos is a further link between Athens and Delphi. Our written sources for the Thyiades are few and late – Pausanias and Plutarch – and they indicate that only Athens and Delphi participate in this rite at Delphi;[39] indeed, Pausanias is very specific in saying that the Thyiades are Attic women (10.4.3), who dance in the company of women from Delphi and celebrate the orgia, the rites, of Dionysos on Mt. Parnassos. The Attic Thyiades are not known elsewhere; Villanueva Puig posits that the Athenian Thyiades are a group similar to that which existed at Delphi in Pausanias' time.[40] We cannot know when the first Athenian women went to Delphi as Thyiades,[41] but Henrichs places the joint worship of Athenian and Delphian Thyiades on Mt. Parnassos by the mid-fifth century at the latest because of literary evidence mentioning such rites.[42] Ironically, it was during the time of the temple's construction that the cult of the Muses at Delphi went into some decline.[43]

Athenian sculptors, Athenian marble, partial Athenian funding, the inclusion of the Thyiades, and the Athenian sponsorship of the earlier temple speak in favor of Athenian dominance in the choice of the fourth-century temple's pedimental themes, which, I believe, were intended to assert Athens' claims to primacy both in the sanctuary at Delphi and in the Greek world more generally speaking.

Further indication of this flexing of Athenian muscles is an incident in c. 339, which, as already noted, is the terminus ante quem for the decision concerning the pedimental themes: the Athenians provoked the Thebans by renewing a dedication of gold or gilt shields taken from the Persians at Plataia, which they erected in the blank exterior metopes on the north side of the temple of Apollo, together with a dedicatory inscription that stated that the spoils came from the Medes and the Thebans, who colluded with them.[44] According to contemporary authors, this gesture was orchestrated by an anti-Theban faction in Athens and was intended to ruin the possibility of an Athenian–Theban alliance, which was being promoted by Demosthenes, against Philip II of Macedon,[45] who, in this scenario, is equated with the Persian enemy. Athens, in fact, had good reason to be suspicious of Thebes, which had invited Philip II to win Hellenic status by carrying out the will of Apollo, which, according to Thebes, was to destroy Phocis, in the Third Sacred War (356–346). Philip obliged. According to the Athenian orator Aischines, the Athenians erred in making this religious dedication – they apparently put up the shields before the religious ceremony itself – which was a sacrilege. The Thebans had their revenge: at the gathering of the Amphictyony of the following year, the Thebans asked that the Athenians be fined 50 talents for their impiety.[46] While the Athenians may have had to pay a price for their strategy, it is clear from this account that the Athenians were already in a strong position in the Amphictyony: they could never have put up the shields – much less on the main temple in the sanctuary – without official Amphictyonic approval.[47]

Political maneuvering using visual means at Delphi was not new, nor was it the first or last time Athens would play a primary role. If we briefly review other, earlier Athenian monuments at Delphi, we can see that the Temple's sculptures were part of a long-established Athenian practice of offering sumptuous structures and monuments in order to ingratiate themselves with the god and his powerful oracle and to claim a special leadership role in the Hellenic world (Figs. 107, 109). For the visitor to the temple in the fourth century,[48] the conventional route would be up the Sacred Way, past the earlier treasuries and monuments, including the Marathon Base dedicated by the Athenians, which was among the first monuments a fourth-century visitor to the site would have encountered.[49] Its exact placement is unknown, but Pausanias' account (10.10.1–2) suggests that it was toward the entrance of the sanctuary, where later, several other military thank offerings from Sparta, Argos, and Arkadia, modeled after the Marathon Base – and designed to challenge and outdo it – were placed.[50] Pausanias tells us that the base was a dedication to celebrate the victory at Marathon. No certain blocks of this monument can be ascertained, though several possibilities have been suggested.[51] Pausanias relates that the Athenians erected the monument to celebrate the victory at Marathon, and this probably occurred in the second quarter of the fifth century B.C.: its over-life-size bronze statues included Apollo, the Athenian general Miltiades, victor at Marathon, being crowned by Athena, and the Athenian eponymous heroes.[52] This is the earliest attested portrayal of Athens' ten eponymous heroes, who were, according to legend, selected with the help of the Delphic oracle.[53] Surely the statue of Miltiades could only be placed here among the gods after his death, and since Pausanias tells us that the sculptor was Pheidias, the monument was probably created sometime in the second quarter of the fifth century B.C., maybe at the instigation of Miltiades' son, Kimon,[54] after his own victory over the Persians at Eurymedon in 465.[55] It is noteworthy that this appearance – perhaps the earliest portrayal of the heroes – takes place at Delphi, not in Athens, and the purpose of this portrayal is to honor the victory at Marathon in a Panhellenic sanctuary (so seen by everyone), to honor Miltiades' role in it, and to exalt Miltiades to the ranks of the eponymous heroes and gods.[56]

As the visitor approached the first bend in the path, yet another Athenian monument was prominently situated to catch the visitors' attention: the Parian marble Athenian Treasury, built just after the Battle of Marathon in 490 (Figs. 85–91).[57] This monument has been discussed at some length in Chapter 3 in the context of the sculptures on the Hephaisteion in Athens, which share many features with those on the treasury. It might be useful to compare the labors of Herakles shown on the Athenian Treasury with those on the Temple of Zeus at Olympia, another Panhellenic sanctuary (Figs. 13, 14, 16). As noted in Chapter 1, the inclusion of the Augean stables and Stymphalian birds labors on the Temple of Zeus at Olympia seemed to refer to local interests; these labors are nowhere to be seen on the Athenian Treasury (nor on the Hephaisteion). Other labors, regardless of where they were imagined to have taken place, seem to possess Panhellenic appeal, such as the Nemean lion or Keryneian hind. So far as we can tell from the extant remains (some metopes survive to only a very small degree), the Hydra, Augean Stables, and Stymphalian birds, Kerberos, the Cretan bull, the Erymanthian boar, and the Apples of the Hesperides are not depicted on the Athenian Treasury (or on the Hephaisteion). Instead, one sees

Herakles' fights with the Centaur Pholos and with Kyknos, and his rustling the cattle of Geryon, which stretches over three metopes before concluding in the battle with Geryon in two. Scholars have posited that the emphasis on the Geryon tale, which also sometimes includes the adventure with Pholos, may be related to Delphi's role in the founding of western colonies,[58] but such an explanation defies logic when one recalls that Athens, the patron of the treasury, was not a colonizing power in the archaic period. The sculpted pediments survive only in poor condition: on the east was a frontal group of figures – Athena in the center flanked by Herakles and Theseus – between two chariots; on the west, a fighting group.[59] This is the very first occasion when these two heroes are depicted on the same monument, and the use of Herakles on this building, together with Theseus, suggests an Athenian attempt to claim Herakles, a Panhellenic hero, as the Athenians' own.[60]

Another Athenian monument lies just next to the treasury: a base that once held sculptures (first ten, later thirteen after an extension of the base) juts out from the southern foundations of the Treasury (Figs. 85, 86). It bears a fragmentary inscription, which is noted by Pausanias (10.11.5) and indicates that the base and the sculptures on it were an Athenian dedication from the spoils of Marathon, so the base must date after 490.[61] Were the base and treasury planned as a single monument after Marathon? Recent study has revealed that the base actually extends from the foundations not only on the south but also on the west; the front horizontal slabs of the base, that is, the slabs that bear the inscription, appear to have been added later. This evidence confounds the date of the Athenian Treasury and this base, but there is no question as to the patrons of both monuments.

Just beyond the Treasury, en route to the temple, is the Stoa or Portico of the Athenians, a dedication by the Athenians as indicated by the inscription written on the stylobate, which states that the dedication of the stoa and weapons and a ship's prow were spoils from a naval victory (Fig. 123). Although we do not know precisely which battle was commemorated here, it is thought that it was a campaign against the Persians, and some have suggested that Kimon dedicated the prows and ropes from victories against the Persians in 479/8, when he pursued these enemies out of Greece and back to Asia.[62] The Ionic Parian marble stoa

123. Delphi, Stoa of the Athenians. Photo: author.

was 31.60 m long and had a depth of 3.73 m, with seven columns to carry
the wooden entablature, so this was an imposing structure.

These earlier structures, especially focused on the battle of Marathon,
were intended to demonstrate Athens' leadership role in this spectacular
victory over the Persians, and more generally speaking, to underscore
Athens' hegemony in the mid-fifth century b.c.[63] If we round the bend
to the Temple of Apollo and the monuments nearby and fast forward to
the fourth century, we can see a similar pattern: monuments responding
to each other, with notable roles played by Athens and – in the fourth
century – Macedonia.

In 338, Greek losses against Philip at Chaironeia were shared by
Thebes, which, in the end, joined the Athenians in resisting him. At Delphi in 338–334 b.c., Daochos of Pharsalos, a Thessalian hieromnemon on
the Amphictyonic Council from 338–334, erected a limestone base just
over 11 m, on which stood eight Parian marble statues above inscribed
blocks, which described the deeds and achievements of the family of
Daochos (Figs. 109, 124–126).[64] Daochos was loyal to Philip II, and
the monument was a thank offering from Macedonia to Apollo, who

124. Delphi Museum, Daochos Monument, c. 338–334 B.C. Photo: Ph. Collet, École Française d'Athènes.

appeared, seated and playing a lyre, on this monument.[65] Arranged before him from left to right were the most recent family members to the most ancient ancestors of Daochos.[66] Daochos' family members shown together in the presence of a god might seem remarkable, but in its use of celebrated mortals in divine company, the Daochos Base clearly was intended to echo an earlier predecessor, the Athenian Marathon Base near the entrance to the sanctuary. But the Daochos Monument endeavors to rival, perhaps even to surpass, its model by ranking *Daochos'* own ancestors – not legendary figures – as heroes and placing them in the company of Apollo and furthermore, strives to rebut Athens' claims to greatness in celebrating the victory at Chaironeia, in which the Athenians were

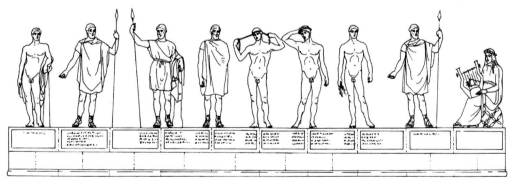

125. Delphi, Daochos Monument, c. 338–334 B.C. Reconstruction by A. F. Stewart, drawing by C. Smith.

126. Delphi, Town Hall, Model of Apollo sanctuary. Photo: H. R. Goette.

severely trounced. It is useful to recall that the Philippeion at Olympia, discussed in Chapter 1, was being constructed at the very same time (Figs. 3, 6); there, too, the emphasis is on exalting living leaders to a higher realm, although in the Philippeion (unlike the Daochos Monument), gods are absent, and only living family members are shown. But the intention to elevate them to the ranks of the gods is made clear by their material gilding or chryselephantine, if we can believe Pausanias, that is, materials reserved for divine images, and their isolation in a structure in the Altis at Olympia.

This bid for Macedonian supremacy at Delphi did not go unchecked. Perhaps even before the Daochos Monument was completed in c. 334, the Athenians began work on a towering akanthos column just to the northeast of the temple (Figs. 109, 126–128). When it was dedicated in c. 330, probably at the Pythiad,[67] the 9-m-high column of Pentelic marble

127. Delphi, Akanthos Monument, c. 334–330 B.C. Photo: c. Ph. Collet, École Française d'Athènes.

128. Delphi, Akanthos Monument, c. 334–330 B.C. reconstruction. Drawing: Ph. Collet, École Française d'Athènes.

towered over all the surrounding monuments, save the temple, which was in its last stages of construction, and partially blocked the view of the Daochos base,[68] thus diminishing its impact.[69] Toward the top of the column, three female dancers, wearing kalathiskoi on their heads, swirl around the support for a tripod.[70] The raised arms of the dancers seemed to suspend the tripod cauldron above them, bringing the original height of the whole monument to 13–14 m.[71] A fragmentary inscription on the base identifies the donors as the demos of the Athenians τοῦ δήμου] τοῦ Ἀθηναίων, in the genitive,[72] and a partial inscription of ΠΑΝ..., restored as Pankrates of Argos, helps to date the column, since we know from building accounts that Pankrates also worked on the fourth-century temple, which, by now, was nearing completion.[73] The identity of the figures is unknown, though three Thyiades and the three daughters of Kekrops, an early king of Athens, have been suggested, the latter because of the Athenian sponsorship.[74]

In the midst of this landscape of claim and counterclaim stood the centerpiece of the sanctuary, the temple to Apollo, which was rebuilt and decorated anew in the fourth century with Apollo and his Muses on the east pediment, and Dionysos, god of theater in the guise of the poetic/musical Apollo,[75] together with his Thyiades, in the west pediment. The visual merging of the two gods is paralleled in contemporary literature: a hymn commissioned from Philodamos of Skarpheia in c. 340–339 B.C. – just when work on the pediments was beginning – to celebrate the Theoxenia, a Delphic festival.[76] The hymn welcomes Dionysos to Apollo's sanctuary at Delphi and, extraordinarily, employs the paian form traditionally associated with Apollo.[77] According to Philodamos, the Muses, crowned with Dionysiac ivy, dance a circular dance in Dionysos' honor, and Dionysos is referred to as a god of healing; this circular dance conjures up images of the dithyramb usually associated with Dionysos but not the Apollonine Muses.[78] In short, Philodamos' hymn mixes the two deities' traditionally separate realms and merges Dionysos with Apollo.[79] Scholars, in fact, have wondered if Philodamos' hymn and the pediments were conceived in tandem, since they accord thematically – Dionysiac and Apollonine imagery fuse.[80] This is unlikely, since the final planning for the pediments' themes and compositions would have to have been settled several years before their installation.

But the poem says more, whose significance has been overlooked by scholars:

> O blessed be that generation of mortals
> O happy that race of men
> Which build an ageless,
> Ever-inviolate shrine for Lord Apollo!
> Cry "Io Bacchus, Ie Paian!"
> A golden temple with golden statues.
> (Translation: A. Stewart)

> Ὦ μάκαρ ὀλβία τε
> κείνων γε[νεὰ] βροτῶν ἀγήρων
> ἀμίαντον ἃ κτίσηι
> ναὸ[ν ἄ]νακ[τι] Φοίβωι,
> Εὐοῖ ὦ ἰὸ Βάκχ', ὦ ἰὲ Π[αιάν]·
> χρύσεον χρυσέοις τύποις . . .

Considering the Temple of Apollo's legendary past as first a temple of laurel, then one of wax and feathers, and finally one of bronze, it would not be so strange to hear of a temple of gold, even though no such thing was ever built. The fourth-century temple, with its Athenian sculptors, Athenian marble, and partial Athenian funding, was splendid in its day (for example, building accounts describe payments made for ivory for the monumental door). It was being built just as the hymn was produced in 340/339. It would be perfectly in keeping with an illustrious series of Athenian public monuments at Delphi, designed to invoke Athenian accomplishments, power, and close contact with Delphi. In fact, Pindar, *Pythian* 8, says that the third temple of bronze was constructed by Athena and Hephaistos,[81] the two principal deities of Athens and the gods of techne, implying Athenian responsibility for a third temple on the site, and scholars also have posited that the fourth temple, the precursor to the Alkmaionid temple, was of Athenian workmanship based on the Parian marble rooftiles and other elements of the architecture recovered from this structure, so yet another, earlier, temple seems to be credited to Athens.[82]

Thus, while there can be no certainty about Athenian responsibility for the fourth temple of Apollo at Delphi, given such a lengthy and distinguished pedigree of Athenian patronage, together with the contemporary political situation and the politically charged nature of the site, it seems a plausible hypothesis. It is noteworthy that Athens also dedicated two others buildings at Delphi as the sixth temple of Apollo was being built: a *hoplotheke* just to the west of the temple in c. 332–321, an elaborate display place for captured armor, like the Stoa of the Athenians, and a gymnasion of c. 330 just outside the Athena Pronoia sanctuary,[83] dedicated to Athena, patron goddess of Athens. The gymnasium seems to have been constructed in conjunction with the upcoming Pythian games,[84] which raises the question of whether the push to complete the temple, finally, may have been motivated by the same impulse. Read in its physical and political context, the fourth-century Temple of Apollo appears as a successor to the fifth-century Athenian monuments that trumpeted the Athenian contribution to the fight against the Persian barbarians, but in the fourth century B.C., the threat was much closer and every bit as menacing.

As at Olympia, here at Delphi, architectural and freestanding monuments exhibit a shift from the mythological to the historical, from the heroic past to the heroic present (or recent past) in an effort to liken the human to the heroic. To be sure, mythological narratives continue to decorate large-scale buildings elsewhere, particularly the tombs of rulers of Asia Minor. But rather than relying on proximity to greatness, as depicted on other structures, to make the visual link between historical individual and great hero, the rulers of Asia Minor get right to the point, employing myth on their own monuments to heroize themselves.

CHAPTER FIVE

THE CULT OF THE INDIVIDUAL AND
THE REALM OF THE DEAD

In this chapter, we move from the mainland of Greece to the fringes, which was probably the route followed by Greek sculptors at the end of the fifth and into the fourth centuries B.C. as commissions on the mainland dwindled while those in Asia Minor increased. In Asia Minor, Greek and Near Eastern artistic and religious concerns mingled to produce extraordinary monuments devoted to the commemoration of a single ruler, such as the Nereid Monument at Xanthos in Lycia of c. 390–380 (Fig. 144) or the later Mausoleion at Halikarnassos of c. 360–350 B.C. This chapter examines the Heroon at Gjölbaschi-Trysa of c. 380–370 B.C., a richly decorated tomb for a Lycian dynast (Figs. 129, 130). While this topic may seem a sharp departure from the preceding chapters devoted to temples in large mainland sanctuaries, it offers the opportunity to better delineate our reading of Greek myth and to compare its use and interpretation in an area far from the center of the Classical Greek world, away from the mainland but still under Greek influence. In addition, the Heroon differs from the earlier monuments discussed in that it is funerary art – designed for a private individual though public in its placement.

Mainland Greece had had heroa and temples, but monumental architecture was reserved for deities – historical figures were not usually the subject of worship, though there are exceptions: Olympic victors; heroes, such as Pelops, who had a legendary past, perhaps rooted in history; and Macedonian rulers. The heroon was usually – though not always – constructed over or near the presumed location of the hero's burial: in the case of Pelops, for example, no burial has been found under the Pelopion

129. Vienna, Ephesos-museum, Model of Trysa Heroon. Photo: H. R. Goette.

at Olympia, although written evidence makes it clear that the Greeks regarded this site as his tomb. This eschewal of monumental structures for all but a few can be explained in part because the polis system in the classical period was based on some form of group government, rather than the rule of a single individual. This was not the case in Asia Minor, where the concept of monarchy had a long, deep-rooted history, where sole rulers controlled large territories, and where the practice of ruler cult, in which humans were exalted to the ranks of the divine sometimes before and almost always after death, was a long-standing tradition.

Lycia, the region in which Trysa is located, was under the control of the Persian king in the fourth century, who administered the area by means of local rulers, satraps. Although governed by Persia, Trysa's dynast was clearly interested in Greek culture and art and engaged Greek artists – or at least artists intimately familiar with Greek myths and standard visual compositions – to carve the sculptures adorning his heroon,[1] which almost certainly was begun before his death. The identity of the Trysa dynast is unknown to us. No inscriptions survive to identify the

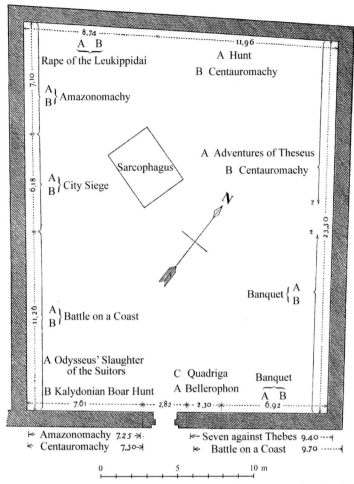

130. Drawing of temenos and frieze themes, Trysa heroon. Reproduced and adapted from O. Benndorf, "Das Heroon von Gjölbaschi-Trysa," *JKSW* 9 (1889) 55, Abb. 37.

deceased or patron, and the date of the monument is established solely on the basis of stylistic comparison of the friezes to other monuments, that is c. 380–370,[2] though some have placed the monument as late as c. 360.[3] The heroon had a polygonal limestone temenos wall (21.65 × 26.54 × 22.70 × 25.50 m), whose southern entrance wall was singled out with more elegant masonry and was the only wall to include a decorated band (Figs. 129, 130).[4] The interior walls and the exterior southern wall were sculpted with superimposed relief friezes (now in the Kunsthistorisches Museum in Vienna).[5] The walls enclosed a landscaped area that included a large sarcophagus for the ruler and his spouse; other, smaller sarcophagi; an altar;[6] a wooden structure for funeral cult in the southeast

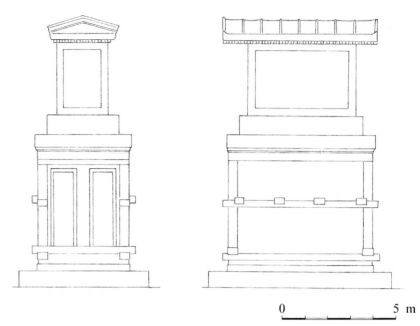

131. Reconstruction of Trysa ruler's sarcophagus. Reproduced and adapted with permission from T. Marksteiner, *Trysa: Eine zentrallykische Niederlassung im Wandel der Zeit* (Vienna, 2002) Abb. 180.

corner; and perhaps yet another structure in the northwest corner.[7] The ruler's rectangular, 7-m-high sarcophagus was placed in the northern portion of the enclosed area and survives only in fragments. It was of two superimposed parts, a common format in the Eastern world: the ruler and perhaps his family were entombed in the upper portion, while the lower portion may have been reserved for slaves or servants (Fig. 131). Its upper shape, in the form of a house, imitates timber construction,[8] and fragmentary sculptured reliefs of three different banqueting scenes have been reconstructed on it: family symposion, male symposion, and funerary banquet.[9] Nearly life-size fragments of three-dimensional fingers from two hands, all of marble, suggest that there may have been cult statues for the ruler and his wife.[10] A necropolis lay outside the precinct to the east, where several other sarcophagi, such as the Dereimis-Aischylos sarcophagus (Kunsthistorisches Museum, Vienna), were found.

The limestone relief friezes, originally painted (a few traces have been detected) and now badly weathered, were arranged in two superimposed tiers at the top of the temenos walls, whose height reaches 3.16 m; the stretch of extant friezes, about 210 m in total length of an original 243 m, is interrupted by the doorway in the southern wall. The placement of

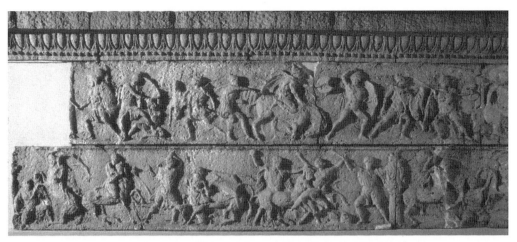

132. Vienna, Kunsthistorisches Museum, Trysa Heroon, c. 380–370 B.C., exterior south wall, Amazonomachy above Centauromachy. Photo: Kunsthistorisches Museum, Vienna.

sculpted friezes both above each other and lining the tops of walls is uncommon in Greek art.[11] Because the friezes were found in situ and were carefully documented, we are certain of their arrangement (Fig. 130). Viewing the monument as a visitor approaching from the south, the reliefs at the west side of the doorway in the southern exterior wall depict the Amazonomachy above and the Centauromachy in the frieze below (Fig. 132). Contrary to all other depictions seen thus far, the Centauromachy includes not only women but also the Kaineus episode, usually mutually exclusive motifs indicating different variants of this myth. To the east of the doorway, the battle of the Seven against Thebes overseen by Zeus seated on a rock is placed above a battle – unidentified – taking place at a ship's landing, where a ruler, probably the dynast of Trysa,[12] oversees the fray (Figs. 133a, 133b); in these two friezes, the figures of Zeus above and the ruler below form a visual parallel. The dynast's troops seem to be winning, since they advance from the left as victors usually do in Greek architectural sculpture. The battle's composition has no clear parallel in the Greek mythological repertoire known from earlier vases and sculpture, and instead finds its closest parallels in Lycian and Near Eastern iconography (see *Nereid Monument* below).[13]

Inside the temenos, facing the southern wall at the east (to the left of the door), one sees several reliefs of both mythological and nonmythological images that many – though not all[14] – scholars associate with the Trysa ruler, as a kind of biographical summary of his life and deeds. Their reasoning partly relies on the fact that these reliefs were placed

a

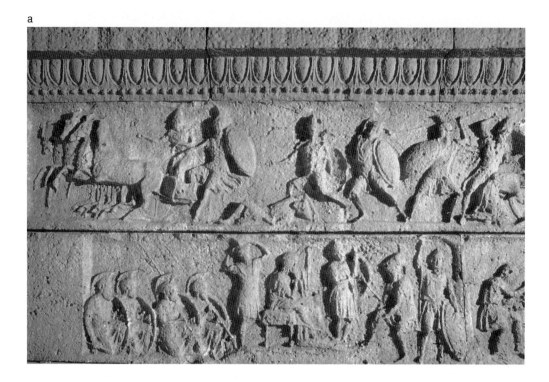

b

133. (a–b) Vienna, Kunsthistorisches Museum, Trysa Heroon, c. 380–370 B.C., exterior south wall, Seven against Thebes, battle. Photo: Kunsthistorisches Museum, Vienna.

in this corner of the temenos, where a banqueting structure once stood (more below).[15] At the viewer's left, two males, whom scholars identify as the Trysa ruler because of his "idealized" appearance,[16] in profile, together with a charioteer, stand in a quadriga, the image of the noble and energetic ruler. Below, at the viewer's left, a man carries off a woman, who wears an Eastern-style pointed cap and gesticulates in protest,

a

b

c

134. (a–c) Vienna, Kunsthistorisches Museum, Trysa Heroon, c. 380–370 B.C., interior south wall, chariot scene, abduction, Bellerophon fighting the Chimaira. Photo: Kunsthistorisches Museum, Vienna.

a1

a2

135. (a–b) Vienna, Kunsthistorisches Museum, Trysa Heroon, c. 380–370 B.C., interior south wall, Odysseus slaughtering the suitors, Kalydonian boar hunt. Photo: Kunsthistorisches Museum, Vienna.

presumably the dynast choosing his wife, and at the right is a scene of Bellerophon riding Pegasos, the winged horse born from Medusa's severed neck, and fighting the fantastic Chimaira, a hybrid creature whose feline body sprouts a goat's head along the spine and whose tail terminates in a snake's head (Figs. 134a–134c); according to scholars, Bellerophon is a reference to the ruler's ancestry (see below). On the other side of the doorway, Odysseus slaughters Penelope's suitors banqueting in his palace on Ithaka in the frieze above,[17] while the hunt for the ferocious Kalydonian boar appears in the lower frieze (Figs. 135a, 135b). In the former, Penelope and her maidservants look on as her husband, accompanied by their son, draws his bow to attack the frightened suitors, who have consumed his household goods and tormented his family in his long absence. The Kalydonian boar hunt was instigated by the king of Kalydon, whose land was ravaged by a wild boar sent by Artemis as punishment for his failure to include her in a sacrificial offering. The king's son, Meleager, enlisted numerous heroes, including Peleus (Achilles' father) and the Dioskouroi, as well as the female devotee of Artemis, Atalanta, to join this noble and dangerous enterprise.[18]

b

135b *(continued)*

The friezes on the interior of the western wall differ in format. At the southern end, four large ships' prows fill the full height of the two superimposed friezes, and then the friezes divide horizontally into two parallel compositions on the south wall. A man stands, his hand raised to his chin, in the leftmost ship as a battle rages nearby (Fig. 136). Although the friezes beyond the ships are spatially divided, some think that the upper frieze images take place in the background of the battle featured below, which is understood as occurring in the foreground; in other words, the two friezes are compositionally united.[19] In the midst of this battle, a commander of troops, presumably the dynast, appears together

136. Vienna, Kunsthistorisches Museum, Trysa Heroon, c. 380–370 B.C., west wall, southern portion. Photo: Kunsthistorisches Museum, Vienna.

137. Vienna, Kunsthistorisches Museum, Trysa Heroon, c. 380–370 B.C., west wall, city siege. Photo: Kunsthistorisches Museum, Vienna.

with a charioteer in a quadriga, a visual parallel to the ruler in the chariot on the south wall, but here, he gestures excitedly as if to urge his troops, approaching from the left, forward; in this instance, he is the aggressor, landing and conquering.[20] The middle of the west interior wall reunites the parallel friezes into a single city siege scene extending the height of the two superimposed friezes, and this depiction is apparently unconnected to the battle on the coast at the left: a fortified city is under attack, an event watched by the city's ruler, who sits on the ramparts, together with a servant, who shades him with a parasol (originally painted but now vanished), while another servant and a panther rest at his feet (Fig. 137). His wife, also shaded by a parasol (now in relief) held by a servant, sits nearby. An animal sacrifice to ensure a favorable outcome in the battle occurs near the ruler. Inhabitants with their belongings flee outside the city walls.[21] The significance of the city-siege images on the interior west wall with their emphasis on the depiction of architecture are enhanced by their situation parallel to the actual fortified walls of the citadel of Trysa rising above and behind the temenos, suggesting that perhaps Trysa itself had successfully withstood a siege under the guidance of its deceased ruler.[22] Some scholars have interpreted the city siege relief as a

138. Vienna, Kunsthistorisches Museum, Trysa Heroon, c. 380–370 B.C., west wall, northern portion, Amazonomachy. Photo: Kunsthistorisches Museum, Vienna.

depiction of the sack of Troy, and while this cannot be ruled out,[23] there is no iconographic parallel for the Ilioupersis that finds compositional matches here. What is more, the two situations are not parallel: Troy was successfully sacked, whereas the Trysa dynast's city – if, in fact, this is what is depicted – is attacked, but there is no indication of the outcome.[24] Others, however, see this as a scene from the myths concerning Bellerophon or view the repetition of the ruler, who appears several times on the west frieze, as references to Bellerophon, ancestor of the Trysa dynast.[25]

An Amazonomachy, familiar from the Parthenon west metopes (see Chapter 2), concludes the images on the north end of the western interior wall (Fig. 138); once again, the theme occupies two parallel friezes, which might be read as foreground and background of the same scene. One of the male warriors, who wears a helmet with a crest in the form of a winged animal and occupies a central position, has been identified as Bellerophon by some scholars.[26]

The friezes on the interior north wall depict, from left (west) to right, the rape of the daughters of Leukippos in both top and bottom friezes, then a hunt scene above a Centauromachy. The two daughters of Leukippos were cousins of the Spartan Diouskouroi, Kastor and Polydeukes, and were engaged to be married to Idas and Lynkeus, two Messenians. The Dioskouroi abducted the women just before the wedding took place. The abduction on quadrigas recalls the scene on the interior south wall, where a woman is carried off by a man, perhaps the dynast, on foot. To the east (right) of the Leukippidai scene, one sees a large building, depicted in some detail, alarmed women, and preparations for a banquet (butchering of animals, large cauldrons). Some celebrants at the banquet, the agitated women, react to the abduction, while others seem unaware of the event. The hunt scene is not compositionally similar to known mythological hunts. Wide spacing between human figures, both mounted and on foot, and animals – goat, bear, and panther – in the hunt distinguish this frieze from others discussed thus far, though the wide spacing recurs in the north wall's Centauromachy below and in earlier Eastern art.[27] The hunters flanking a poised feline anticipate later Macedonian compositions, such as the lion hunt mosaic in Pella of the late fourth century B.C.,[28] which themselves derive from Eastern royal artistic traditions. The Centauromachy begins at the east end of the north wall, then continues round the corner to the east wall. Unlike the Centauromachy on the exterior south wall, that on the eastern wall has no women or Kaineus episode, and the Centaurs use rocks, not vessels, as weapons; these features suggest that this is not the Thessalian wedding but instead the Heraklean adventure against Pholos.

On the east wall, the Centauromachy frieze is topped by at least one adventure of Perseus, his beheading Medusa; lacunae on both sides of this block may have been filled with other deeds of Perseus. The deeds of Perseus and the Centauromachy yield to the deeds of Theseus, which fill both top and bottom friezes with lacunae among them. From what remains, we can see that Theseus retrieves his father Aigeus' sword and sandals from under a rock, hurls Skiron off his rock, combats Sinis, and slays the Minotaur; curiously, the frieze below the Skiron and Sinis scenes are filled with very large marine animals – a turtle, fish, a dolphin (Fig. 139). Moving to the south, on the eastern interior wall, both top and bottom friezes conclude with themes of banqueting by men, and women and boys dancing to music (Figs. 140). A wooden structure with two rooms once stood at the corner of the eastern and southern interior walls, as attested by postholes in the extant stone blocks and the shifting of the frieze one course lower at this point to accommodate the structure. Scholars speculate that funerary cult activities, including banquets, occurred here.[29] A second area for the deposition of offerings may have been added in the northwest corner of the temenos at a later time.[30] The banqueting and dancing friezes, which are clearly divided into two horizontal friezes, though their action may interconnect,[31] round

139. Vienna, Kunsthistorisches Museum, Trysa Heroon, c. 380–370 B.C., east wall, deeds of Theseus. Photo: Kunsthistorisches Museum, Vienna.

the corner and terminate on the southern interior wall adjacent to the abduction and chariot scenes featuring the dynast.

The exterior lintel of the doorway is adorned by four winged-bull pro-tomes separated by rosettes[32] and a centrally placed Gorgon's head, all in low relief (Fig. 141). Below are two enthroned couples, each member of the couple facing the other, together with attendants, two dogs, and a goose. Oberleitner interprets the bulls and Gorgon above as apotropaic figures keeping watch over the heroized dead and his family depicted below them, but offers no evidence to support this claim.[33] On the inte-rior of the lintel, eight nude, bearded figures of the Egyptian god Bes dance, sit, or play musical instruments across the length of the lintel; life-size dancing figures, wearing open baskets on their heads and short tunics, appear on the door jambs, recalling the dancers on the interior

140. Vienna, Kunsthistorisches Museum, Trysa Heroon, c. 380–370 B.C., east wall, banqueting and dancing. Photo: Kunsthistorisches Museum, Vienna.

141. Vienna, Kunsthistorisches Museum, Trysa Heroon, c. 380–370 B.C., exterior lintel of the doorway. Reproduced from O. Benndorf and G. Niemann, "Das Heroon von Gjölbaschi-Trysa," *JKSW* 9 (1889)Taf. VI.

eastern and southern walls (Fig. 142).[34] Wooden doors once were fitted into the doorway to secure the area but some accommodation – steps or a ladder – was needed to bridge the 2-m gap between the ground level and the threshold.[35]

   In the absence of written documentation with which to interpret the monument, we must rely heavily on comparative evidence. The form of this monument, a (slightly irregular) rectangular wall surrounding a sarcophagus and wooden structure, is unusual, and scholars have looked to both the Greek and Eastern worlds for precedents. Superimposed friezes, such as the fragmentary marble stele with stacked battles from

142. Vienna, Kunsthistorisches Museum, Trysa Heroon, c. 380–370 B.C., interior doorway. Reproduced from O. Benndorf and G. Niemann, "Das Heroon von Gjölbaschi-Trysa," *JKSW* 9 (1889) Taf. VI.

the late fifth century B.C., now in Eleusis,[36] occasionally occur on the Greek mainland, but are not so common as they are in Asia Minor, where this arrangement is used on funerary stelai from the sixth century B.C. onward or on Lycian grave monuments,[37] such as a marble funerary stele from the first half of the fifth century with a banqueting scene above a file of animals.[38] In the Asia Minor examples, the friezes sometimes are at the top edge of a longer, smoothed vertical surface,[39] a position that corresponds to that of the Trysa heroon friezes. Scholars disagree as to whether the combination of tomb and enclosure wall temenos at Trysa derives from a local or imported tradition.[40] The use of a temenos around a tomb appears in the pre-Hellenistic mainland Greek world only in connection with hero cult. As for Asia Minor, comparisons can be made with the temenos surrounding Pillar 5 of the fifth century B.C. in Apollonia and the temenos at Phellos, which is contemporary with the Trysa heroon.[41]

The architectural precedents for the Trysa heroon may be Eastern in part, but much of the sculptural decoration clearly is based on Greek models. This has led scholars to suggest that for both its form and its decoration, the Trysa heroon takes its inspiration from an earlier heroon, the Theseion in Athens,[42] which was decorated with paintings of an Amazonomachy and Centauromachy in the 470s B.C. Before this time, the Amazonomachy had never been used as sculptural decoration in a funerary context, and its combination with the Centauromachy at the Theseion and again at Trysa has lent support to this proposal.[43] Beyond this, however, the claim has never received full argumentation or explanation, but is certainly worth considering, because so much of the Trysa heroon's mythological sculptural program uses the same compositions and motifs as one sees in Attic vase painting, sculpture,[44] and perhaps monumental wall paintings, which are now lost to us but known from written descriptions and possibly from reflections in vase painting.

The Heroon at Trysa is extraordinary for its use of so many Greek myths on a single monument, which is unprecedented in any sculptural monuments in Lycia or anywhere else save for extraordinary curiosities, such as the Chest of Kypselos of the sixth century B.C. at Olympia; the throne of Apollo at Amyklai, erected by the Lakedaimonians at the end of the sixth century B.C. and attributed to the sculptor Bathykles of Magnesia; or the throne of the Pheidian Zeus at Olympia of c. 430. Zeus' throne at Olympia was already discussed in Chapter 1, where the presence of the Centauromachy and Amazonomachy were noted; beyond these two themes, none recur at Trysa, and while the Chest of Kypselos was sumptuously decorated, it shares no myths with the Trysa heroon.

The Amyklai throne, however, is more promising as a possible influence on the Trysa heroon in terms of mythological subject matter and function. This extraordinary monument, known only from small architectural fragments and literary descriptions (Paus. 3.18.9–3.19.5), supported the cult statue of Apollo Amyklai, which was built over a site recognized as the heroon of Hyakinthos, one of Apollo's lovers, who was honored by the Hyakinthia festival in nearby Sparta. From the scrappy evidence, the throne seems to have towered upward in several stages like many Eastern tombs, such as the Nereid Monument (Fig. 144),[45] and was lavishly decorated with many myths including several featured on the Trysa heroon: the rape of the Leukippidai, Bellerophon killing the Chimaira, Perseus slaying Medusa, Theseus fighting the Minotaur, the Kalydonian boar hunt, and the Centauromachy (the adventure of Herakles and Pholos). Pausanias, however, mentions one peculiarity of the throne: Magnesian dancers – presumably contemporary figures – are featured in the friezes (3.18.14); the use of nonmythological figures in such public religious art at the end of the sixth century is unheard of in mainland Greece,[46] though they do occur in Asia Minor, the origin of the sculptor, Bathykles. Do the dancers on the doorway of the Trysa heroon resemble them? Hyakinthos gave his name to one month of the calendar in Spartan colonies as far east as Kos and Rhodes[47] – not Lycia but perhaps close enough for some awareness in Lycia of this hero and his heroon at Amyklai, which may have served as a model for the ruler's heroon at Trysa. Yet none of the myths shared with the Trysa heroon appear on the actual *altar* to Hyakinthos, but are described as adorning the throne supporting the Apollo cult statue.

The use of Greek myths (and so many of them) in nonmainland funerary architectural sculpture makes for a good comparison with what we have observed about myth in architectural sculpture on the mainland. Let us first look at each individual mythological theme to see how and where it is used on the mainland and western Greece in monumental form, primarily in the Classical period, and then return to the question of the relationship of the Trysa heroon to the Theseion in Athens. Nearly all these myths appear in vase painting, and while vase painting may be a tool for accessing lost monumental works, our focus here will be on architectural sculpture and wall painting rather than on vase painting.[48]

Some myths found at Trysa, such as the Centauromachy, Amazonomachy, and adventures of Theseus, have a long history of use, both together and separately, on mainland monumental architecture, as we have observed, not only in Athens on the Parthenon (and we might recall the Amazonomachy sculpted in relief on the shield of the Athena Parthenos statue within the Parthenon) or Hephaisteion, but elsewhere in Attika – the Centauromachy and deeds of Theseus appear on the frieze slabs from the Temple of Poseidon at Sounion of c. 430, for example.

Some themes also appear at other locations on the mainland, such as the Temple of Apollo at Bassai of c. 400–390 B.C., where both the Amazonomachy with Herakles (identified by his lion skin on British Museum 541) and the Centauromachy decorate the interior frieze of the cella (Fig. 143), or Olympia, where the Centauromachy fills the west pediment of the Temple of Zeus, and the Amazonomachy with Theseus and Herakles (presumably Herakles' retrieval of the girdle of the Amazon queen) adorns the throne of the cult statue within. We might also recall the use of Theseus in several monuments in the Athenian Agora – attacking Skiron as an akroterion of the Royal Stoa in the Athenian Agora (see Chapter 3), and fighting Amazons and present at the Battle of Marathon in paintings in the Stoa Poikile in the Athenian Agora – and Theseus' defeat of the Minotaur was the subject for a sculptural group on the Athenian Akropolis (see Chapter 2).

Other myths at the Trysa heroon, however, such as the Kalydonian boar hunt, are rarely used in architectural sculpture, either on the mainland or in western Greece. The fact that the latter group of myths – those not commonly used in architectural sculpture – appears at Trysa is intriguing and can serve as a control on tracking possible influences on the Trysa heroon: we would expect to see myths commonly used in architectural sculpture elsewhere also at Trysa, but when myths occur at the Trysa heroon that rarely appear in monumental public form elsewhere, it may be especially useful to note where they occur, when, and in which contexts. These less commonly used myths are documented in vase painting, earlier free-standing sculpture, and in some cases, monumental wall painting. The Seven against Thebes, for example, was the subject of the free-standing Argive sculptural dedication of c. 450 B.C. at Delphi (Paus. 10.10.3–4) and another in the Agora of Argos (Paus. 2.20.5), and also appeared on the Amyklai throne.

The Kalydonian boar hunt – at least a boar hunt that clearly can be identified as the Kalydonian boar hunt – was used in earlier vase painting and on the fifth-century Melian painted terracotta reliefs, which decorated tombs or were used as grave gifts,[49] and scholars have argued that a wall painting of the Kalydonian boar hunt produced by the Circle of Polygnotos of c. 460 is responsible for a series of compositional innovations that take place in the standard Attic vase painting depiction of this myth in the mid-fifth century;[50] Athens has been proposed as the

143. London, British Museum 524, Bassai, Temple of Apollo, Centauromachy. Photo: author.

location of such a painting, if it existed. Additionally, the theme was used as the sculptural decoration for the east pediment of the Temple of Athena Alea at Tegea in the 340s, as known from Pausanias (8.45.5-7) and the fragmentary remains,[51] but this postdates the Trysa heroon. The Kalydonian boar hunt may also have appeared in the metopes from the Sikyonian monopteros at Delphi of c. 560 B.C., some of which were reused in the foundations of the Sikyonian Treasury at Delphi when it was rebuilt after c. 548 B.C. However, the identification of the boar in the extant metope with the Kalydonian boar is impossible to establish with certainty.

The Rape of the Leukippidai had a long tradition in Attic vase painting and was also the subject of various free-standing sculptural groups, appeared on the throne at Amyklai, and was also painted by Polygnotos in the sanctuary of the Dioskouroi in Athens, according to Pausanias 1.18.1. Unlike many of the other themes depicted at Trysa, it may have surviving precedents in architectural sculpture on the mainland: on the Siphnian Treasury at Delphi of c. 525 B.C. if the abduction on the south frieze is, in fact, that of the Leukippidai (this is debated); in Magna Graecia at Silaris (Foce del Sele), where the theme is one of several proposed for two metopes from the Treasury of the Heraion of c. 550-525 B.C.;[52] and possibly at the Nereid Monument of c. 390-380 B.C. in nearby Xanthos, where two akroteria groups have been identified as abductions, possibly those of the Leukippidai (Fig. 144).[53]

Perseus beheading Medusa also was occasionally used as architectural sculpture, as attested by the limestone metope from Temple C at Selinus of c. 530–510 B.C. (now in the Palermo Museum) and possibly a marble akroterion from a building on the sixth-century Athenian Akropolis.[54] Earlier depictions include numerous vase paintings and free-standing sculpture, such as the statue by Myron of c. 450 B.C. on the Athenian Akropolis (no longer extant but known from Paus. 1.23.7 and Pliny, *HN* 34.57), and the theme recurs on the contemporary carved throne for the cult statue by Thrasymedes of Paros in the Temple of Asklepios at Epidauros (c. 380 B.C.), which is attested only by Pausanias (2.27.2). Pausanias also (1.22.7) describes a monumental wall painting of Perseus beheading Medusa in the Pinakotheke of the Propylaia on the Athenian Akropolis, but the date of the painting cannot be determined beyond establishing that it dates between the completion of the building in c. 432 B.C. and Pausanias' lifetime in the second century A.D. (Figs. 40–42).

Especially intriguing is the fact that some uncommon myths that are used at Trysa appear in the *same* unusual combinations in mainland settings, as well. For example, the Seven against Thebes and Odysseus slaughtering the suitors, both highly unusual topics for architectural sculpture, once existed in combination as wall paintings (now lost) made by Onasias and Polygnotos, respectively, for the pronaos wall of the Temple of Athena Areia at Plataia of c. 475–450 B.C. (Paus. 9.4.2, who, however, indicates that Odysseus has completed his vengeful actions).[55] Bellerophon and the Chimaira, while occasionally the subject of akroteria on mainland buildings,[56] were relatively uncommon in architectural sculpture, but appeared on painted Melian reliefs, some of which may have been used as decoration for tombs or as grave gifts,[57] and were paired with the Perseus scene on the aforementioned cult statue at Epidauros.

Curiously, the Heroon omits one myth we have come to expect from Classical architectural sculpture on the mainland – the Gigantomachy, which was ubiquitous on Archaic and Classical temples and treasuries. It may be that this myth was considered inappropriate for a private tomb, that this theme should ornament temples or altars to gods, not monuments to men. Alternatively, the iconography and meaning of Greek gods may have been of little importance or attraction to this Lycian

144. London, British Museum, Xanthos, Nereid Monument, c. 390–380 B.C.
Photo: H. R. Goette.

dynast and his people, whose gods were not Greek and whose familiarity
with Greek myth was restricted to tales known from major monuments
and wall painting via pattern-books[58] or through small-scale portable
objects, such as vases, gems, or metalwork, not from first-hand exposure
to major monuments.

What is evident from this brief excursus is that a number of the Trysa
myths, well known or not, appear in monumental form on the mainland, both as architectural sculpture and as monumental wall painting:
perhaps the Kalydonian boar hunt, but certainly the rape of the Leukippidai, Odysseus slaughtering the suitors, the Seven against Thebes,
Perseus with the head of Medusa, Bellerophon slaying the Chimaira, the
adventures of Theseus, Centauromachy, and Amazonomachy. Moreover,
all of these themes, save the Plataia paintings of the Seven against Thebes
and Odysseus slaughtering the suitors, appear in fifth-century Athens in

monumental form, either as sculpture – architectural and free-standing – on the Akropolis, or as monumental paintings in the Agora or in buildings near the Akropolis. Several of these monumental wall paintings were by Polygnotos of Thasos, who worked in Athens, where he became an Athenian citizen in the mid-fifth century or so (Harp. *Lexicon*, s.v. Polygnotos), or by one of his peers.

This can scarcely be a coincidence, especially in the case of the myths less commonly used in monumental form, such as Bellerophon and the Chimaira, the rape of the Leukippidai, or Odysseus slaughtering the suitors. With the weight of the evidence, it seems plausible that mythological depictions in monumental form – painted or sculpted – from the Greek mainland, particularly from Athens, exerted some measure of influence on the decoration of the Trysa heroon. This is especially likely because the deeds of Theseus are seen nowhere else in Lycian art. Was the Theseion in Athens influential on the Trysa heroon, as some scholars have suggested? While the Theseion has not been precisely located nor any remains found, the use of the terms *temenos*, *hieron*, and *sekos* to describe the structure suggest an enclosure of some sort.[59] Polygnotos painted a Centauromachy and Amazonomachy onto the walls of the Theseion (Paus. 1.17.2), and it is noteworthy that Pausanias' account places the sanctuary of the Dioskouroi, adorned by a Polygnotan painting of the rape of the Leukippidai, very close to the Theseion and below the shrine of Aglauros (1.18.2), which we know was on the east slope of the Akropolis; thus, the Theseion and shrine of the Dioskouroi must have been east of the Akropolis (see Chapter 3). The subsequent combination of these themes in a funerary context at Trysa and the first instance of the use of the Amazonomachy in a sepulchral context suggest that the designer of the Trysa sculptural program was aware of the Theseion's decoration. However, without knowing more about the precise form of the Theseion and the disposition of its decoration, it is impossible to draw a clear connection between the two heroa – that of Theseus and the Trysa dynast's. Nevertheless, influence from Athenian monuments, at least for a large part of the sculpture, is highly probable.

Greek myths, however, are not the only subject of sculpture on the Heroon, where other Greek and Near Eastern elements are combined or even intermingle. The kalathiskos dancers on the interior of the doorway have close parallels in earlier Greek sculpture[60] and vase painting and in the later kalathiskos dancers on the akanthos column at Delphi of c. 330 B.C. (see Chapter 4, Figs. 127, 128).[61] Yet the use of life-size figures flanking doorways has a long Near Eastern history,[62] and kalathiskos dancers appear on other Lycian monuments.[63] Furthermore, in Greece, the dancers are usually female, but at Trysa, as elsewhere in Lycia, they are male.[64] We also have noted the appearance of purely Eastern elements, such as the winged-bull protomes and Bes on the door lintel – the former derives from Persia,[65] the latter from Egypt, though they are used elsewhere in Lycia.[66] Several of the friezes are devoted to nonmythological themes – or at least representations that have no known correspondence to mythological images in Greek or Near Eastern art: battles and city sieges taking place on coasts, as indicated by ships beached nearby, an abduction, animal hunts, and banqueting. While battle, hunting, abductions, and banqueting are ubiquitous in Greek art, especially on Greek vases of the archaic and classical periods, in both clearly mythological and nonmythological contexts, the combination of these themes on a single monument, the compositions themselves, their style (which varies from the highly skilled, e.g., the foreshortened quadriga in the rape of the Leukippidai, to the less proficient, e.g., Bellerophon and the Chimaira, Fig. 134c),[67] and, as noted above, the disposition of the decoration in superimposed continuous friezes at the top of a wall are more familiar from Lycian art and Eastern art, more generally speaking.[68]

The nearly contemporary Nereid Monument in Xanthos provides a good Lycian parallel for this Greek–Near Eastern blend of themes – mythological and nonmythological (Fig. 144). The tomb's decoration includes friezes of a pitched battle and a city siege (Fig. 145), which appear on two superimposed friezes (the city siege above) at the top of its base (like the Trysa heroon's friezes at the top of the temenos wall); the eponymous Nereids in the intercolumniations; a hunt scene (prey: bear, boar, Fig. 146), banquet preparations, and a battle (some warriors mounted, some on foot) on three of the four sides of the architrave (a procession of figures carrying garments fills the third); a battle in one pediment, the dynast and his wife seated opposite each other surrounded by other figures in the other (note the presence of a sleeping dog under the dynast's chair and another, very alert dog in the corner of the pediment, Fig. 147); abductions for the central akroteria; and a banqueting scene together with an animal sacrifice on the frieze running around the top

145. London, British Museum 871c-877-872, Xanthos, Nereid Monument, c. 390–380 B.C., city-siege and battle friezes. Photo: H. R. Goette.

146. London, British Museum 889, Xanthos, Nereid Monument, c. 390–380 B.C., hunt frieze. Photo: © Copyright the Trustees of the British Museum.

147. London, British Museum 924, Xanthos, Nereid Monument, c. 390–380 B.C., east pediment. Photo: © Copyright the Trustees of the British Museum.

148. London, British Museum 898, Xanthos, Nereid Monument, c. 390–380 B.C., banqueting frieze. Photo: H. R. Goette.

of the wall in the interior of the cella (Figs. 148, 149, 150a, 150b).[69] The themes of the dynast victorious in battle, the seated royal couple with dogs, the use of parasols for the dynast, and nonmythological scenes of city siege, banquet, and land battle derive from an Asia Minor tradition,[70] and specific compositional motifs on the Nereid Monument also appear at the Trysa heroon, such as a seated ruler accompanied by a servant shading him with a parasol (British Museum 879) or the ruler and his wife seated and facing each other (Figs. 137, 147).[71] Yet the style of the sculpture on the two monuments is distinctly different – the Nereid Monument tends to use taller, more elongated figures and more transparent drapery, and shows greater similarities to mainland Greek sculpture.

Why were particular Greek myths chosen for the Trysa heroon? Eastern associations of some of the myths may have appealed to the Trysa dynast. Greek monster-slayers, such as Bellerophon, Herakles, and others, can be

149. London, British Museum 899, Xanthos, Nereid Monument, c. 390–380 B.C., banqueting frieze. Photo: H. R. Goette.

traced back to Near Eastern mythology, where heroes, such as Gilgamesh, were already slaying monsters millennia earlier; the fantastic creatures – the Chimaira and Pegasos – are also Near Eastern imports and had particular significance for the Lycians. Greek authors indicate that the Lycians regarded Bellerophon as the founder of their royal line (Apollod. 2.3.2) and that the hero was ordered to kill the Chimaira by the king of Lycia (Hom. *Il.* 6.179–182). In the Classical period, Perseus beheading Medusa and Bellerophon killing the Chimaira appear elsewhere in Lycian monuments as, for example, at the Heroon of Perikles of c. 370–350 B.C. at Limyra.[72] According to the literary tradition, Perseus constructed Mycenaean structures in Argos using Lycian architects and was an ancestor of a Persian royal family (Hdt. 7.61; Apollod. 2.4.5); modern scholars, therefore, believe that the Lycians regarded him as an ancestor of Lycian kings.[73]

What of the remaining myths and nonmythological scenes? Scholars have argued persuasively that the Near Eastern scenes – the battles and city siege – represent accomplishments of the ruler's lifetime, and that the banqueting scenes refer to the actual funerary banquet held at Trysa at the time of the ruler's interment and on subsequent festival days in his honor.[74] Moreover, the juxtaposition of mythological and generic themes, their placement within the temenos and in relationship to the fortified city of Trysa rising behind the temenos, contribute to the meaning of an overall program: the Greek myths without obvious Eastern associations were not chosen randomly but paired with nonmythological Eastern scenes to liken the deceased ruler to Greek heroes who perform valorous deeds; according to this line of reasoning, the ruler and his achievements (withstanding the city siege, for example) are heroized by visual metaphor and juxtaposition.[75] The deceased therefore can expect an afterlife existence worthy of heroes, including veneration at his burial spot. For example, the rape of the Leukippidai and Centauromachy, the Seven against Thebes, and the Kalydonian boar hunt parallel the nonmythological scenes of abduction, city-siege, and hunt; in the case of the abductions and hunts, the mythological and generic scenes appear on opposite interior walls – north and south – inviting the viewer to make visual connections across space. The deceased ruler's accomplishments (battles, hunt) and his family (abduction) are exalted by these parallels to the mythological sphere, thus heroizing and ennobling

a

b

150. (a–b) London, British Museum 904/905, Xanthos, Nereid Monument, c. 390–380 B.C., sacrifice frieze. Photo: © Copyright the Trustees of the British Museum.

his and his family's history. Likewise, the representation of Odysseus slaughtering the suitors is a banquet that mirrors the generic banquet depicted in the southeast corner, and the latter, in turn, reflects actual funerary banquets held in a wooden enclosure within the temenos.[76] This is not to say that the plan was to create a direct connection between the scene of Odysseus slaughtering the suitors and the banquet – after all there are no suitors to be slaughtered at the banquet in honor of the ruler – but simply to heroize by visual analogy: the message is that the ruler had significant achievements just as these heroes of Greek myth did. Thus, the deeds of Perseus and Theseus are intended as mythological parallels for the ruler's own accomplishments, which also are depicted on the interior walls. The Amazonomachy does not fit so neatly into this scheme of mythological/nonmythological groups but one might construe it as another battle scene, parallel to the battles on the exterior south and interior west walls.

At the Trysa Heroon, myths familiar to the reader from monuments discussed in previous chapters resonate with new meanings particular to Eastern social, political, and funerary situations. The Amazonomachy and Centauromachy that formerly adorned temples or treasuries in sanctuaries, for example, the Temple of Zeus at Olympia, the Parthenon and Hephaisteion in Athens, the Athenian Treasury at Delphi, the Temple of Poseidon at Sounion, and the temple of Apollo at Bassai, or decorated vases appear in funerary contexts for the first time in the fourth century, where the theme of Kaineus' death, perhaps suitable for funerary contexts, is always included in the Centauromachy.[77] As discussed earlier in this book, scholars frequently interpret the Amazonomachy and Centauromachy as signifying the conquest of foreign or uncivilized forces, but this cannot be the case at Trysa since the foreigner or uncivilized is now the patron! Instead, the choice to use the Amazonomachy in Lycia may have been because Bellerophon, ancestor of the Lycian rulers and perhaps an analogue for the Trysa dynast, defeated the Amazons during an expedition in Lycia (Hom. *Il.* 6.186). Perhaps it is *this* Amazonmachy that is depicted on the interior west wall, a mythological parallel to the Trysa dynast's battle adjacent to it. The Centauromachy on the Trysa heroon is the first or among the first instances of the use of this theme on a structure that one can firmly identify as funerary (another nearly contemporary example is the Lycian sarcophagus of c. 380 from Sidon[78]), a practice that spreads regionally in Lycia – the Centauromachy recurs on the Ptolemaion, another heroon, of the early third century B.C. at nearby Limyra[79] – and elsewhere, such as the frieze from a Tarentine tomb of the mid-fourth century B.C. [80] and the Mausoleion at Belevi[81] of the first half of the third century B.C. The Centauromachy, together with the Amazonomachy, appear on the metopes of the Tholos in the sanctuary of Athena Pronaia of the fourth century B.C. at Delphi, a structure that some have recognized as a heroon,[82] and again on the frieze slabs of the Mausoleion at Halikarnassos, another funerary context. In this respect, as in many others, the monument at Trysa is a landmark.

Motifs familiar from the mainland take on new meanings in Lycia. The hero Theseus, who was so ubiquitous on the monuments of the mainland, particularly in Athens, may not signify a heroic ideal of the same sort for his Eastern viewers, where his journey and his ability to slay monsters may matter much more than his early kingship of Athens. In the realm of the Greek sixth- and fifth-century polis, hunting scenes reflected aristocratic or heroic activities closely linked to prowess in warfare, and hunting sometimes was used as a rite of passage. In the East (and also in Macedonia), hunting imagery is particular to royalty: Assyrian reliefs of the seventh century B.C. demonstrate an association between royal hunting and valor in battle; Persian imperial art, such as reliefs from the Hall of a Hundred Columns at Persepolis of the fifth century B.C., depicts the king fighting in hand-to-paw combat with lions and other animals,[83] and on Persian cylinder seals of the Classical period, one sees the king hunting lions, either from a chariot or on foot.[84] It is not only the Greek myths themselves that are borrowed from the mainland but also, in some cases, their composition, conglomeration, and even context, often from monumental painting and sculpture.

We have noted the use of Greek myths elsewhere in Lycia – at the heroon of Perikles in Limyra and at the Nereid Monument at Xanthos. In each case, the dynasts for whom these tombs were built apparently aimed to draw likenesses between themselves and heroes, expecting (and presumably receiving) worship after their death (there is no evidence that such activity occurred during their lives). Excavations at the Mausoleion at Halikarnassos in nearby Caria reveal an enormous deposit of animal sacrifices that occurred at the time of burial,[85] recollecting the monumental funerals of Homeric heroes, such as that of Patroklos, which is described in *Iliad* 23. On the tombs of Asia Minor rulers and particularly at the Trysa heroon, myth, so often serving political, didactic, or religious purposes on the mainland, is used to exalt human rulers to the ranks of heroes and gods.

This lofty view of Eastern rulers (and it has a long history – one might consider Egyptian pharaohs, for example) was to have a profound effect on Alexander the Great (356–323 B.C.), whose imagery both during and after his lifetime was marked by heroizing poses and imagery, though he was not the first to receive godlike status during his lifetime; his father Philip II had already represented himself as such in public monuments and festivals.[86] A small bronze statuette from Alexandria, now in Paris (Louvre B370), is believed to copy an original large-scale portrait

151. Paris, Musée du Louvre B370, bronze figurine of Alexander the Great. Photo: H. R. Goette.

of Alexander by his court sculptor, Lysippos (Fig. 151); here Alexander is shown in heroic nudity and steps forward, holding a spear in his upraised right hand. Scholars posit that the image relies on the fifth-century Doryphoros of Polykleitos, which may represent the great Homeric hero Achilles, whom Alexander regarded as a model for himself.[87] Coins issued during his lifetime portray a youthful visage with the lion skin of Herakles, the Panhellenic hero, on the obverse (Fig. 38); by means of juxtaposition, the viewer associates the hero with the ruler.[88] Coins minted in Egypt and in Thrace after his death portrayed Alexander with the ram's

152. Naples, Museo Nazionale 5026, bronze statuette of Demetrios Poliorcetes. Photo: Koppermann, Deutsches Archäologisches Institut, Rom, Neg. D-DAI-Rom 1959.0763.

horns of Zeus Ammon, thus likening the ruler to an Eastern god, who would appeal to both Greeks or Macedonians living in Egypt and to the local inhabitants; such depictions multiply after his death, when his images are endowed with the attributes of Dionysos and Herakles.

Alexander's successors continued to exploit and develop the concept of the ruler as hero or god; Demetrios Poliorketes (336–283 B.C.), for example, not only affected Alexander's famed anastole and breathless expression, but also adopted attributes and poses associated with the god Poseidon, and received cult in his lifetime (Fig. 152). Thus, while Eastern rulers, such as the Trysa dynast, may have borrowed Greek myths to liken themselves to mythological heroes, Greco-Macedonian rulers from the time of Philip II on also learned from the East by adopting and fully exploiting the practice of elevating the ruler, both living and dead, to a heroic or divine level (whether Greek or not), and combining this practice with religious and political concerns. In this way, they created new variations on old themes.

CONCLUSION

Greek myth is infinitely variable in its details and contexts, but as architectural sculpture must be recognizable and speak to a contemporary viewer. The Centauromachy and Amazonomachy are ubiquitous in architectural sculpture after their first use in 470–456 and c. 490 B.C., respectively, and like the labors of Herakles, also have Panhellenic appeal in spite of their being set in specific locales, such as Thessaly, the Black Sea region, or the Athenian Akropolis. What's more, their protagonists have the narrative advantage of being immediately recognizable – the appearance of a Centaur instantly signals "myth." Details indicate which narratives are intended, though it is important to bear in mind that myths are never fixed but mutable. The inclusion of Kaineus (e.g., on the west frieze of the Hephaisteion) or women (e.g., the Parthenon south metopes) or the types of weapons (branches or crockery) wielded by the Centaurs can determine which variant of the myth is intended. Likewise, female warriors can only be the Amazons; the appearance of Herakles, as at the Temple of Apollo at Bassai, or the inclusion of architectural features, as one sees on the shield of the Athena Parthenos statue in the Parthenon, determine the location and therefore the version of a battle between Greek males and Amazons.

What is striking is the malleability of these myths and their meanings, especially the Centauromachy, and their depictions in a great variety of places and contexts. At Olympia, the Centauromachy is fashioned to address athletes and to strengthen Elean claims to greatness through their genealogical connection to the Lapiths. While both pediments at Olympia deal with ideas of weddings or marriage, other themes not only are present but also dominate – athletics and noble behavior, for example. The Centauromachy recurs on the Parthenon south metopes, but in this instance, the stress seems to be on a marriage disrupted and on the chaste reaction of the Lapith women to the Centaurs' boorish advances. Uncertainty about the theme of the middle metopes of the south flank makes it impossible to say more; if they did refer to an early phase in Athens' history, this would accord well with other themes and rituals on the Akropolis, which, among other things, emphasize the importance of women as wives and mothers to the stability and continuity of the city. As part of a larger network of images in the Athenian Agora, the Hephaisteion's west frieze employs a variant of the Centauromachy myth – not the wedding but the combat including Kaineus – to highlight the heroic behavior of Theseus, who is championed elsewhere on the building's north and south metopes, and in the Agora more generally. The two Centauromachies on the wall of the Trysa Heroon differ from each other and from the previous examples. The exterior south wall Centauromachy apparently shows the wedding with Centaurs attacking Lapith women and using vessels as weapons while the Lapith men fight them off, but two Centaurs also pound Kaineus into the earth in this same frieze; it is not clear if this signals a change in locale or is simply a continuation of the same scene but with the inclusion of an atypical motif. The north wall Centauromachy employs only combats between Lapiths and Centaurs – no women, no Kaineus – in other words, the details that would have made a clear statement about place or mythical variant are absent, perhaps intentionally to generalize this fight between human and half-human/half-animal combatants. In this funerary context, the myth seems to be combined with other mythological (rape of the Leukippidai) and nonmythological abductions (dynast and woman on interior south wall) to liken the ruler to mythological heroes – the Lapiths – and thereby exalt the ruler to heroic rank.

The Amazonomachy appears already in the Athenian Treasury metopes, where elsewhere on the building, one sees the labors of Herakles and Theseus. The monument at Delphi seems to have been a thank offering for victory at Marathon. Discrete episodes of the Amazonomachy that result in Herakles' attack on their queen appear, among other places (e.g., a metope from Temple E at Selinus of c. 470 B.C.), on the Temple of Zeus at Olympia and the Hephaisteion in the context of Herakles' other labors. An extended Amazonomachy recurs without Herakles, so far as we can tell, in the Parthenon west metopes; because of the location of the building itself, we perhaps can conclude that the Amazonomachy alluded to is the attack on the Akropolis. The Parthenon, like the Athenian Treasury at Delphi, has also been construed as a memorial to Marathon, but the prevalence of females in other areas of the temple's sculptures and on the Akropolis more generally allows the Amazonomachy to be viewed as resistance to the society of manly, uncontrolled women, who are not domesticated by marriage or civilized society (defined, in this case, by the Athenian point of view). When we see the Amazonomachy again at Trysa, it is in a private funerary context, juxtaposed to a city-siege scene, perhaps fighting Bellerophon, ancestor of the Lycian dynasts. If the adjacent city-siege really depicts the dynast as victor, one might construe the Amazonomachy's presence as a means of heroizing the dynast by visual association.

Other myths, such as the Ilioupersis, are not so well represented in architectural sculpture, though they flourish in other media, such as vase painting, and the local association of some myths, such as the labors of Theseus and the myth of Pelops' chariot race with Oinomaos, are so strong and so peculiar to a given place (Attika, Olympia) that their use on monumental architecture is sharply circumscribed (the myth of Pelops' race with Oinomaos is used only this one time at Olympia as architectural sculpture). When we find the labors of Theseus in a non-Athenian context, such as the Trysa Heroon, which was not commissioned by an Athenian, some special explanation must be sought – either sculptors from the mainland or influence from Athens in particular, which is precisely what one sees at Trysa.

In every case, context determines meaning and what elements of a myth are stressed: religious rituals, oracular consultations, and hero cult; events, such as athletics; and other monuments, such as military or athletic victory monuments, shrines, altars, and treasuries, all contribute to the meanings and interpretations available to the viewer, who looks not only up at sculpture, but all around, who experiences the images within a three-dimensional active world and not as monuments affixed to a wall in a museum, isolated from their original context.

153. Naples, Museo Nazionale 6015, Dying Gaul, Roman copy. Photo: Koppermann, Deutsches Archäologisches Institut, Rom, Neg. D-DAI-Rom 1993.0544.

The durability of Greek myth in architectural sculpture persists through the Hellenistic period; in some ways, this is surprising considering the proliferation of images of individual rulers, many of whom are publicly likened to heroes and gods in visual form, as well as in terms of address and sometimes hero worship. The Gigantomachy, which was used repeatedly as architectural sculpture in the sixth and fifth centuries B.C., vanishes from this format in the fourth century, but experiences a revival in the third and second centuries, particularly under the Attalid kings of Pergamon. A free-standing rendition of this myth composed part of the Lesser Attalid dedication of c. 200 B.C. on the Athenian Akropolis, and a dazzling and overwhelming Gigantomachy is carved in very high relief all around the marble socle frieze of the Altar of Zeus of c. 160 B.C. The Attalid dedication on the Athenian Akropolis stood along the south side of the Parthenon (Paus. 1.25.2; Plut. *Ant.* 60.4) and included numerous freestanding statues, about two-thirds life size, of Giants, Amazons, Gauls, and Persians (Fig. 153),[1] all of whom meet defeat at the hands of an unseen enemy (or at least we have no indication that there was a sculpted victor). These figures, known now only in Roman copies scattered in museums throughout Europe, were placed on bases near the southeast Akropolis wall. This grand votive offering would have resonated – thematically – with the metopes of the Parthenon, where one sees Giants and Amazons, and with the shield and sandals of the Athena Parthenos statue within. The theme of Persian defeat is an echo of the Parthenon itself, which, in part, commemorates the Greek victory over the Persians in the Persian Wars, while simultaneously analogizing this Greek victory to the recent Attalid victory over the Gauls. This is not the only Attalid dedication in Athens, but one of many designed to leave the Attalids' mark on the city, to stake their claim to be the true inheritors of Athens' glorious legacy.

The Altar of Zeus was originally located on the Akropolis of Pergamon (and was mostly transported to Berlin in the nineteenth century), where it was dedicated as a military thank offering to Zeus and Athena (although there is much dispute as to all the functions of this monument, Figs. 154, 155).[2] Each of its four sides appears to be devoted to deities of different realms: night and the underworld, light and day, the marine world and Dionysos and his followers, and Olympian deities, so that the ordering of deities already asserts a measure of order in this battle against the threatening chaos of the Giants. After ascending the stairs to reach the interior of the shrine and the altar itself, one faces another relief frieze around the interior wall, which depicts the life of Telephos (Fig. 156), founder of Pergamon and ancestor of the Attalids, who is repeated throughout the frieze in various vignettes, a different narrative strategy from the more conventional continuous frieze on the exterior (though one is loath to describe the Gigantomachy frieze as "conventional," since its size and technical details are extraordinary), where each figure is shown only once in a composition that appears to possess a unity of time and place. Here at the Altar, the viewer moves from the chaos and tumult of the outside frieze to the relative tranquility of the interior frieze, from the divine cosmos to the human world, a reversal of what one might expect in a religious structure. The closest analogy that exists in an earlier monument is on the Parthenon, where the exterior east metopes also depict the Gigantomachy, while the Ionic frieze running round the cella portrays a religious procession, perhaps composed of actual – though generic – Athenians (comparable to the local hero Telephos). For the erudite viewer, this comparison may have come to mind already when approaching the Altar, which was approached from its rear or eastern side, where the Olympians Athena and Zeus are poised

154. Berlin, Pergamonmuseum, Altar of Zeus, c. 180–160 B.C. Photo: H. R. Goette.

in a visual quotation from the west pediment of the Parthenon (Figs. 46a and 157), also the first side visible to a visitor on the Akropolis, another shrine to Athena. This appears to be another Pergamene effort to style itself as a new Athens.

155. Berlin, Pergamonmuseum, Altar of Zeus, model. Photo: H. R. Goette.

156. Berlin, Pergamonmuseum, Altar of Zeus, c. 180–160 B.C., Telephos frieze. Photo: H. R. Goette.

Like many other Hellenistic cities, Pergamon engaged in ruler cult for Alexander the Great, as well as for earlier Attalid kings. As we have seen, this is fully in keeping with developments from the time of Philip II on, as various rulers likened their predecessors or themselves to mythological heroes and gods in public ceremonies, on coinage, in sculpture, and religious ritual. Using myth as a political tool is nothing new, as we have seen, but the elision of the boundary between actual mortal and mythological hero is a relatively late development for Greek culture. Special mortals, such as Olympic victors, received hero worship even in their lifetime, but this was highly unusual; rulers were another matter altogether.

157. Berlin, Pergamonmuseum, Altar of Zeus, c. 180–160 B.C., east frieze. Photo: H. R. Goette.

158. Sperlonga, Polyphemos group reconstruction. Photo: reproduced and adapted with permission from B. Andreae, ed., *Odysseus: Mythos und Erinnerung* (Mainz 1999) 200–201.

Once established, however, the practice of likening rulers to heroes, gods – and Alexander the Great – gained strength and accelerated in the Roman world, where leaders and rulers, such as Pompey and Augustus, styled themselves after Alexander the Great, or, as did Claudius and others, appeared in heroic or divine attire in their portraiture, particularly outside of Italy. Greek mythological narratives lived on largely in Roman private art: sarcophagi and wall painting in Pompeii and elsewhere; certainly, in the case of painting, these images were designed to impress, to display one's erudition and knowledge of the Greek world, perhaps to inspire conversation and contemplation. But Greek myth also occasionally appears in imperial contexts, such as the grotto of Tiberius at Sperlonga, where over-life-size three-dimensional marble sculptures of episodes during the travels of Odysseus on his return to Greece, were exhibited in a rocky, watery setting (Fig. 158): one had to travel by boat to move from sculpture to sculpture in this water-flooded grotto and in this fashion, relive the journey of Odysseus. This Greek myth is a curious choice for a Roman context, but it was the destruction of Troy and the escape of Aineias, of course, that led to the establishment of the Roman people in Italy and ultimately to their domination of the world – including Greece, which was responsible for sacking Troy. Here, Greek myth is used to underscore Roman superiority for the amusement of a Roman audience.

159. Rome, Museo Centrale Montemartini, fifth-century B.C. pediment sculptures of the Amazonomachy from the Temple of Apollo Sosianus, Rome, c. 30–20 B.C. Photo: H. R. Goette.

But Sperlonga, wall painting, and the mythological sarcophagi are largely exceptions: rather than using Greek myths or adapting them as they did in the case of the Trojan War cycle to explain and highlight their origins, their government, their civic ideology, and their piety – many of the same reasons that Greeks employed myths – the Romans instead tended to focus on an individual's actual biography and attainments, or an emperor's achievements. These may have been expressed through Greek myth if we accept the argument regarding architectural sculpture on the Temple of Apollo Sosianus in Rome. In 32 B.C., the Roman Consul Sosius vowed the rebuilding of the Temple of Apollo *in circo* or the Temple of Apollo Sosianus. Scholars posit that as part of the temple's decorative program executed in c. 30 B.C., Sosius employed a sculpted Amazonomachy, made of Parian marble, taken from a fifth-century B.C. Greek building as the Apollo temple's pedimental decoration (Fig. 159).[3] According to this interpretation, the theme of the Amazonomachy – here the version of Herakles' acquisition of Hippolyte's girdle – that once signified the Greek triumph over Eastern, perhaps Persian, forces, is transformed in its Roman context into a symbol for the Roman defeat of the Egyptians, specifically Octavian's defeat of Kleopatra at the Battle of Actium in 31 B.C.[4] In this view, Herakles and Theseus are identified with Octavian, and Hippolyte signifies Kleopatra. In this instance, not only was Greek myth used in Roman art, but an actual Greek depiction of a myth was transported to Rome and reused on a public building.

But the use of Greek mythological narratives for Roman public building is uncommon. Greek myth lives on in Roman literature, such as Ovid's *Metamorphoses* or Virgil's *Aeneid*, but certainly in the latter instance, serves purely Roman aims to legitimize and glorify the imperial rule established by Augustus. When mythological figures other than Aineias and his family were employed in imperial art, they tended to be plucked or detached from narrative contexts and used in emblematic ways.

Although this study has confined itself only to the Classical period and has dealt almost exclusively with mainland and Lycian developments, much more remains to be done even within these confines. Questions about mainland monuments not located in such well-explored and well-published sites could be queried in the manner suggested here, so long as there is sufficient evidence to reconstruct a context, and one could certainly extend the investigation to western Greek sites, as well, or move the scope backward or forward in time, for example, Archaic Delphi, or the Hellenistic or Roman phase of Olympia (a project that I am engaged in). One might extend the breadth to consider how Roman Athens deployed Greek myth and earlier monuments to facilitate Roman claims or ideology. Likewise, one might consider regional variants on familiar myths: do Arkadian sites, for example, relate a myth differently or use a different variant than do neighboring Achaian or Lakonian sites? One sees variation even within a single polis, so one would expect regional variation – the task would be to define the differences, and then explain them.

Pragmatic concerns about the physical composition of a depiction of a myth and how issues of space and medium affect narrative have been explored to some degree, but a closer examination of how composition affects not only the form but the meaning perceived by the viewer deserves more study. Differences between a relief frieze and a painting on the curving surface of a vase, between viewing a frieze laterally while the viewer moves, as opposed to turning a vase in one's hand or circling round it, affect the perception of narrative, which can also influence one's understanding and conception of a given myth. Indeed, one might well ask whatever inspired anyone to paint a Greek myth on a terracotta pot, which seems an overly complicated kind of ornament, or to decorate a building with elaborate mythological narratives in sculpted form. Why not just use repeated decorative moldings, which are easier and less costly? Clearly in the case of monumental architecture, mythological narratives or images were meant to be seen, to be perceived, not simply by the gods but by their mortal worshippers, whose thinking and imagination, whose understanding of the order of things, in turn, shaped the sculptured adornment of their world.

NOTES

1 The Temple of Zeus at Olympia, Heroic Models, and the Panhellenic Sanctuary

1. See Howie (1991, 69) for Pelops as ruler of the Peloponnese; and Herrmann (1980, 59) for Pelops as a Peloponnesian hero. See also Sinn 1991, 48–49; Lacroix 1976. Zeus is credited with the foundation of the games in honor of his victory over Kronos (Paus. 5.7.10). On the founding of the Olympic games and the first event(s), see Burkert (1983, 94–96), who maintains that the *stadion* was "the preeminent agon" at Olympia (96) but does not specify when this was the case.
2. A list of victims killed by Oinomaos is preserved in Hes. frag. 259 M-W, but the circumstances of their deaths are not. See Howie (1991) for Pindar's account and the literary tradition. Bulle (1939, 210ff.) and Shapiro (1994, 78–83) discuss the relationship between the poem and the Olympia sculptures, a connection made originally by Winter in 1925.
3. On the literary tradition, see Barringer 2005b.
4. For a complete account of the literary sources, see Howie 1991; *LIMC* V, 435, s.v. Hippodameia I [M. Pipili]. Another version has Hippodameia bribe Myrtilos with sexual favors; it is not attested until the Hellenistic period although Howie (1991, 92ff.) speculates that Pindar's audience knew this variant.
5. Cf. Stewart (1983, 134), who also thinks that the cheating version is Pherekydes' invention. In favor of an earlier date for a version involving the corruption of Myrtilos, see Howie 1991, 57–59, 99–100 and passim; Hurwit 1987, 7ff.; Becatti in 1939 as reported in Säflund 1970, 36. Other ancient authors who recount this version or variants on it: Eur. *Or.* 988ff.; Ap. Rhod. 1.752–758 and the scholia *ad loc*; Diod. 4.73 in which Oinomaos kills himself after Pelops wins the race by bribing Myrtilos.
6. Patay-Horváth (2004) questions the identity of the figures in the east pediment and argues that the identification of the scene as the preparations for the chariot race of Pelops and Oinomaos is a later development. He does not, however, offer anything more specific for the identity of the original composition than that Figure G portrayed a local hero of some importance.
7. An account doubted by Patay-Horváth (2004, 26–27), who does not believe that the spoils from Pisa could have financed such a splendid structure.

8. Sinn (1994, 592; 1991, 50) cites Jacoby; Knell 1990, 79–80. On the motivation for erecting the temple, see recently, Pimpinelli (1994, 402–405), who provides further bibliography.

9. On worship at the Pelopion and its relationship to that of Zeus at the ash altar, see Antonaccio 1995, 170–176; Burkert 1983, 97ff. Tulunay (1998, 453) states that new excavations reveal that Pelops' stature was nearly as great as Zeus' at Olympia.

10. On the myth, see *LIMC* VIII, 671–721, s.v. Kentauroi et Kentaurides (M. Leventopoulou et al.).

11. His left hand presumably held a bow and arrow (Tersini 1987, 141). Tulunay (1998, 454), however, thinks the bow was a fourth-century B.C. addition by someone who misunderstood the original figure, whom he names as Anatolian Pelops holding a *kentron*. Pausanias (5.10.8) identifies him as Perithoos, and other scholars have adhered to this suggestion (Lapalus 1947, 175–179), but Herakles and a youthful Zeus Areios (Kardara 1970; Dörpfeld, Weege, and Dornseiff, as reported in Lapalus 1947, 174) have also been proposed. Sinn (1994, 593–594) summarizes the various arguments and concludes, as have others, that the figure is Apollo.

12. Sinn (2000, 58, 69) claims that the victorious athletes were crowned in the temple's pronaos but offers no citations to support this statement.

13. See Barringer 2005b, 220–221 for a discussion and bibliography.

14. Sinn 2000, 60. Others see the sculptures as expressive of Olympian claims about territorial control or civil strife.

15. E.g., Stewart (1997, 192–193), who does not accept the cheating version as influential on the pediment but does make the case for divine admonition; Knell 1990, 87 re: west pediment; Raschke 1988, 47; Belloni 1987, 270; Tersini 1987, 140; Stewart 1983, 134. Contra: Sinn (1994, 598–599), who also notes that Simon has proven that the Centauromachy on the Parthenon's south metopes cannot allude to the Persian Wars (598). Simon (1968, 165–166) and Bulle (1939, 217–218) recognize the theme of hubris and consequent vengeance in the west pediment and with regard to Zeus but do not link it to the Persian Wars. Cohen (1994) reads the use of Herakles' club instead of his bow as an anti-Persian statement (the Persians were regarded as great archers) in the aftermath of the Persian Wars.

16. Sinn (1994, 599–600) points to an inscription that describes how a board of arbiters at Olympia mediated civil strife between Athens and Boeotia, the only existing evidence for Olympia's arbitration.

17. Sinn 1991, 60. Kyrieleis (1997, 24) also offers a political explanation for the choice of Pelops in the temple's decoration; he briefly states that the Eleans promoted Pelops in an effort to justify and extend their expansionist policies. Likewise, Raschke (1988) argues that the pediments and metopes refer to the democratization of Elis and the Olympic games. See also Pimpinelli (1994, 406ff.), who, drawing heavily on Pindar, views the sculptures, especially the metopes, as expressions of nature overcome by culture (the νόμος of Zeus) and posits a political reading concerning Elis' claims to power.

18. Cf. Raschke (1988, 48) who briefly states that the viewer of both the temple and surrounding athletic statues was inspired "to emulate an idealized arete."

19. For a brief overview of the excavation history, see Pimpinelli 1994, 350–351.

20. See also Kyrieleis (2006b, 186), who points out that the roof was also of Parian marble and required the largest order of marble from Paros ever made in the Peloponnese until then.

21. On the marble, see now Herrmann 2000; Rehak 1998, 194.

22. See *LIMC* 5, 5–6, s.v. Herakles [J. Boardman] for a discussion of the labors and their treatment in literature.

23. A recent study and reconstruction of the chest is offered by Splitter 2000. See Arafat (1995) for the Heraion's function.

24. See Splitter 2000, 16–22.

25. Splitter 2000, 21.

26. On the transfer of artistic motifs from Athens to Olympia, see, e.g., Raschke (1988, 46–47), who posits that the Eleans appropriated Athenian symbols when they adopted a democracy along the lines of that in Athens after 471. For the date of the original group of the Tyrannicides, see the lucid summary in Shapiro 1994, 124; and also Raubitschek 1940, 58 n. 2.

27. E.g., Florence, Museo Archeologico Etrusco 4209, *ABV* 76, no. 1; *Para* 29; *Addenda²* 21. Also on a bronze relief of c. 650–625 B.C. from Olympia (Mallwitz and Herrmann 1980, 77–78, no. 42). See also *LIMC* VIII, 671–721, s.v. Kentauroi et Kentaurides [M. Leventopoulou et al.].

28. The equine nature of both pediments is noteworthy, as are Hippodameia's name ("horse tamer") and the fact that Perithoos' wife is sometimes named as Hippodameia, too (e.g., Hom. *Il.* 2.742). The importance of horses and chariot racing at Olympia was not limited to the fifth century; the numerous bronze dedications of horses at Olympia date back to the Geometric period. Mallwitz (1988, 81–85) notes that all such votives were damaged, which is unusual for bronzes. It is also remarkable that a number of divinities honored at Olympia are linked to horses via the suffix Hippios/Hippia (see Paus. 5.15.5–6). See also Lacroix (1976, 330–331), who points out the importance of horses to Elis and also notes their connection with Hippodameia's name.

29. Robertson 1975, 280–281; Barron 1972.

30. Heiden 2003. Lapalus (1947, 171) accepts it as the Thessalian myth but cites von Wilamowitz-Moellendorf's idea that the pediment portrays the Centaurs of Mount Pholoe attacking the daughters of Dexamenos (note 2). Holloway (1967, 97–98) refutes von Wilamowitz-Moellendorf's proposal.

31. Rehak 1998, 199.

32. By contrast, Raschke (1988, 41–45) takes the opposite view: that the statues on the temple are meant to emulate statues of Olympic victors in the Altis.

33. Sinn 1994, 596–598, 1991, 40–51.

34. Ael. *NA* 5.17; Philostr. *De Gymnastica* 17. Dillon (2000) responds to criticisms of the accuracy of Pausanias' text and argues that the exclusion of married women derives from a myth concerning Hippodameia after her marriage (Paus. 6.20.7). Burkert (1983, 100) is right to point out that the presence of a representative of Demeter at Olympia unites Pelops, Zeus, and Demeter, who were joined in the myth of Tantalos' infanticide.

35. Dillon 2000, 458, 461–462, 468; Steiner 1998, 140–143. On the Pindar passage, see, e.g., Perysinakis 1990, 43–44; and more generally on the ode and its association of wedding and athletics, Carson 1982. See also Achilles Tatius 1.18.

36. On the date, see Scanlon 2002, 110–117; and Serwint (1993, 405–406), who summarizes previous scholarship.

37. The girls may have worn a man's *exomis* (Serwint 1993, followed by Scanlon 2002, 108) although Scanlon (1984, 79–81) earlier suggested a short chiton like those worn by Amazons, Spartan girls, and participants in the Arkteia. Serwint (1993, 407–408, Fig. 1) and others (e.g., Scanlon 2002, 101–102, 116) associate two statues of female runners, a Lakonian(?) bronze statuette (London, British Museum 208) and a Roman marble copy (Rome, Vatican, Museo Pio-Clementino inv. 2784), with Heraia participants.

38. E.g., Scanlon 2002, 98–99, 101, 119–120; Dillon 2000, 460; Clark 1998, 21; des Bouvrie 1995, 62–63. Cf. Calame 1997, 115–116; Serwint 1993; Scanlon 1984, 79, 83–85, 90.

39. Scanlon 2002, 101–107, 111; Bonfante 1989, 559.

40. Men certainly watched Spartan girls exercise in the nude. See Dillon (2000, 465–466), who also notes that Plut. *Mor.* 249d reports that suitors on Keos watched *parthenoi* performing sports and dances but does not mention nudity. Indeed, Dillon goes so far as to claim that female athletics were a Dorian feature (466).

41. As inspired by the Heraia runners, according to Scanlon 2002, 108.

42. Säflund (1970, 42) reports that Floriani Squarciapino (1955) pointed out that Hippodameia's gesture links her to Hera, who is often characterized by the same gesture.

43. Stehle and Day (1996, 105) maintain that Hippodameia and Pelops are counterparts: both are heroic patrons of athletics and revered as such by women and men, respectively.

44. The arguments are summarized in Trianti 2002; Kyrieleis 1997, 13–14; and Tersini 1987, 140–142. See also Stewart 1983, 135–136; Säflund (1970) for a summary and another reconstruction; and Simon 1968. Note that the current arrangement of the figures in the Olympia Museum (Fig. 7) differs from the reconstruction presented in Fig. 8.

45. E.g., Kyrieleis 1997, 21–22; Simon 1968, 155. See now the description of the current arrangement of figures in the Olympia Museum, together with an account of new fragments, their position, and technical observations in Trianti (2002), who makes the argument that Zeus looks to his left, where she places Pelops (294–297).

46. See Splitter 2000, 23–24 for a reconstruction of this portion of the chest.

47. Göttingen, Georg-August-Universität J22, *ABV* 508, 1; Splitter 2000, 24. See Barringer 2005b, 222 n. 31 for further bibliography.

48. Athens, National Museum 595 (CC968) attributed to the Sappho Painter; *LIMC* 7, 20 no. 5, s.v. Oinomaos [I. Triantis]; *LIMC* 7, 284 no. 12, s.v. Pelops [I. Triantis]. See Barringer 2005b, 222 n. 31 for further bibliography.

49. E.g., Osborne 1998, 171–172; Spivey 1996, 34; Hurwit 1987; Pollitt 1972, 34; Frickenhaus in 1923 as cited in Säflund 1970, 31.

50. Stewart (1997, 260) suggests that the prominence of the two seers may be a political gesture on the part of Elis to link itself to Sparta. For the identities of the seers, see Bulle 1939, 213ff.; and Simon (1968, 157–162), who counts Figure E as yet a third seer, Melampus, and explores their links to Zeus.

51. On the identity of the river gods, see Simon 1968, 162–165.

52. Cf. Kyrieleis' (1997, 19–20) observation regarding Sterope's mourning gesture. Several scholars have suggested that the two seers' visages are portraits of contemporary priests descended from Iamos and Klytios. See Bulle 1939, 213; Säflund 1970, 41. Stewart (1983, 139–140) regards the seers' expressions as

registering apprehension and horror but as responses to Oinomaos' defeat, not to cheating. Cf. Simon, 1968, 158.

53. For others who find a cheating version on the pediment incredible: Hirschfeld, Loeschke, Six, all reported in Säflund 1970; von Wilamowitz-Moellendorff 1922, 414 n. 1. While it could be argued that cheating in this instance would be justified by Oinomaos' cruel or obstructive behavior, thus allowing Pelops to maintain heroic stature, such an ambiguous reading is not supported by surrounding monuments and practices at Olympia, which exhibit clear disapproval of cheating, nor is official art likely to have encouraged such a multivalent reading of Pelops.

54. The earliest Zanes base can be dated to the early fourth century B.C. See Mallwitz 1972, 74–75.

55. Robertson (1975, 271) mentions that the bases of the monument were partially covered by dumped material from the construction of the Temple of Zeus, hence the date. On the Achaian dedication, see Kyrieleis 1997, 18; Eckstein 1969, 27–32.

56. *LIMC* 7, 284–285 nos. 8–11, 17, 25, 29, s.v. Pelops [I. Triantis].

57. For a discussion of whether this armor was integral to the original composition or a later addition, see the discussion in Barringer 2005b, 226 n.43.

58. Cf. des Bouvrie 1995, 63, 67; Scanlon 1988.

59. Des Bouvrie (1995, 67) gives the date. The armed race began at the Pythian Games at Delphi in c. 480.

60. Scanlon 1988, 233ff.

61. On the oracle, see Sinn (1991), who dates its inception at least to the eighth century B.C. and notes its new prominence in the seventh century B.C. for west Greek colonists (46ff.).

62. Scanlon (1988) gathers the written evidence.

63. Pl. *Prt.* 326b–c; Plut. *Mor.* 639D-E; and Philostr. *De Gymastica*. See also Serwint 1993, 417.

64. Kurke 1993, 133–137.

65. Barringer 2001, 2–46 with further bibliography; Golden 1998, 23–28; Scanlon 1988, 235–238.

66. Golden 1998, 12ff., 91ff. with further bibliography; Nagy 1979, 117.

67. For recent discoveries at the site of the Pelopion, including a Mycenaean grave beneath it, see Kyrieleis 2006a. Kyrieleis (2002, 219) and Antonaccio (1993, 62) place the foundation of the Pelops cult in the archaic period. Herrmann (1980, 62–66) claims that the Pelops myth, the Pelopion, and the Olympic competition date to the Mycenaean period. Heilmeyer (1972) claims that the earliest votives are Protogeometric and therefore dates the instigation of cult worship in the tenth century B.C. The earliest votives seem intended for Zeus; Hera's worship may not have begun until the fifth century. See Moustaka 2002. Serwint (1993, 405–406) summarizes challenges to the traditional founding date of 776 B.C. for the Olympic games and notes that recent scholarship places it in 704 B.C. on the basis of fill from wells near the stadium. Cf. Mallwitz (1988), who dates the inception of the games to c. 704 but the cult back at least to the Protogeometric period.

68. Cf. Scanlon 1988, 237–240.

69. Scanlon 1988, 240.

70. Noted by Scanlon 1988, 243.

71. Perysinakis 1990.

72. Moreover, Hera, who is honored by a temple at Olympia, was worshiped elsewhere, for example, at Argos, by rituals flavored with military overtones, such as military processions and contests for which armor was awarded as prizes: Pind. *Nem.* 10.22–23. See also Burkert (1983) 163 for further references.
73. Trans. F. Nisetich, Baltimore, 1980.
74. E.g., Simon (1968, 148–149) with discussion of previous scholarship. Contra: Patay-Horváth (2004, 23–24), who repeats and expands some of the same points in Patay-Horváth 2005.
75. In this passage, Pausanias also describes the footrace held by Danaos to marry off his daughters.
76. On the parallels between the Heraia and the Olympic games, see Scanlon 2002, 111–112; Golden 1998, 129–131; des Bouvrie, 1995; Scanlon 1984.
77. Stadia for girls also existed elsewhere in the Classical period. See, e.g., Dillon 2000; Serwint 1993, 417ff.
78. Probably added later: see Robertson (1975, 284ff.) for a discussion of date and authorship.
79. See Lapatin (2001, 84–85), who briefly discusses the importance of Nike in the iconography of the Zeus statue and posits that many of the myths incorporated in the Pheidian image at Olympia concern the punishment of hubris.
80. Cf. also Pimpinelli 1994, 379, 405–410, and passim; and Geertman (1982, 74–75) on the geographical distribution of the labors.
81. Cf. also Holloway 1967, 99–101.
82. Herakles' mares were also victorious in the Olympic games, according to Pausanias 5.8.3.
83. Pimpinelli 1994, 354; Raschke 1988, 43–44.
84. Pimpinelli 1994, 353.
85. For a recent publication, see Kosmopoulou 2002, 73–74, 77, 200–202, Figs. 55–57. Relief sculpture is conjectured for the fourth side, perhaps Poulydamas with the steer or with the horse-drawn chariot mentioned by Paus. 6.5.6. The inscribed base on which Poulydamas' statue survives has been recovered: see Taeuber 1997. No remains of the statue itself can be certainly identified with the base but Moreno (1995, 94–95) speculates on stylistic grounds that a marble head in Copenhagen with cauliflower ears (Ny Carlsberg Glyptotek inv. 118) may be a copy of that of Poulydamas by Lysippos, while Schauenburg (1963) identifies marble heads in Rome and Magdeburg as deriving from the Poulydamas type.
86. Attic red-figure amphora of c. 520 B.C. in London, British Museum B193, attributed to the Andokides Painter. *ARV* 4, 8; *Addenda*¹ 149.
87. Also noted by Sinn 1991, 48.
88. Kosmopoulou 2002, 200.
89. A free-standing group of Herakles shooting the Nemean lion by the sculptor Nikodamos of Mainalos was dedicated by Hippotion of Taranto and placed against the wall of the Altis (Paus. 5.25.7). The group is lost but the inscribed base, with cuttings for the lion, survives, together with its inscription. Presumably, Herakles appeared on a second adjacent base. See *OlBer* 6, 6. Taeuber (1997, 242–243) adds another level to the allusion: he thinks that Poulydamas is likened not only to Herakles, but also to Alexander, who appears as a lion hunter in artistic representations and also "conquered" the Persian king. This seems to push the evidence rather far, since Alexander is always shown hunting with others and using conventional weapons, not wrestling the lion, and the Persian empire was impressed, not destroyed, by Poulydamas.

90. On the extraordinary stature of athletic victors, see Kurke (1993), who also provides citations.
91. Kurke 1993, 141–149.
92. For a recent discussion of Theagenes' statue, see Jones 1998.
93. Grandjean and Salviat 2000, 73–76; Chamoux 1979, 143–153. Chamoux restores an altar atop the four-stepped base. Some scholars, e.g., Bentz and Mann (2001, 240), have seen the flourishing of these cults in the fifth century as linked to elite culture, also exemplified by epinician poetry in the first quarter of the century, under threat, and as a desire to exalt aristocratic achievement. Others explain the phenomenon as motivated by specific political circumstances in each city that made it advantageous to promote an Olympic victor as a civic figure. See Bohringer 1979. Another point of view disavows any connection between the foundation of the cult and the fact that the recipient was an Olympic victor. See Bentz and Mann 2001, 235. This strains credibility: why would Herodotos, Pausanias, and other authors mention the Olympic victory if it were not an important factor?
94. On the power of victors' statues, see Kurke 1993, 149–153.
95. Taeuber 1997, 242–243; Moreno 1974, 10–11.
96. Cf. Pind. *Nem.* 8.85–87, where losers cannot even earn a smile or laughter from their mothers, *Ol.* 8.65–69, and frag. 229.
97. On the issue of athletes' social status, see Pleket 1992; Raschke 1988, 47. On the cultural values associated with athletics as revealed by Pindar, see Lee 1983.
98. Translation by F. Nisetich, Baltimore 1980.
99. Translation by W. H. Race, Loeb edition.
100. Translation by F. Nisetich, Baltimore 1980, and W. H. Race, Loeb edition.
101. Paus. 5.10.2, 5.11.1–11; Strabo 8.3.30; Dio Chrys. *Or.* 12.50–52.
102. On the statue of Zeus, see now Lapatin 2001, 79–88. On the base, see Kosmopoulou 2002, 240–242.
103. For a recent treatment of the Philippeion, see Schultz (2007), who convincingly argues that the entire design was Philip's alone and that the building was completed before his death in 336.
104. See Lapatin 2001, 115–119 for the Philippeion statues.
105. Schultz (2007) argues against the testimony of Pausanias here, believing the bases to have been prepared for marble statues, which were probably gilt at some point; even if this is the case, Schultz also points out that marble portraits of living individuals in sanctuaries would have been heroizing at this time.
106. Lapatin 2001, 118.
107. See Schultz (2007) with further bibliography, which also adresses Philip's divine pretensions. See also *ThesCRA* 2, 164–167, which assembles the literary and material evidence for the heroization and divinization of Philip.
108. Lapatin 2001, 117.

2 The Athenian Akropolis, Female Power, and State Religion

1. For a recent and thorough presentation with ample bibliography, see Hurwit 1999.
2. For the Gigantomachy suggestion and a review of the evidence, see the unpublished doctoral dissertation: Shear 2001, 29–71.

3. The xoanon resided on the north part of the Akropolis in the Old Temple of Athena in the sixth and and part of the fifth century B.C., then was moved to the Erechtheion, when it was constructed in the last years of the fifth century B.C. See now Ferrari (2002a), who suggests that the Old Temple of Athena was still standing and housed the statue after the Persian Wars.

4. Hurwit 2004, 106.

5. Hurwit 2004, 107. Hurwit (2004, 112) also makes the case that the temple "functioned principally as a treasury, as a votive and as a symbol."

6. And a third frieze may have been planned and partially executed; see infra n. 47.

7. See Korres 1994b; Korres 1994c.

8. Though at least one scholar has suggested that they were Corinthian, not Ionic. See Pedersen 1989.

9. E.g., Pollitt 2000, 224–225; Palagia 1998, 40; Castriota 1992, 148–149.

10. Cf. Pollitt 2000, 225.

11. A minority view maintains that the metopes depict Greeks fighting Persians, but a close examination of the sculptures themselves at eye level clearly indicates that the figures are females, thus Amazons. See Wesenberg 1983b for further discussion. For careful descriptions and discussions of the metopes, including the identification of the scenes, see Brommer 1967, 3–22.

12. E.g., *LIMC* 1, 587 nos. 1–3, 597 nos. 168–174, among many other examples.

13. For citations and a catalog of objects, see *LIMC* 1, 586–653 [P. Devambez].

14. E.g., Attic black-figure skyphos fragments, Athens, National Museum, published in Graef and Langlotz 1925, 466, pl. 22.

15. For the variants, see *LIMC* 1, 639ff., s.v. Amazones [P. Devambez].

16. Most recently, see Mostratos (2004), who summarizes previous scholarship and provides a new reconstruction of his own.

17. The literary evidence is collected in *LIMC* 1, 191–196, s.v. Gigantes [F. Vian].

18. E.g., *LIMC* 1, 215–217, nos. 104–108, 112–113, 119, s.v. Gigantes [F. Vian]

19. The written sources do not date before the last quarter of the fifth century B.C. but this was presumably an old practice. See *LIMC* 1, 210, s.v. Gigantes [F. Vian] for the testimony.

20. *LIMC* 8, 650–651, s.v. Ilioupersis [M. Pipili] provides the literary testimony, and lists which episodes are treated by each author.

21. *LIMC* 8, 651–652, nos. 1, 5, s.v. Ilioupersis [M. Pipili].

22. Brommer 1967, 48–51.

23. Brommer 1967, 54.

24. Brommer 1967, 42.

25. Brommer 1967, 43.

26. Brommer (1967, 52, 66) discusses the various identifications made until then.

27. Brommer 1967, 97–109.

28. Schwab (2005, 174), who cites Westervelt, personal communication, as the author of this idea.

29. Robertson 1984.

30. Simon 1975.

31. Wesenberg 1983a.

32. Korres 1994b, 68–69.

33. E.g., Attic black-figure plaque fragments, Athens, National Museum, Akropolis 1.2553, Graef and Langlotz 1925, 2553, pl. 108.

34. Metope S27: Stewart 1990, 155. Metope S32: Boardman 1985a, 105. West frieze figure: Harrison (1984, 234), who sees this scene as a visual analogue for the *synoikismos* or unification of Attika. Contra: Pollitt 1997, 55–57.

35. Hurwit 1999, 130.
36. Kaltsas 2002, 96–97 n. 169.
37. E.g., Neils 1987, 46.
38. Neils (1987, 108) suggests that the Kritios Boy (Athens, Akropolis Museum 698) may be Theseus on the basis of his hairstyle.
39. See Plut. *Kim.* 8.5–6, *Thes.* 36; Paus. 1.17.6.
40. Metope E9: Boardman 1985b, 232. Metope E11: Brommer 1967, 34.
41. E.g., Kreuzer 2005, 194–195; Lapatin 2001, 67; Hurwit 1999, 169; Blundell 1998, 55; Korres 1994c, 33; Castriota 1992, 41–58, 137–138, 141–183, and passim (he provides a list of scholars who endorse this view on p. 282 n. 15); Shapiro 1989, 149. Wesenberg (1983b, 206 n. 22) presents bibliography until 1983 and differentiates the issue of a metaphorical use of myth in place of reality from parallel political contexts (206–208).
42. Questioning the prevailing view, see Ridgway 1999, 154, 164. Korres (1994a, 58) interprets the metopes as images of Agon, rather than showing victors and vanquished.
43. Shapiro 2006; Eaverly 1995, 100–106.
44. The juxtaposition of an Amazonomachy and a fighting Centaur on fragments of an Attic red-figure kylix of c. 500–475 B.C. from Tarquinia attributed to the Kleophrades Painter suggests an analogous relationship between Amazons, who fight against Herakles and another Greek, and Centaurs, one of whom, galloping while brandishing a long branch, serves as an Amazon shield device. See Paris, Cabinet des Médailles 535, 699, *ARV*² 191, 103; *Addenda*² 189. For a brief history of the scholarship on Amazons from the nineteenth century onward, see Stewart (1995), who also emphasizes the Amazons' status as parthenoi.
45. *ARV*² 189, 74; 1632; *Para* 341; *Addenda*² 189.
46. E.g., Neils 2001; Jenkins 1994. For excellent illustrations and commentary, see Brommer 1977.
47. Korres (1994a, 94–95 n. 28; 1994b) speculates that in the original design, i.e., with a standard Doric frieze over the pronaos and opisthodomos prostyle columns, a continuous Ionic frieze was planned directly atop the cella wall.
48. On the identity of the bearded males on the east frieze, see Neils (2001, 158–161), who summarizes the various identifications, including marshals, magistrates, and eponymous heroes, and concludes that the best identification may be that they are embodiments of Attika's *phylai* (161).
49. Blundell (1998, 62–63) suggests that the sixteen women carrying objects on the east frieze may be ergastinai.
50. Contra: Harrison (1984), who argues that each side represents a different time period.
51. Neils 2005, 216–218.
52. Pollitt 1997, 53–55.
53. Boardman (1977; 1984) argued for the one immediately preceding the Greek victory over the Persians at the Battle of Marathon in 490, a victory for which Athenians were largely responsible, effectively making the frieze and the building a type of heroon to these war heroes. See also Boardman 1999. Holloway (1966) argues that the frieze depicts the statues on the Akropolis destroyed by the Persians animated and participating in the Panathenaic procession, a view that has found no acceptance to my knowledge.
54. Kardara 1961.
55. Brommer 1977, 145–150.

80. On korai, see the recent studies by Karakasi 2003; Keesling 2003. Numerous small late archaic and early classical bronze figures of a striding Athena Promachos (Athena at the head of battle, in keeping with her role as warrior goddess), her right arm wielding a spear, were dedicated on the Akropolis. Athena Nike (victory) was honored by a shrine and altar on the southwest bastion of the Akropolis for centuries before an Ionic temple was built for this purpose c. 437–424. See Mark 1993, and the review of it by Wesenberg 1998. Ziro (1994) offers a revision of the chronology. Athenians worshipped Athena Hygieia (health) on the Akropolis, as indicated by an altar and statue base near the Propylaia of the 420s, but the cult dates back to the late archaic period. See Hurwit 2004, 192–194; Ridgway 1992, 137–138.

81. See Keesling 2003, 97–121, on this issue with further bibliography. She believes that the korai found on the Akropolis mostly depict Athena.

82. Keesling 2003, 124.

83. E.g., Raubitschek 1949, 234–235 no. 201 of c. 500, 320–321 no. 297 of c. 475–450, 398–399 no. 369 dated just before c. 480, 406 no. 378 of c. 450; Dillon 2001, 14–18. On the treasuries from the Akropolis, see Harris 1995, especially 225–228.

84. Harris 1995, 236.

85. See Dillon 2001, 37–41, for kanephoroi.

86. For a recent treatment of this sanctuary and its cult statue by Praxiteles (of which the head, Akropolis 1352, survives), see Despinis 1997.

87. E.g., Kahil 1981. Contra: Hamilton 1989. Ferrari (2002b, 166–176) challenges the commonly held view that the krateriskoi depict elements of the Arkteia ritual. Fragmentary krateriskoi have been found outside of a typically Artemisian context: in the cave of Pan at Vari and in the cave at Eleusis. See Schörner and Goette 2004, 114, Taf. 50:4; 118.

88. Ferrari (2002b, 166, 176–177) suggests that all Athenian aristocratic girls were *eligible*, which is undoubtedly true.

89. Dillon 2001, 20; Cole 1998.

90. Dillon 2001, 19–20; Cole 1998, 32–42. The records of offerings to Artemis Brauronia may be duplicates of those kept at Brauron, and therefore, the offerings should be understood as having been made there and not on the Akropolis. See Linders 1972, especially 70–73. For other testimony of premarital offerings or *proteleia* to Artemis, see Oakley and Sinos 1993, 133 n.6.

91. Deacy (1997) draws similarities between Athena and the typical parthenos, mythological or actual, but Athena is a goddess and therefore is anything but typical; her androgyny is "socially" permissible only because of her special status.

3 Making Heroes in the Athenian Agora

1. The question of whether this building was the Theseion or the temple to Hephaistos and Athena was a preoccupation of earlier scholars. For a summary of the controversy, see Reber 1998, 32. But the identification has been challenged again recently by Wetzel (1996), who claims that the structure does not accord with temple architecture and planning and therefore we should not think of this structure as a temple.

2. Date of 449 for initiation of construction: Dinsmoor (1975, 180) on the basis that it must be just before the Parthenon and the potsherds found among

stonemasons' chips; Thompson and Wycherley 1972, 142–143; Boersma (1964, 102–106) as part of a larger Kimonian building program (cf. Cruciani and Fiorini [1998], who broaden the dates to c. 450–445 but accept the Kimonian patronage). Ridgway (1981, 27) and Morgan (1962a, 219) put it at c. 450. For 460: Reber (1998, 32, 47) reviews the evidence and proposals, and advocates a date for the beginning of construction just after the Ephialtic reforms of 462/1. Camp (2001, 103) places the beginning of construction c. 460–450 B.C., and Delivorrias (1997b, 95) thinks it was no earlier than 454/453 B.C.

3.   Dinsmoor (1975, 180) claims that Pentelic was used for the building, Parian for the sculpture, and Thompson (1949, 233) assigned both Parian and Pentelic sculpture to the Pentelic and Parian marble building. See also Scheffer 1996, 182. Delivorrias (1997b, 87) declares the controversy to be over: all the architectural sculpture was made of Parian marble.

4.   Delivorrias (1997b, 84) and Neils (1987, 127) place them in the 450s. On the metopes, see also Morgan 1962a.

5.   On the controversial date of the building, see Fittschen 2003, 12–15; Rolley 1999, 218–219; Amandry 1998; Maass 1993, 174. The style of its architectural details and sculpture suggests a date in the late sixth or early fifth century B.C. but an inscribed base associated with it points to a post-Marathon date. Amandry (1998) also argues that the statues did not belong to the original dedication but were placed on the base sometime later.

6.   Thompson (1962, 340–341) discusses the possibilities, including a Hesperid (also advocated by Morgan 1962a, 212), and weighs in in favor of Athena. He is followed in this identification by Ridgway (1981, 29–30).

7.   Knell 1990, 130, 133. Ralf von den Hoff also pointed out to me that compositional elements seem to be efforts to liken Herakles to Theseus. I am currently investigating these possibilities.

8.   Neils 1987, 126–127; Thompson 1962, 341; Morgan (1962a, 212–214) discusses the identification of the adventures and the problematic Periphetes and Prokrustes metopes.

9.   See *LIMC* 7, 922, s.v. Theseus [Neils] for the literary tradition.

10. Florence, Museo Archeologico 4209, *ABV* 76, 1; *Para* 29; *Addenda*[2] 21.

11. See Xen. *An.* 5.3.4–5; and Maass 1993, 168–170. On the controversial ordering of the metopes and their placement around the building, see Hoffelner (1988), who reviews the scholarship and offers his own reconstruction, giving the south and north sides to Theseus, and the east and west to Herakles.

12. On the akroteria, see De la Coste-Messelière 1957, 182–187. Other parallels between the Athenian Treasury at Delphi and the Hephaisteion sculptures are striking: the use of a single narrative stretched across two metopes occurs not only in the east metope of Herakles fighting Geryon on the Hephaisteion but also on the Monopteros of Sikyon at Delphi, where the ship of the Argonauts occupies two metopes. Likewise, the assembly of gods watching the combatants on the Hephaisteion east frieze finds a parallel on the east frieze of the Siphnian Treasury at Delphi, where the gods observe and discuss the battle between Achilles and Memnon. See Knell 1990, 18–38.

13. See, for example, Felten 1984, 58; Ridgway 1981, 88. Delivorrias (1997b, 95) objects to a date between 430 and 420 B.C. and instead places them between 436 and 431 B.C. Von Bockelberg (1979, 48) assigns them to c. 430–425.

14. Boersma 1964, 106.

15. See, for example, Cohen 1983.

16. Thompson (1949, 244–247) interprets him as Zeus in a depiction of the introduction of Herakles to Olympos. See also Thompson (1962, 344–345), who identifies the eastern akroteria as Hesperides and agrees with Harrison's interpretation of the west pediment as the Centauromachy at the wedding of Perithoos (see Kotsidu [1995, 98], who also concurs with Harrison's hypothesis). Morgan (1963), however, interprets the east pediment as the birth of Athena. Scheffer (1996) thinks that the east pediment portrays the return of Hephaistos and believes that the enthroned figure was Hera, and Simon (1998, 199) accepts this proposal. On sculptures assigned to the pediments, see Delivorrias 1997b, 96–100; Thompson 1949.

17. Berlin, Staatliche Museen F2273, ARV^2 174, 31, $Addenda^2$ 184; Florence, Museo Archeologico 81 600, $LIMC$ 4, 633 no. 44, s.v. Hephaistos [A. Hermary and A. Jacquemin].

18. Fragmentary Attic red-figure cup, Berlin, Staatliche Museen F2294, ARV^2 400, 1, *Para* 370, $Addenda^2$ 230; Attic white-ground alabastron, Brussels, Musées Royaux d'Art et d'Histoire 2314, $LIMC$ 4, 632 no. 12, s.v. Hephaistos [A. Hermary and A. Jacquemin].

19. Wyatt and Edmonson 1984. Two series of letter forms exist, one of c. 460–450 B.C., another c. 420 B.C., which together demonstrate a delay in the construction process.

20. $LIMC$ 4, 634–636 no. 67–81, s.v. Hephaistos [A. Hermary and A. Jacquemin].

21. See, e.g, Kosmopoulou (2002, 129), who summarizes the evidence and provides bibliography; $LIMC$ 4, s.v Hephaistos [A. Hermary and A. Jacquemin] 634–635 no. 67; $LIMC$ 2, s.v. Athena [P. Demargne] 979 n. 241. Brommer (1978, 75–90) neatly illustrates and discusses the various reconstructions and offers one of his own.

22. On the myth of Erichthonios and his original identification with Erechtheus, see $LIMC$ 4, s.v. Erechtheus [U. Kron], 923–9251. According to Kron, the two mythological figures were only clearly differentiated in the second half of the fifth century. See also $LIMC$ 4, s.v. Hephaistos [A. Hermary and A. Jacquemin], 629. Robertson (1985) dates the inception of the myth of Erichthonios' birth from Hephaistos' pursuit of Athena to the mid-sixth century B.C. and is firm in distinguishing Erichthonios from Erechtheus (254–256). For the base showing the birth of Erichthonios, see Harrison (1977, 137–178), who accepts Papaspyridi-Karusu's reconstruction of 1954–1955, and more recently Delivorrias (1997a), who offers a somewhat different reconstruction based on the rather startling idea that Athena and Hephaistos enjoyed a *hieros gamos* and would place the scene in the sanctuary of Aphrodite in the Gardens. On the reconstruction of the baby held in Athena's arms, see Palagia 2000, 68–74. For a summary of other views of the subject of the cult statue base and a recent survey of the evidence, see Kosmopoulou (2002, 126–130, 242–244), who favors the birth of Erichthonios on the base. Based on the cuttings on the presumed orthostate blocks of Eleusinian limestone, twelve figures were attached to the base.

23. For recent treatments of this myth and the issue of autochthony in fifth-century Athens, see, e.g., Cohen 2000, 82–103; Shapiro 1998.

24. For example, Reber 1998, 35, 45; Knell 1990, 134–138; Felten 1984, 58; Thompson 1962, 343.

25. Delivorrias 1997b, 87.

26. Cf. Dinsmoor 1975, 181; and Thompson (1962, 342–343), who also remarks on the effort to unify the parts of the east porch. But see Morgan (1962a), who

27. For example, Harrison 2005, 122; Reber 1998, 45; Von Bockelberg 1979, 27; Morgan 1962b, 222, 223, 226.
28. Thompson (1962, 347) briefly mentions the suitability of the Hephaisteion's Theseus imagery for the building's location near the west side of the Agora.
29. Miller (1995) identifies this structure as the Old Metroon.
30. See Shear (1994, 231–241) for the dates of the initial constructions of the Old Bouleuterion and the Royal Stoa.
31. Camp (1986, 100) places their length at 25 m, while Miller (1995, 145) estimates their total length as more than 37 m. A fifth row of benches may once have existed; see Miller 1995, 147 n. 38. Thompson and Wycherley (1972, 149) also mention a ramp that was built running from the Agora up to the east façade of the temple on the Kolonos Agoraios but offer no explanation or evidence.
32. Arguing against Thompson (1937, 220), who puts their construction at c. 450 and after the Hephaisteion, Miller (1995, 147) thinks that the benches preceded the construction of the Hephaisteion and dates them to the time of the construction of the Tholos. For the purposes of this discussion, the coordinated construction of Hephaisteion with the benches is the key point, whichever came first.
33. Boegehold 1967.
34. Miller 1995, 145–156.
35. Wycherley and Thompson 1972, 149; Boegehold (1967, 118–119) estimates that an additional hundred persons could be seated on the hillside below the benches in addition to a minimum of 400 on the benches. Miller (1995, 147) places the seating capacity at about 400, while Camp (1986, 100) provides the more modest estimate of at least 200.
36. The fence is restored by Miller (1995, 149–151) to demarcate his hypothetical Bouleuterion from the rest of the Agora. On the history of the shrine of Apollo, see Hedrick 1988.
37. For example, Von den Hoff 2001.
38. Cruciani and Fiorini 1998, 124–125.
39. Ajootian 1998, 3ff.; Reber 1998, 35–36, 44.
40. For example, Reber 1998, 44; Knell 1990, 132, 138. See also Cruciani and Fiorini 1998, 124, on the metopes.
41. On the Centauromachy, see *LIMC* 8, s.v., Kentauroi et Kentaurides [M. Leventopoulou] 671–710, esp. 689 no. 213.
42. Von den Hoff 2003c, 24–25; Von den Hoff 2001, 79, 83–85. Von den Hoff (2001, 85, 88) notes the Hephaisteion's divergence from this model.
43. Von den Hoff 2003b, 33. For the issue of ephebes in the fifth-century, see the summary of scholarship in Barringer 2001, 47–59.
44. Von den Hoff 2003a, 19–21; Von den Hoff 2003b, 34; Von den Hoff 2003c, 25.
45. Von den Hoff 2003b, 33–34; Bugh 1990, 20.
46. Contra: Bugh 1990. According to the second-century inscriptions, the events included *euandria, euoplia,* torch race, gymnastic, and equestrian competitions. See Bugh 1990, 22ff.
47. Bugh 1990, 22–24.
48. An alternate tradition, Hom. *Il.* 18.382, has him married to Charis (Grace), and Hesiod, *Theogony* 945–946, names his wife as Aglaia. See Shapiro 1995, 10–11.

49. *LIMC* 4, 630, s.v. Hephaistos [A. Hermary and A. Jacquemin] collects the sources. See also Robertson 1985, 273–276.

50. Shapiro (1995, 1–2) notes that none of the literary or epigraphical evidence for the cult of Hephaistos dates before the last third of the fifth century B.C. though archaeological evidence for cult prior to that time can be inferred, e.g., the later worship of Hephaistos in the Erechtheion. See also Robertson (1985, 270–271), who discusses a marble throne inscribed to the priest of Hephaistos in the Erechtheion (*IG* II² 4982+5166); the lettering suggests a date in the fourth or third century B.C.

51. On the Apaturia, see Hdt. 1.147; Deubner 1956, 232–234, who cites Harpokration (n. 10) for the information pertaining to Hephaistos.

52. Simon 1983, 53; Deubner 1956, 212–213. See also Hdt. 8.98, who mentions a lampadedromia in honor of Hephaistos, and Robertson's (1985, 286) comment on this passage; Robertson posits that the torch race predates *IG* I³ 82 and the end of Herodotos' working life. Sekunda (1990, 155–156) assumes that the Hephaisteia torch race was a relay race, based on Herodotos' description at 8.98.

53. Harrison 1977b, 414–416; Deubner 1956, 213. Harrison also explores the thematic connections between the Chalkeia and Hephaisteia and posits their celebration close to one another in time in the Athenian calendar (415).

54. Papaspyridi-Karusu (1954–1955, 74) suggests that the torches were lit at the anvil next to the statue of Hephaistos in the temple.

55. Robertson (1985, esp. 258–265, 284–287) discusses the Hephaisteion at the Academy, where he locates the myth of Hephaistos' pursuit of Athena and the start of the torch race of the Hephaisteia. According to Robertson, the myth is an aition for the bringing of new fire to the Akropolis from the Academy, which occurred at the Panathenaia.

56. *IG* I³ 36; Robertson 1985, 284. Harrison (1977, 414) proposes that fire was brought from the Academy to the temple, as in other torch races for other festivals, to make it available to households and craftsmen, who would take new fire at the Hephaisteia.

57. Shear 1994, 237–241; Nicholls 1970, 120–123 discusses terracotta fragments that might pertain to this group.

58. Shear 1994, 239–240. Thompson and Wycherley (1972, 83–90) describe the building and mention fragments of the terracotta akroterion (85).

59. Ar. *Lys.* 678 and Arr. *Anab.* 7.13.5 both state that Mikon painted an Amazonomachy but do not locate the painting; Plut. *Kim.* 4.6–7 mentions that Polygnotos has a painting in the Stoa Poikile but does not name the subjects. See Camp 2001, 67–68.

60. Camp (2001, 104) provides the date.

61. See Chapter 2.

62. See Reber 1998, 43, for ancient citations.

63. For example, Ar. *Eq.* 1311–1312; Plut. *Thes.* 36.4; Robertson 1998, 297–298; Christensen 1984. On the possible location of the Theseion, see, e.g., Hurwit 1999, 101; Robertson 1998, 295–298; Shear 1994, 228.

64. Cf. Shear 1994, 228.

65. Camp 1994, 10; Neils 1992, 18; Shear 1975, 362–365.

66. Athen. 9.402f. citing Mnesimachos, a Middle Comedy writer. See Ajootian 1998, 4–8; Camp (1994, 10) who posits this practice in the sixth century B.C.

67. Thompson and Wycherley 1972, 145.

68. Cf. Ridgway (2005, 114), who argues for the rarity of cult images in bronze and points out the suitability of this medium for the image of Hephaistos in the Hephaisteion.

69. Kotsidu (1995, 100) takes this idea further and claims that the temple specifically addresses this group and, citing Kraterinos 263 and Pherekrates 134, points out that the Kolonos Hill is where the workers received their wages.

70. Reber 1998, 46–47.

71. Cf. Bérard (1976, 111), who also suggests this possibility. On the Chalkeia, see Parker 2005, 464–465; Robertson 1985, 271; Simon 1983, 38–39; Deubner 1956, 35–36, who cites the *Suda*, Harpokration (Phanodemus *FGrH* 325F 18), and *IG* 2² 674, 16, *IG* 2² 930, 3, and *IG* 2² 990, 2. Kotsidu (1995, n. 53) cites modern scholars who claim that the Chalkeia was celebrated on the Akropolis and that Hephaistos was added to Athena Ergane as an object of veneration only later. On Athena Ergane, see Consoli 2004; Hurwit 2004, 27–34; Ridgway 1992.

72. On the passage of Sophokles and the association of the *liknon* with Athena Ergane, see Bérard (1976), who believes that a fragment of an Attic red-figure neck amphora of c. 485–455 B.C. attributed to the Pan Painter, which was dedicated on the Athenian Akropolis, depicts the Chalkeia; Deubner 1956, 36.

73. Simon 1983, 383–389. Shapiro (1995, 3) suggests that the nine months echoes the gestation period of Erichthonios, and I think he is right.

74. According to Kotsidu (1995, 101 and n. 53), Athena Hephaisteia is first mentioned in *IG* II² 223 of the mid-fourth century B.C. but the name appears as a votive dedication on a terracotta plaque (Berlin, Antikensammlung 2759) of the late fifth century from Athens.

75. Cf. Pl. *Leg.* 11.921d–e, which refers to strategoi as craftsmen (δημιουργοί) of another sort, the former sacred to Athena and Ares, the latter sacred to Athena and Hephaistos.

76. I would like to thank Lucy Grig for suggesting this possibility to me.

77. I thank the anonymous reader for Cambridge University Press for this idea.

78. Felten 1984, 60–64, followed by Simon 1998, 197–201; Delivorrias 1997b, 84, 89–90; Kotsidu 1995, 98–99; Knell (1990, 136–137), who sees the battle as an analogue for the Persian Wars (cf. Cruciani and Fiorini [1998], who argue that both friezes are mythological metaphors for the Battle of Marathon and the victory over the Persians).

79. Müller (1833) followed by Harrison (2005, 121–123), who identifies Hephaistos as V, 24 seated among the gods; Reber (1998, 41–43), who views the theme as a mythological analogue of the expulsion of the aristocracy, tyrants, and antidemocratic elements by the people; Neils 1987, 126; and Thompson 1962.

80. See Dörig 1985, 67–73, for a summary of views with bibliography and an interpretation of his own.

81. *LIMC* 7, 935–936, s.v. Theseus [J. Neils].

82. For the exomis, together with literary citations for it, see Serwint 1993, 416–417. For the cult statue, see Harrison 1977a, 146–150.

83. Dörig 1985, 69. If an earthquake is intended by these rock-throwers, a metaphorical reading that may be too far-fetched for this period of time, it might be worthwhile considering one inspiration: earthquakes in 426(?) in Athens, Euboia, and Boeotia (Thuk. 3.87. 3.89), which were apparently devastating. Coming on the heels of a two-year plague, which, according to Thuk. 3.87, reduced the hoplites

by 4,400 and the cavalry by 300 (not to mention thousands of other civilians) in the midst of a war, it must have seemed like the end of the world. Earthquakes forced the Spartans to turn back from invading Attika in 426(?) and produced a tidal wave in Euboia. Earthquakes near the island of Atalante (note the resemblance to the name Atlantis) near Opuntian Locris produced a tidal wave that destroyed an Athenian fort and destroyed two ships tethered to the shore (Thuk. 3.89). Earthquake damage in Athens c. 425 is confirmed by the archaeological record – a massive amount of pottery in a deposit from c. 425 found in the Athenian Agora; part of the northeast corner of the Parthenon, including almost one-third of the east side, moved 2.5 cm to the north, which required repairs; and damage was also done to building Z in the Kerameikos and to the Themistoklean wall. See Rotroff and Oakley 1992, 51–57. It is Poseidon who is connected with earthquakes, at least on the mainland. Interestingly, it is Poseidon whom Plato (*Kritias* 113c) names as the god allotted to Atlantis (just as Athena and Hephaistos were allotted to Athens); he was worshipped in a temple covered with silver and gold, while all the rest, save a roof of ivory, was made of orichalcum, another metal, next in value only to gold (*Kritias* 114e, 116d).

84. Vidal-Naquet (1981, 207) certainly thinks Plato refers to the Hephaisteion in the Agora; and Robertson (1985, 270) takes Plato's reference to indicate that the cult on the Kolonos Hill is earlier than the mid-fifth century.

85. Cruciani and Fiorini 1998, 82; Wycherley and Thompson 1972, 149.

86. Shapiro (1998, 135) refers to the two gods as parents of Erichthonios, who, together with the child, form a "'holy family,'" and elsewhere (1995, 11–13) discusses Hephaistos' connections to marriage.

87. Thompson (1962, 343) observes that the prominence of Athena and the similarity of combatants make it likely that this is a scene of civil strife. Müller 1833, 3–4, acknowledges that he had considered the Atlantis battle as a possibility but dismissed it because of the lack of evidence for the myth earlier than Plato's account.

88. Procl. *In Ti.* 1.85.10–15 (*ad Tim.* 243–25d) states that the battle of Athenians against the inhabitants of Atlantis was embroidered on Athena's peplos given to the goddess in the Lesser Panathenaia, a parallel to the gods' defeat of the giants woven into the peplos for the Greater Panathenaia. Proclus' fifth-century A.D. testimony has been doubted; see the discussion in Mansfield 1985, 93–94 n.35.

89. Rome, Vatican 344 of c. 540 B.C. *ABV* 145, 13, 686; *Para* 60; *Addenda*² 40.

90. Cf. Neer 2004, 76, who draws the same conclusion.

91. Woodford 1971.

92. See the inscription published by Vanderpool 1942.

4 Myth and Religion at Delphi

1. For the date of the inception of Apollo's oracle, see Jacquemin 1999, 23–24.

2. Paus. 10.5.9–13, who cites Pindar as saying that the bronze temple had gold Charmers (Κηληδόνες) above the pediment. See also Strabo 9.3.9. For other sources on the legendary temples, see the discussion by Sourvinou-Inwood (1991, 192–216), who explains that the Keledones had the gift of prophecy and are "mythical prefigurations of the human female prophetess" at the temple (201–202).

3. On the Muses and their cult at Delphi, see Parke 1981, 104–107.

4. Poros blocks, probably from the Alkmaionid temple, were incorporated into part of the south wall of the sanctuary in the fourth century. See Maass (1993, 92, 110–111), who points out that the earthquake only damaged a part of the sanctuary and that the treasuries, the Stoa of the Athenians, the Naxian column, and the monument to the Messenians remained standing.

5. For this chronology, see Croissant 1996, 129.

6. On the construction dates, see, e.g., Neumann-Hartmann 2004, 19 for a brief summary; Croissant 2003, 61; Croissant 1996, 129–130; Flashar 1992, 61–62; Amandry 1989, 27; Bousquet 1977.

7. Although the head, inv. 2380, attributed to Dionysos in the west pediment, is not of Pentelic but perhaps of island marble. See Croissant 2003, 85.

8. See Croissant 2003 for a full catalogue. The figures' being hollowed out in the back makes attribution of fragments somewhat easier; the only exception to this is the figure of Apollo, whose back is solid. See Rolley 1999, 379.

9. Although the first excavations at Delphi, conducted by the French, were begun in 1892, the fragmentary sculptures were not correctly identified with the fourth-century B.C. temple until 1971. Croissant 2003, 3.

10. Croissant 2003.

11. Croissant (2003, 86) discusses the evidence for the kithara and offers a reconstruction. For a much earlier parallel, see Stibbe (1992), who suggests that the figure playing a kithara in the tondo of a Lakonian cup is Dionysos.

12. The head: Delphi, inv. 2380, discovered between the western edge of the temenos and the Treasury of Athenians, is joined to the torso, inv. 1344, discovered in the opisthodomos. See Croissant (2003, 30, 86–87), who discusses the controversial joining of the head to the body, a join that he endorses. Flashar (1992, 60–70) questions it, as does Palagia (*LIMC* 201 no. 101, s.v. Apollo), both of who identify it as Apollo.

13. Scholars had been puzzled by Pausanias' mention of a setting Helios, but Croissant (2003, 33) convincingly determined that this term was poetically used to refer to the cardinal direction, the west pediment, as he recorded the figures that he observed there.

14. Croissant (2003, 165) also draws this contrast.

15. Croissant 2003, 165. Also noted by Villanueva Puig 1986, 38.

16. See Shapiro (1996), who discusses the use of Apollonine imagery on fifth-century Athenian vase painting; Villanueva Puig 1986, 39; and Queyrel (1984, 156–158), who concentrates on Dionysiac and Apollonine scenes by the Pothos Painter, and the merging of Dionysiac imagery with that of Apollo in his work. Moreover, the two deities are worshipped together at other sites, as well. See Detienne 2001, 149ff. See also Croissant 1996. Villanueva Puig (1986, 40–41) gathers and discusses the literary passages, along with the evidence for Dionysiac worship at Delphi long before the fifth century (43–46). The connection between Athens and Delphi in Athenian tragedy, specifically the *Ion* and the *Eumenides*, is explored by Vogt 1998. Neumann-Hartmann (2004, 21) follows Furley and Bremer (2001, 1.126–128) in interpreting Philodamos' paian (see below) to indicate that Dionysos only achieved a permanent place (not a temporary one) in the sanctuary in the fourth century B.C. and goes on to claim that the paian celebrates the Delphic oracle that commanded the change in cult practice.

17. St. Petersburg, Hermitage Museum St. 1807, *ARV*² 1185, 7.

18. Supra n. 16; Metzger 1951, 177–186.
19. Croissant 2003, 178; 1996.
20. Villanueva Puig 1986, 40–41; McInerney (1997, 265), who also discusses the Corycian cave as a cult place of Thyiades (276–283).
21. McInerney 1997, 265; Vogt 1998.
22. Croissant (2003, 150), for example, points to the Apollo Patroos in the Agora and an Apollo Kitharodos on a pelike by the Marsyas Painter. See also Rolley 1999, 380.
23. On the reconstruction, see Croissant 2003, 67–71.
24. Contra: Croissant (2003, 164), who sees a similarity in attitude of the Muses and Thyiades in the temple's pediments.
25. Cf. Croissant 2003, 165.
26. Despinis (2000) has suggested that a Parian marble satyr, 33 cm high, belongs to the eastern pediment of the archaic Temple of Dionysos, c. 500–480 B.C., on the south slope of the Akropolis and that the satyr may have been part of a Gigantomachy that included Dionysos. Gigantomachies would normally include Dionysos but perhaps in this instance – because the temple is dedicated to him – his role was more prominent than in other Gigantomachies. Dionysos also appears reclining on a kline in a symposion relief on a pediment of poros from a late sixth-century temple on Corcyra. Here, however, the scene may have been of the return of Hephaistos in which Dionysos would be a supporting figure. See *LIMC* 3, 456 no. 370, s.v. Dionysos [C. Gasparri].
27. For example, Rolley (1999, 380) points out that it was at the time of the construction of temple of Apollo at Delphi that Athenians, at the initiative of Lykourgos, rebuilt the theater and instituted the Pythiad in 330–325. Vollgraf (1927), thinking that Philodamos' hymn had been composed in 335, believed that the poem and pediments were efforts by Alexander the Great to impose a Thracian-Macedonian version of Dionysiac cult on Delphi. See Croissant 2003, 166.
28. Strauss Clay 1996. Contra: Croissant 2003, 172–173.
29. Croissant 1996, 133–137. But note that the date of the theater's construction is controversial. Cf. Strauss Clay 1996.
30. Croissant (2003, 179–180) emphasizes the Athenian motive to take a leadership role against Macedonia but does not focus on the religious motive asserted here. For the historical circumstances, see Markle (1981, 72–76), who discusses the change in Athenian policy toward Philip from conciliatory to wary and openly defensive in 343 and 342, when they sent embassies into central and southern Greece to seek alliances and encourage opposition to Philip.
31. On the date of the Alkmaionid temple, see now Childs (1993), who dates the structure and its sculptures to c. 530 on the basis of their similarity to the Siphnian Treasury sculptures. For the temple and its reconstructed pediments, see Picard and De la Coste-Messelière 1931, 15–74.
32. Noted by many, e.g., Knell 1990, 44–51.
33. Maass 1993, 104, 108; Knell 1990, 47–49.
34. Davies (2001, 222) summarizes the information from the surviving accounts.
35. Jacquemin 1999, 57.
36. Croissant (1996, 134) thinks that the Athenians wished to use the tyrant's authority to reinforce their power in the Amphictyony. See also Croissant (2003, 175) and Davies (2001, 218–221) for a discussion of the temple's financing based on extant accounts from the 360s and 350s. Elsewhere, Davies (1998, 12–13) argues that Peloponnesian Dorians tried to exert influence to be represented

among the naopai to counterbalance their small numbers on the Amphictyony, and that Peloponnesians received most of the business as contractors and suppliers but the chronological scope of the latter claim is unclear. He makes no mention of the Athenian sculptors contracted to work on the temple. He does point out, however, that the creation of *tamiai* officers at Delphi in perhaps 337 appears to reflect a desire to strengthen the power of the Amphictyony and to render it useful for indirect Macedonian control (14).

37. Cf. Croissant (2003, 174–175), who also draws connections between Athenian involvement in the Alkmaionid temple and that of the fourth century.

38. Cf. Croissant 1996, 134–135.

39. Villanueva Puig (1986) gathers and discusses the evidence.

40. On the Delphic Thyiades, see Sourvinou-Inwood 2005, 211–240.

41. Villanueva Puig 1986, 36.

42. Henrichs 1978. Bremer (1996, 90) makes no distinction between Thyiades and Maenads.

43. Parke 1981, 108.

44. Aisch. *In Ctes.* 116 describes how the Athenians, renewal of their dedication offended the Thebans, whose collaboration with the Persians was recalled by this gesture. This act led to the Fourth Sacred War, which resulted in Macedonian domination of the Greek cities. See Bommelaer 1991, 180. Cf. Paus. 10.19.4, who mentions gold armor taken from the enemy and dedicated by Athenians on the architrave but does not draw the connection with Thebes. See the discussion of this passage by Jacquemin 1999, 58 n. 159; Parke 1939.

45. See Roux 1979, 30–33; Parke 1939, 73–75.

46. Roux 1979, 30.

47. Parke (1939, 75–76) speculates that the shields were promptly removed and replaced later not only because of the impiety but also because to leave them up would have been incongruous with Athens' efforts a short time later to create an alliance with the Thebans against the Macedonians.

48. On the decline of the oracle's power in the fourth century and later, see Arnush 2005.

49. See Despinis and Harrison 2001; Stähler 1991.

50. Despinis and Harrison (2001, 119–121) draw a connection between the Spartan monument honoring Lysander's victory at Aigospotamos and the Marathon Base. Pausanias 10.9.7 says that Poseidon crowned Lysander on this monument, and Despinis and Harrison believe that the same kind of motif existed previously on the Marathon Base, Athena crowning Miltiades. Stähler (1991, 198–199) also sees the Lysander monument as a rejoinder to the Marathon Base, but sees it in terms of Spartan reassertion of control over the Thracian Chersonnese.

51. Vidal-Naquet 1967, 287–290.

52. Erechtheus, Kekrops, Pandion, Leos, Antiochos, Aegeus, Akamas, Kodros, Theseus, and Philaios, as well as Demetrios, Antigonos, and Ptolemy III Euergetes, who were granted eponymous hero status in the Hellenistic period; the first two were probably added to the base in 307/306 and Ptolemy III in 224/223. The restoration of the name "Philaios" in Pausanias is controversial; see Vidal-Naquet 1967, 284–287.

53. *Ath. Pol.* 21.6.

54. See, for example, Despinis and Harrison 2001, 109–110, 121; Stähler 1991, 192; Vidal-Naquet 1967, 282–284.

55. Maass 1993, 190–191. Though this is the earliest known portrayal of the Athenian eponymous heroes, those originally featured on the monument do not accord with the ten heroes created by Kleisthenes' reforms (Ajax, Oineus, and Hippothoon are omitted; and Kodros, Theseus, and Philaios are additions). See Vidal-Naquet 1967.

56. Cf. Despinis and Harrison 2001, 121.

57. See Chapter 3, n. 5 and infra pp. 116–121. Neer (2004, 84–86) argues that the Geryon metopes on the Athenian Treasury were meant to echo the same theme, which he believes appeared on the Alkmaionid Apollo Temple. Though it would support the argument made here, our current knowledge about the two structures does not permit certainty about this.

58. *LIMC* 5, 84, s.v. Herakles [P. Brize].

59. For the pediment fragments and their reconstruction, see De la Coste-Messelière 1957, 167–181.

60. Political readings that view Herakles as representative of Peisistratos or the Alkmaionid family, a powerful aristocratic Athenian clan, and Theseus of the democracy see the building as depicting the usurpation of the Peisistratid political symbol by the Athenian democracy, or as a two-stage building process, which begins by emphasizing Herakles but is completed with an emphasis on Theseus. See, e.g., Williams 1983, 140.

61. See Chapter 3, n. 5. Raubitschek (1974) argues that the Marathon Base with eponymous heroes that Pausanias describes (and scholars locate toward the entry of the sanctuary) is, in fact, the same as the socle that projects from the Athenian Treasury that once bore statues; according to this line of argument, the base near the Treasury was erected in the Kimonian period, and lengthened and given additional statues and recarved inscriptions in the Hellenistic period. Then at a later point, the statues were removed and placed on a socle near the entrance to the sanctuary, which is where Pausanias saw them; the inscribed base that he describes at 10.11.5 was the statueless socle adjacent to the Athenian Treasury. In other words, there are not two such statue dedications from Marathon but one.

62. Bommelaer 1991, 149.

63. We could also add a private Athenian dedication, the bronze palm-tree of Eurymedon inserted into a cylindrical hole with a diameter of 0.38 m. A gilt statue of Athena, gilt dates, and gilt owls were borne by the tree, which commemorates the naval victory and scattering of the Persians near the Eurymedon River by the Athenian Kimon in 465. The palm evokes the earlier Corinthian Treasury at Delphi, which included a bronze palm, a suitable motif for Apollo. Paus. 10.15.4–5 and Plut. *Nikias* 13.3 report seeing the monument, so it was not destroyed in the earthquake of 373, which damaged the nearby sixth-century temple of Apollo.

64. This date is the general scholarly consensus, but Geominy (1998) downdates the monuments to c. 287–277 B.C. Jacquemin and Laroche 2001 reconstruct the monument not as a single line of statue bases in a U-shaped structure but as a rectangular structure with a single line of bases at the north and four discreet bases at the south and an entrance at the west but believe that the monument was destroyed by a natural disaster during the installation of the statues. On the inscriptions, see Ebert 1972, 137–145 nos. 43–45.

65. On this Apollo, now recognized in inv. 10950, see Croissant 2003, 70–71; Picard 1991, 98–100. Themelis (1976) placed this Apollo in the east pediment of the

fourth-century temple, an attribution that is no longer credible, although he considers the possibility of the Daochos Monument and discards it in Themelis (1979). Taeuber (1997, 240–243) considers this monument in relationship to Thessalian politics and monuments elsewhere, including the Poulydamas base of c. 330 B.C. at Olympia (Figs. 35–37).

66. Rolley 1999, 326. See also Jacquemin and Laroche 2001.

67. Jacquemin 1999, 315; Rolley 1999, 381; Maass 1993, 202. See Amandry 1990 for a recent treatment of the Pythian festival.

68. Croissant (1996, 139) notes that the column was erected among Thessalian monuments, which it dwarfs in size and splendor, as if to outdo the loyal servants of Macedon. The Daochos monument may not have been finished when it was partially covered by a landslide, and the construction of the Kalathiskos monument would have blocked much of the view of whatever was left standing. See Jacquemin and Laroche 2001; Rolley 1999, 326.

69. Picard 1991, 88, asserts that the akanthos column is a project of Lykourgos, designed to restore the prestige of the Athenians after Chaironeia.

70. For precedents for the kalathiskos dancers, see Rolley 1999, 153.

71. Maass 1993, 202.

72. Pouilloux 1976, 139–140 no. 462. The genitive form prompted Jacquemin (1999, 58) to suggest that the dedication was not an official one made by the Athenian state but a private one made in the name of the Athenian demos. See also Pouilloux and Roux 1963, 140–141.

73. Croissant 1996, 138; Bommelaer 1991, 200; Pouilloux and Roux 1963, 123–124.

74. On their identity, see Rolley 1999, 382; Croissant 1996, 139; Maass 1993, 202; Villanueva Puig 1986, 40. On the dancers as Aglaurides and other proposed identities, see *LIMC* 1, 283–284 n. 42, s.v. Aglauros, Herse, Pandrosos [U. Kron], which also claims that they are *not* Aglaurides. Pouilloux and Roux (1963, 145) speculate that because of the monument's location near the tomb of Neoptolemos, the use of the akanthos plant, the dancers, their dance, and their facial expressions, the monument may have some relationship with the tomb of Neoptolemos. For the association of akanthos plant and the funerary realm, see Blech 1982, 98–99, esp. no. 83.

75. Croissant (2003, 169) suggests that Dionysos is shown with a kithara to indicate that music pacifies the Dionysiac world, which is accomplished by Dionysos himself under the inspiration of Apollo.

76. The stone inscription, found at Delphi, survives in 25 fragments. See Furley and Bremer 2001, 2.52–84 for the text and commentary, 1.121–128 for a translation and discussion of the paian and its novelties, and a description of its discovery and composition. The hymn was regarded by earlier scholars, especially Vollgraf, as commissioned by Alexander in an attempt to impose a Thracian-Macedonian Bacchus on the Delphic clergy, but this interpretation was based on a misunderstanding of the poem's date (see Croissant 2003, 166). Neumann-Hartmann (2004) offers a recent study, which reviews previous scholarship and the data concerning the date of the paian and of the temple, in an attempt to discern the patron of the hymn and the influence of the Fourth Sacred War on its creation.

77. Though not exclusively so. See Sourvinou-Inwood (2005, 165), who discusses this in the course of arguing against the radical division of Apollo and Dionysos presented in Plutarch's *De E apud Delphos*. See also Stewart (1982) for a discussion of the fusion of the two gods in both the hymn and in the pediment.

78. Bremer 1996, 89.
79. See, for example, Bremer 1996.
80. Croissant 1996, 129–130. Vollgraf restores Athens as the destination of the "ivy-tressed choruses" from Delphi at line 150, which would certainly support the argument presented here, but the text is very fragmentary. But see Neumann-Hartmann (2004), who argues that the paian was commissioned to create unity among the Amphictyony in its device of having Dionysos travel through the several lands represented in the Amphictyony before arriving at Delphi and in Apollo's call for the completion of the temple. According to this argument, the actions of the Athenians against the Thebans, which had occurred before the paian's performance, indicate that the Athenians could not have been among the patrons of the paian, since they were not interested in created a unified Amphictyony. As my line of argument shows, I think that the paian does not call for unity of the Amphictyony and does not introduce Dionysos to Delphi (this had been done at least over a century before) but instead specifically praises Athens and Delphi.
81. Davies (2001, 210) dismisses Pindar's evidence as "worthless, disfigured by myth and fantasy." This seems overly harsh.
82. Maass 1993, 104; Ohnesorg 1993, 12.
83. Cf. Croissant 1996, 138.
84. Amandry 2000, 15.

5 The Cult of the Individual and the Realm of the Dead

1. My preliminary thoughts on the Heroon appear in Barringer 2001, 192–201. Oberleitner (1994) provides the most recent detailed monograph on the subject.
2. On the date, see Oberleitner 1994, 56–61.
3. Fedak 1990, 91.
4. Fedak 1990, 89. A detailed analysis of the architecture is available in Marksteiner (2002, 138–144).
5. For an account of the removal of the reliefs to the museum in the nineteenth century, see Szemethy 2005.
6. Marksteiner 2002, 166.
7. Marksteiner 2002, 183, who thinks it unlikely; Oberleitner 1994, 19; Benndorf and Niemann 1889, 41–42.
8. Fedak 1990, 88.
9. Marksteiner 2002, 167–175.
10. See Marksteiner 2002, 165; Benndorf and Niemann 1889, 37 fig. 24.
11. Though Robertson 1975, 405, is willing to allow that Greek heroa may have had interior paintings, which provided a model for the Trysa heroon.
12. Oberleitner 1994, 27.
13. Eichler 1950, 14–15.
14. Against the idea of the images as biography: Borchhardt 1976, 142.
15. Oberleitner 1994, 29, 55; Eichler 1950, 12. Oberleitner (1994, 55) connects the deeds of Theseus more vaguely to the Trysa ruler; their presence simply reflects the greatness of the Trysa ruler.
16. Oberleitner 1994, 28. Contra: Borchhardt 1976, 142.
17. Gschwantler (2002, 133–134) and Oberleitner (1994, 30–32) claim that the Odysseus scenes take their inspiration from Homer's *Odyssey*.
18. See Barringer 2001, 147–171; Barringer 1996.

19. Oberleitner 1994, 33. On the spatial relationships in the Trysa friezes, see Eichler 1950, 22–26.
20. Oberleitner 1994, 34.
21. Jacobs (1987, 61–64) thoroughly analyzes the city siege scene and determines that it does not derive from Assyrian prototypes, as Childs has argued.
22. For example, Oberleitner 1994, 42.
23. Jacobs (1987, 61–62) summarizes the history of this idea, first posited by Benndorf and Niemann in 1889. See also Borchhardt 1990, 168; Borchhardt 1976, 143.
24. Ridgway (1997, 92, 107 n. 29), Oberleitner (1994, 42–43), and Jacobs (1987, 62) point out the difficulties with such a thesis.
25. Koepp 1907.
26. Oberleitner 1994, 38.
27. For example, a Cypriot sarcophagus with a hunting scene in relief of c. 500–450 B.C., New York, Metropolitan Museum of Art 74.51.2451, Cesnola Collection. See Barringer 2001, fig. 97.
28. See Dunbabin 1999, fig. 9.
29. For example, Oberleitner 1994, 48.
30. Supra n. 7.
31. Oberleitner (1994, 48) speculates that they are meant to be read in the same spatial field and that the action of the upper frieze is in front of or behind that of the lower.
32. The use of rosettes as architectural decoration of a funerary structure recalls the rosettes on the south porch architrave of the Erechtheion on the Athenian Akropolis, which marks the legendary place of Kekrops' tomb. See Scholl 1995, 208. Lycian parallels occur at Sidyma, where lions' heads replace the bulls' heads, and at the heroon of Perikles of c.370 at Limyra. See Szemethy 2005, 72; Ridgway 1997, 94; Eichler 1950, 8.
33. Oberleitner 1994, 22; and Ridgway 1997, 89, states that the figures are "obviously apotropaic in function."
34. These dancers bear a strong resemblance to those of the Kalathiskos monument at Delphi, which dates c. 330 B.C. Of the heroon dancers, Oberleitner (1994, 22) says only that "Der Tanz an der Türgewänden gehört dem Bereich des Totenkultes an." But Robertson (1975, 405) links them to the dancers who performed at the Karneia festival in honor of Apollo at Sparta and elsewhere in the Peloponnese. Ridgway (1997, 90) identifies one of them as bearded, and therefore male.
35. Fedak 1990, 90.
36. Archaeological Museum MA 51. See Rolley 1999, fig. 139.
37. Eichler 1950, 14.
38. Basmahane Museum 4338 from Ödemiş. See Pfuhl and Möbius 1977–1979, 10, Taf. 2:6.
39. See, for example, Pfuhl and Möbius 1977–1979, 8–9, 30–31, Taf. 1:2, 19:73–74.
40. Marksteiner 2002, 180–181.
41. Marksteiner 2002, 181–182, with further bibliography.
42. Berns (2002, 128) claims that Theseus' grave in Athens, as known from Pausanias 1.17.2–6, was the inspiration for the Heroon, but offers no explanation or support for this remark. He apparently has picked up the suggestion first made by Thompson (1966, 42 n. 8, 47) that the rectangular enclosure in the

Agora that he identifies as the Theseion was the model, both in form and for the sculptural themes, of the Trysa heroon. See also Childs and Demargne 1989, 263, 275; Abramson 1978, 139–144; Benndorf and Niemann, 1889, 250.

43. Childs and Demarge 1989, 262–263, 275.
44. Eichler (1950, 10–43) examines precedents in vase painting and sculpture.
45. Fedak 1990, 38–39.
46. Noted also by Martin 1976, 209.
47. *LIMC* 5, 546, s.v. Hyakinthos [L. and F. Villard].
48. Moreover, Eichler (1950) has already done much of this work.
49. Infra n. 57.
50. Barringer 2001, 147–161, 183–190, with further bibliography.
51. See Stewart 1977, 14–32.
52. Conti 1994, 75–76.
53. Childs and Demargne (1989, 298–299) summarize the various identifications and argue against the Leukippidai.
54. For the Akropolis akroterion (Athens, Akropolis Museum 3799), see *LIMC* 7, 341 no. 149, s.v. Perseus [L. Jones Roccos]. For the Selinus metope, see Marconi 2007, 142–150.
55. On the historical circumstances surrounding the creation of these paintings and their subjects, see Castriota (1992, 63–76), who argues for Athenian influence in the choice of subject and its portrayal. I find his arguments that the Thebans are portrayed as Medizers by Athenian patrons to be unpersuasive.
56. The theme has been suggested for the central akroterion of the Temple of Athena Nike on the Athenian Akropolis, but see Schultz (2001), who argues against this.
57. Stilp 2006, 67–71; *LIMC* 7, 224 nos. 160–162, s.v. Pegasos [C. Lochin]. Stilp claims that they were never used as tomb ornaments but only as grave goods in these funerary contexts.
58. Ridgway 1997, 88, 93.
59. Abramson 1978, 137.
60. Eichler (1950, 10) and other scholars suggest that the Trysa dancers derive from the famed Lakonian dancers of Kallimachos, a fifth-century sculptor; the work, now lost, is known from Pliny's account (*HN* 34.92), and scholars have endeavored to perceive the work through Roman copies.
61. Rolley 1999, 152–153, with further bibliography.
62. Eichler 1950, 10.
63. Eichler 1950, 10–11; Benndorf and Niemann 1889, Taf. XXIX: 1.
64. Eichler 1950, 11.
65. Eichler 1950, 7–8.
66. Eichler 1950, 9.
67. Cf. Oberleitner 1994, 56, 60.
68. For a careful discussion of composition and style, see Ridgway (1997, 92–94, 100–101), who notes that the trapezoidal shape of the blocks comprising the precinct wall are characteristic of Lycian tombs. See also, e.g., Barringer 2001, 195, for a brief discussion and further bibliography; Oberleitner 1994, 60; Jacobs 1987, 45; and Eichler 1950, 14–43.
69. The official publication of Childs and Demargne (1989) offers complete photographic documentation.
70. Jacobs 1987, 45; Eichler 1950, 8.

71. Childs and Demargne (1989, 258) tabulate the battle motifs that are repeated in architectural sculpture in Greece and Asia Minor in the fifth and fourth centuries B.C.

72. Borchhardt 1976, 81–97. Beheading of Medusa: as the north central akroterion of the Heroon at Limyra and painted on the south wall of the tomb at Kızılbel of c. 525. Bellerophon killing Chimaira: reconstructed as the south central akroterion of the Heroon at Limyra. See Jacobs 1987, 65, for further bibliography.

73. Borchhardt 1990, 170.

74. See Barringer 2001, 195–196, with further bibliography; Oberleitner 1994, 55, 58 and passim.

75. Marksteiner 2002, 185–186; Ridgway 1997, 91–92, 107 n. 29; Childs and Demargne 1989, 263, 275. Oberleitner (1994, 55 and passim) claims that the Greek myths have associations or exemplify qualities or achievements that Eastern rulers wished to emulate. Jacobs (1987, 66–67), however, argues that the use of Greek myths in Lycia may have been a rebellious gesture against the Persian king.

76. Oberleitner 1994, 48–51, 55. Jacobs (1987, 56), thinks that the banquet draws on the Achaemenid tradition of rulers presiding over banquets for political reasons. Jacobs (1987, 66), however, claims that the defensive battle on the shore against outside invaders depicted on the exterior southern wall finds a correspondence in Odysseus slaughtering the suitors.

77. Ridgway 1999, 155.

78. Istanbul, Archaeological Museum 369. See Barringer 2001, 185, figs. 99–100.

79. See, for example, Borchhardt 1990, 182–183, Abb. 39.

80. Amsterdam, Allard Pierson Museum 1588. See *LIMC* 8 (supp.), s.v. Kentauroi et Kentaurides, 690–691 no. 225.

81. See, for example, *LIMC* 8 (supp.), s.v. Kentauroi et Kentaurides, 690 no. 217.

82. Ridgway 1999, 155.

83. See, for example, Ghirshman 1964, 202–203, figs. 250–253. I thank the anonymous reader for the press for suggesting Persian art as a source of parallels and for the charming phrasing, "hand-to-paw."

84. Ghirshman 1964, 268–269, figs. 329, 332.

85. Jeppesen (1994, 81–82) points out that the sacrificial victims were not burnt or roasted but that the meat was raw at the time of its deposit, and therefore, this was not a traditional hero cult sacrifice, yet still characterizes it as hero cult.

86. Stewart (1993, 95–102) discusses Alexander's divine status.

87. Stewart 1990, 160–161.

88. Stewart (1993, 158–159) argues against prevailing scholarly opinion that the visage surrounded by the lion skin on these coins was intended to be Herakles until after Alexander's death.

Conclusion

1. See now Stewart 2004.

2. Scholars have questioned whether this structure really is an altar and altar enclosure. See recently, Stewart 2000, who also discusses the matter of the honorees of the monument based on the fragmentary dedicatory inscription.

3. Cook 1989; La Rocca 1988a; La Rocca 1988b. La Rocca advocates the Temple of Apollo Daphnephoros at Eretria as the source of the sculpture. Cook (1989)

offers a reconstruction of the Greek pediment from which the sculptures were taken. Contra: Ellinghaus 2004, who provides bibliography. He and others are skeptical that the Roman temple held pedimental sculpture, and doubt that the sculptures restored in the Apollo temple by La Rocca come from a single monument (not necessarily architectural sculpture) or even the same time period.

4. La Rocca 1988a, 123–124; La Rocca 1988b.

WORKS CITED

Abramson, H. 1978. *Greek Hero-Shrines*. Ph.D. diss., U. of California, Berkeley.

Ajootian, A. 1998. "A Day at the Races: The Tyrannicides in the Fifth-century Agora." In *ΣΤΕΦΑΝΟΣ: Studies in Honor of Brunilde Sismondo Ridgway*, edited by K. Hartswick and M. Sturgeon, 1–13. Philadelphia.

Amandry, P. 1989. "La Ruine du temple d'Apollon à Delphes." *Bulletin de la Classe des lettres de l'Académie Royale de Belgique*, 5th series, 75: 26–47.

Amandry, P. 1990. "La Fête des Pythia." *PraktAkAth* 65: 279–317.

Amandry, P. 1998. "Notes de topographie et d'architecture delphiques: X. Le socle 'marathonien' et le trésor des Athéniens." *BCH* 122: 75–90.

Amandry, P. 2000. "La Vie religieuse à Delphes: Bilan d'un siècle de fouilles." In *Delphes: Cent ans après la grande fouille, essai di bilan, BCH* Suppl. 36, edited by A. Jacquemin, 9–21. Paris.

Antonaccio, C. 1993. "The Archaeology of Ancestors." In *Cultural Poetics in Archaic Greece: Cult, Performance, Politics*, edited by C. Dougherty and L. Kurke, 46–70. Cambridge.

Antonaccio, C. 1995. *An Archaeology of Ancestors: Tomb Cult and Hero Cult in Early Greece*. London.

Arafat, K. 1995. "Pausanias and the Temple of Hera at Olympia." *BSA* 90: 461–473.

Arnush, M. 2005. "Pilgrimage to the Oracle of Apollo at Delphi: Patterns of Public and Private Consultation." In *Pilgrimage in Graeco-Roman & Early Christian Antiquity*, edited by J. Elsner and I. Rutherford, 97–110. Oxford.

Barber, E. J. W. 1992. "The Peplos of Athena." In *Goddess and Polis: The Panathenaic Festival in Ancient Athens*, edited by J. Neils, 102–117. Hanover and Princeton.

Barringer, J. M. 1996. "Atalanta as Model: The Hunter and the Hunted." *ClAnt* 15: 48–76.

Barringer, J. M. 2001. *The Hunt in Ancient Greece*. Baltimore and London.

Barringer, J. M. 2005a. "Alkamenes' Prokne and Itys in Context." In *Periklean Athens and Its Legacy: Problems and Perspectives*, edited by J. M. Barringer and J. M. Hurwit, 163–176. Austin.

Barringer, J. M. 2005b. "The Temple of Zeus, Heroes, and Athletes." *Hesperia* 74: 211–241.

Barron, J. P. 1972. "New Light on Old Walls: Murals of the Theseion." *JHS* 92: 20–45.

Belloni, G. G. 1987. "Olimpia: Considerazioni su alcune sculture del tempio di Zeus." *Quaderni Catanesi di Studi Classici e Medievali* 9: 263–296.

Benndorf, O., and G. Niemann. 1889. "Das Heroon von Gjölbaschi-Trysa," *JKSW* 9.

Bentz, M., and C. Mann. 2001. "Zur Heroisierung von Athleten." In *Konstruktionen von Wirklichkeit*, edited by R. von den Hoff and S. Schmidt, 225–240. Stuttgart.

Bérard, C. 1976. "Le Liknon d'Athena." *AntK* 19: 101–114.

Berns, C. 2002. "Ionien und Lykien." In *Die griechische Klassik: Idee oder Wirklichkeit*, 125–131. Mainz.

Blech, M. 1982. *Studien zum Kranz bei den Griechen*. Berlin.

Blundell, S. 1998. "Marriage and the Maiden: Narratives on the Parthenon." In *The Sacred and the Feminine in Ancient Greece*, edited by S. Blundell and M. Williamson, 55–57. New York.

Boardman, J. 1977. "The Parthenon Frieze – Another View." In *Festschrift für Frank Brommer*, edited by U. Hockmann and A. Krug, 39–49. Mainz.

Boardman, J. 1984. "The Parthenon Frieze." In *Parthenon-Kongress Basel, Referate und Berichte, 4. bis 8. April 1982*, edited by E. Berger, 210–215. Mainz.

Boardman, J. 1985a. *Greek Sculpture: The Classical Period*. London.

Boardman, J. 1985b. *The Parthenon and Its Sculptures*. London.

Boardman, J. 1999. "The Parthenon Frieze: A Closer Look." *RA*: 305–330.

Boardman, J. 2001. "Pandora in the Parthenon: A Grace to Mortals." In Καλλίστευμα: μελέτες προς τιμήν της Όλγας Τζάχου-Αλεξανδρή, edited by Α. Αλεξανδρή και Ι. Λεβέντη, 233–244. Athens.

Boegehold, A. 1967. "Philokleon's Court." *Hesperia* 36: 111–120.

Boersma, J. 1964. "On the Political Background of the Hephaisteion." *BaBesch* 39: 101–106.

Bohringer, F. 1979. "Cultes d'athlètes en Grèce classique: Propos politiques, discours mythiques." *RÉA* 81: 11–18.

Bommelaer, J.-F. 1991. *Guide de Delphes: Le Site*. Paris.

Bonfante, L. 1989. "Nudity as a Costume in Classical Art." *AJA* 93: 543–570.

Borchhardt, J. 1976. *Die Bauskulptur des Heroons von Limyra*. Berlin.

Borchhardt, J., ed. 1990. *Götter, Heroen, Herrscher in Lykien*. Vienna and Munich.

Bousquet, J. 1977. "Inscriptions de Delphes: Notes sur les comptes des naopes." *BCH* Suppl. 4: *Études delphiques*: 91–101.

Bremer, J. M. 1996. "A Purposeful Manipulation of Myth: Philodamos' Paian to Dionysos." In *Studi di Teoria e Storia Letteraria in onore di Pieter de Meijer*, edited by D. Aristodemo, C. Maeder, and R. de Rooy, 81–92. Florence.

Brommer, F. 1967. *Die Metopen des Parthenon*. Mainz.

Brommer, F. 1977. *Der Parthenonfries*. Mainz.

Brommer, F. 1978. *Hephaistos*. Mainz am Rhein.

Bugh, G. R. 1990. "The Theseia in Late Hellenistic Athens." *ZPE* 83: 20–35.

Bulle, H. 1939. "Der Ostgiebel des Zeustempels zu Olympia." *JdI* 54: 137–218.

Burkert, W. 1983. *Homo Necans: The Anthropology of Ancient Greek Sacrificial Ritual and Myth*. Translated by P. Bing. Berkeley.

Burkert, W. 1966. "Kekropidensage und Arrhephoria." *Hermes* 94: 1–25.

Calame, C. 1997. *Choruses of Young Women in Ancient Greece*. Translated by D. Collins and J. Orion. Lanham, Md.

Camp, J. M. 1986. *The Athenian Agora*. London.

Camp, J. M. 1994. "Before Democracy: Alkmaionidai and Peisistratidai." In *The Archaeology of Athens and Attica under the Democracy*, edited by W. D. E. Coulson et al., 7–12. Oxford.

Camp, J. M. 1996. "Excavations in the Athenian Agora: 1994 and 1995." *Hesperia* 65: 233–261.

Camp, J. M. 2001. *The Archaeology of Athens*. New Haven and London.

Carson, A. 1982. "Wedding at Noon in Pindar's *Ninth Pythian*." *GRBS* 23: 121–128.

Castriota, D. 1992. *Myth, Ethos, and Actuality: Official Art in Fifth-Century B.C. Athens*. Madison.

Chamoux, F. 1979. *Thasiaca, BCH* Suppl. 5. Paris.

Childs, W. A. P. 1993. "Herodotos, Archaic Chronology, and the Temple of Apollo at Delphi." *JdI* 108: 399–441.

Childs, W. A. P., and P. Demargne. 1989. *Fouilles de Xanthos VIII: Le Monument des Néréides: Le décor sculpté*. Paris.

Christensen, K. A. 1984. "The Theseion: A Slave Refuge at Athens." *AJAH* 9: 23–32.

Clark, I. 1998. "The Gamos of Hera: Myth and Ritual." In *The Sacred and the Feminine in Ancient Greece*, edited by S. Blundell and M. Williamson, 13–26. London and New York.

Cohen, B. 1983. "Paragone: Sculpture versus Painting, Kaineus and the Kleophrades Painter." In *Ancient Greek Art and Iconography*, edited by W. G. Moon, 171–192. Madison.

Cohen, B. 1994. "From Bowman to Clubman: Herakles and Olympia." *ArtB* 86: 695–715.

Cohen, E. 2000. *The Athenian Nation*. Princeton.

Cole, S. 1998. "Domesticating Artemis." In *The Sacred and the Feminine in Ancient Greece*, edited by S. Blundell and M. Williamson, 27–43. London and New York.

Connelly, J. 1996. "Parthenon and Parthenoi: A Mythological Interpretation of the Parthenon Frieze." *AJA* 100: 53–80.

Consoli, V. 2004. "*Atena Ergane*, sorgere di un culto sull'Acropoli di Atene." *ASAtene* 82, series III, 4: 31–60.

Conti, M. C. 1994. *Il più antico fregio dallo Heraion del Sele*. Florence.

Cook, R. M. 1989. "The Pediment of Apollo Sosianus." *AA*: 525–528.

Croissant, F. 1996. "Les Athéniens à Delphes avant et après Chéronée." In *Le IVe siècle av. J.-C.: approches historiographiques*, edited by P. Carlier, 127–139. Nancy.

Croissant, F. 2003. *Fouilles de Delphes IV: Monuments figurés sculpture VII: Les Frontons du temple du IVe siècle*. Athens.

Cruciani, C., and L. Fiorini. 1998. *I Modelli del moderato: La Stoà Poikìle e l'Hephaisteion di Atene nel programma edilizio cimoniano*. Perugia.

Davies, J. K. 1998. "Finance, Administration, and 'Realpolitik': The Case of Fourth-Century Delphi." In *"Modus operandi." Essays in Honour of Geoffrey Rickman*, BICS Suppl. 71, edited by M. Austin, J. Harries, and C. Smith, 1–14. London.

Davies, J. K. 2001. "Rebuilding a Temple: The Economic Effects of Piety." In *Economies beyond Agriculture in the Classical World*, edited by D. J. Mattingly and J. Salmon, 209–229. London and New York.

Deacy, S. 1997. "The Vulnerability of Athena: *Parthenoi* and Rape in Greek Myth." In *Rape in Antiquity*, edited by S. Deacy and K. F. Pierce, 43–63. London.

De la Coste-Messelière, P. 1957. *Fouilles de Delphes IV: Monuments figurés: sculpture, IV: Sculptures du trésor des Athéniens*. Paris.

Delivorrias, A. 1997a. "A New Aphrodite for John." In *Greek Offerings: Essays on Greek Art in Honour of John Boardman*, edited by O. Palagia, 109–118. Oxford.

Delivorrias, A. 1997b. "The Sculpted Decoration of the So-Called Theseion: Old Answers, New Questions." In *The Interpretation of Architectural Sculpture in Greece and Rome*, Studies in the History of Art 49, edited by D. Buitron-Oliver, 83–107. Washington DC.

Des Bouvrie, S. 1995. "Gender and the Games at Olympia." In *Greece & Gender*, Papers from the Norwegian Institute at Athens 2, edited by B. Berggreen and N. Marinatos, 55–74. Bergen.

Despinis, G. 1997. "Zum Athener Brauronion." In *Kult und Kultbauten auf der Akropolis*, Internationales Symposion vom 7. bis 9. Juli 1995, edited by W. Hoepfner, 209–217. Berlin.

Despinis, G. 2000. "Il tempio arcaico di Dionisio Eleutereo." *ASAtene* 74–75 (new series 58–59, 1996–1997): 193–214.

Despinis, G., and E. B. Harrison. 2001. "Vermutungen zum Marathon-Weihgeschenk der Athener in Delphi." *JdI* 116: 103–127.

Detienne, M. 2001. "Forgetting Delphi between Apollo and Dionysus." *CP* 96: 147–158.

Deubner, L. 1956. *Attische Feste*. Berlin.

Dillon, M. 2000. "Did Parthenoi Attend the Olympic Games? Girls and Women Competing, Spectating, and Carrying Out Cult Roles at Greek Religious Festivals." *Hermes* 128: 457–480.

Dillon, M. 2001. *Girls and Women in Classical Greek Religion*. London and New York.

Dinsmoor, W. B. 1975. *The Architecture of Ancient Greece*. Reprint of 3rd ed. (1950). New York.

Dörig, J. 1985. *La Frise est de l'Héphaisteion*. Mainz.

Dontas, G. S. 1983. "The True Aglaurion." *Hesperia* 52: 48–63.

Dunbabin, K. 1999. *Mosaics of the Greek and Roman World*. Cambridge.

Eaverly, M. A. 1995. *Archaic Greek Equestrian Sculpture*. Ann Arbor.

Ebert, J. 1972. *Griechische Epigramme auf Sieger an gymnischen und hippischen Agonen*. Berlin.

Eckstein, F. 1969. *ΑΝΑΘΗΜΑΤΑ*: Studien zu den Weihgeschenken strengen Stils im Heiligtum von Olympia, Berlin.

Eichler, F. 1950. *Die Reliefs des Heroon von Gjölbaschi-Trysa*. Vienna.

Ellinghaus, C. 2004. "Der Giebel des Apollon Sosianus Tempel in Rom – wirklich ein Giebel?" In *Bildergeschichte: Festschrift Klaus Stähler*, edited by J. Gebauer et al., 111–123. Möhnesee.

Fedak, J. 1990. *Monumental Tombs of the Hellenistic Age*. Toronto.

Felten, F. 1984. *Griechische tektonische Friese archaischer und klassischer Zeit*. Waldsassen-Bayern.

Ferrari, G. 2002a. "The Ancient Temple on the Acropolis at Athens." *AJA* 106: 11–35.

Ferrari, G. 2002b. *Figures of Speech: Men and Maidens in Ancient Greece*. Chicago and London.

Fittschen, K. 2003. Review of P. C. Bol, *Die Geschichte der antiken Bildhauerkunst* I, in *GGA* 255: 1–25.

Flashar, M. 1992. *Apollon Kitharodos*. Cologne.

Furley, W., and J. Bremmer. 2001. *Greek Hymns* 1. Tübingen.

Geertman, H. 1982. "Riflessioni sulle metope del tempio di Zeus a Olimpia: Disegno e esecuzione." *BABesch* 57: 70–86.

Geominy, W. 1998. "Zum Daochos-Weihgeschenk." *Klio* 80: 369–402.

Ghirshman, R. 1964. *Persia: From the Origins to Alexander the Great*. London.

Golden, M. 1998. *Sport and Society in Ancient Greece*. Cambridge.

Graef, B., and E. Langlotz. 1925. *Die antiken Vasen von der Akropolis zu Athen*. Berlin.

Grandjean, Y., and F. Salviat. 2000. *Guide de Thasos*. Athens.

Gschwantler, K. 2002. "Das Heroon von Trysa." In *Die griechische Klassik: Idee oder Wirklichkeit*, 131–135. Mainz.

Hamilton, R. 1989. "Alkman and the Athenian Arkteia." *Hesperia* 58: 449–472.

Harris, D. 1995. *The Treasures of the Parthenon and Erechtheion*. Oxford.

Harrison, E. B. 1977a. "Alkamenes' Sculptures for the Hephaisteion: Part I, The Cult Statues." *AJA* 81: 137–178.

Harrison, E. B. 1977b. "Alkamenes' Sculptures for the Hephaisteion: Part III, Iconography and Style." *AJA* 81: 411–26.

Harrison, E. B. 1984. "Time in the Parthenon Frieze." In *Parthenon-Kongress Basel, Referate und Berichte, 4. bis 8. April 1982*, edited by E. Berger, 230–234. Mainz.

Harrison, E. B. 1996. "The Web of History: A Conservative Reading of the Parthenon Frieze." In *Worshipping Athena*, edited by J. Neils, 198–214. Madison.

Harrison, E. B. 2005. "Athena at Pallene and in the Agora of Athens." In *Periklean Athens and Its Legacy: Problems and Perspectives*, edited by J. M. Barringer and J. M. Hurwit, 119–131. Austin.

Hedrick, C. W., Jr. 1988. "The Temple and Cult of Apollo Patroos in Athens." *AJA* 92: 185–210.

Heiden, J. 2003. "Thessalische Lapithen in Elis: Zur Deutung des Westgiebels von Olympia." *AA*: 183–190.

Heilmeyer, W.-D. 1972. *Olympische Forschungen* 7: *Frühe Olympische Tonfiguren*. Berlin.

Henrichs, A. 1978. "Greek Maenadism from Olympias to Messalina." *HSCP* 82: 121–160.

Herrmann, H.-V. 1980. "Pelops in Olympia." In *ΣΤΗΛΗ· Τόμος εις μνήμην Νικολάου Κοντολέοντος*, 59–74, Athens.

Herrmann, K. 2000. "Zur Verwendung des parischen Marmors im Heiligtum von Olympia." In *Paria Lithos: Parian Quarries, Marble and Workshops of Sculpture* (Proceedings of the First International Conference on the Archaeology of Paros and the Cyclades, Paros, 2–5 October 1997), edited by D. U. Schilardi and D. Katsonopoulou, 379–389. Athens.

Hoffelner, K. 1988. "Die Metopen des Athener-Schatzhauses: ein neuer Rekonstruktionsversuch." *AM* 103: 77–117.

Holloway, R. R. 1966. "The Archaic Acropolis and the Parthenon Frieze." *ArtB* 48: 223–226.

Holloway, R. R. 1967. "Panhellenism in the Sculptures of the Zeus Temple at Olympia." *GRBS* 8: 93–101.

Howie, G. 1991. "Pindar's Account of Pelops' Contest with Oenomaus." *Nikephoros* 4: 55–120.

Hurwit, J. M. 1987. "Narrative Resonance in the East Pediment of the Temple of Zeus at Olympia." *ArtB* 69: 6–15.

Hurwit, J. M. 1995. "Beautiful Evil: Pandora and the Athena Parthenos." *AJA* 99: 171–186.

Hurwit, J. M. 1999. *The Athenian Acropolis*. Cambridge.

Hurwit, J. M. 2004. *The Acropolis in the Age of Pericles*. Cambridge.

Jacobs, B. 1987. *Griechische und persische Elemente in der Grabkunst Lykiens zur Zeit der Achämenidenherrschaft*. Josered.

Jacquemin, A. 1999. *Offrandes monumenales à Delphes*. Athens.

Jacquemin, A., and D. Laroche. 2001. "Le Monument de Daochos ou le trésor des Thessaliens." *BCH* 125: 305–332.

Jenkins, I. 1994. *The Parthenon Frieze*. London.

Jeppesen, K. 1994. "Founder Cult and Maussolleion." In *Hektomnid Caria and the Ionian Renaissance*, edited by J. Isager, 73–87. Oxford.

Jones, S. C. 1998. "Statues That Kill and the Gods Who Love Them." In *ΣΤΕΦΑΝΟΣ: Studies in Honor of Brunilde Sismondo Ridgway*, edited by K. J. Hartswick and M. C. Sturgeon, 139–143. Philadelphia.

Kahil, L. 1981. "Le 'Cratérisque' d'Artémis et le Brauronion de l'Acropole." *Hesperia* 50: 253–263.

Kaltsas, N. 2002. *Sculpture in the National Archaeological Museum, Athens*. Translated by D. Hardy. Athens.

Karakasi, K. 2003. *Archaic Korai*. Malibu.

Kardara, C. 1961. "Γλαυκῶπις-ο αρχαίος ναός και το θέμα της ζωφόρου του Παρθενῶνος." *ArchEph*: 61–158.

Kardara, C. P. 1970. "Olympia: Peirithoos Apollo or Zeus Areios?" *ArchDelt* 25: 12–19.

Keesling, C. M. 2003. *The Votive Statues of the Athenian Acropolis*. Cambridge.

Knell, H. 1990. *Mythos und Polis: Bildprogramme griechischer Bauskulptur*. Darmstadt.

Koepp, F. 1907. "Zum Westfries des Heroon von Gjölbaschi." *JdI* 22: 70–77.

Korres, M. 1994a. "The Architecture of the Parthenon." In *The Parthenon and Its Impact on Modern Times*, edited by P. Tournikiotis, 56–97. Athens.

Korres, M. 1994b. "Der Plan des Parthenon." *AM* 109: 53–120.

Korres, M. 1994c. "The Sculptural Adornment of the Parthenon." In *Acropolis Restoration: The CCAM Interventions*, edited by R. Economakis, 29–33. London.

Korres, M. 1997. "Die Athena-Tempel auf der Akropolis." In *Kult und Kultbauten auf der Akropolis*, edited by W. Hoepfner, 218–243. Berlin.

Kosmopoulou, A. 2002. *The Iconography of Sculpted Statue Bases in the Archaic and Classical Periods*. Madison.

Kotsidu, H. 1995. "Zum baupolitischen Hintergrund des Hephaistostempels auf der athener Agora." *Hephaistos* 13: 93–108.

Kreuzer, B. 2005. "Geschlossene Gesellschaft im Parthenon-Westgiebel." *Otium: Festschrift für Volker Michael Strocka*, edited by T. Ganschow et al., 193–200. Remshalden.

Kurke, L. 1993. "The Economy of *Kudos*." In *Cultural Poetics in Archaic Greece: Cult, Performance, Politics*, edited by C. Dougherty and L. Kurke, 131–163. Cambridge.

Kyrieleis, H. 1997. "Zeus and Pelops in the East Pediment of the Temple of Zeus at Olympia." In *The Interpretation of Architectural Sculpture in Greece and Rome*, Studies in the History of Art 49, edited by D. Buitron-Oliver, 13–27. Washington DC.

Kyrieleis, H. 2002. "Zu den Anfängen des Heiligtums von Olympia." In *Olympia, 1875–2000: 125 Jahre deutsche Ausgrabungen: Internationales Symposion, Berlin 9.-11. November 2000*, edited by H. Kyrieleis, 213–220. Berlin.

Kyrieleis, H. 2006a. *Anfänge und Frühzeit des Heiligtums von Olympia: die Ausgrabungen am Pelopion 1987–1996*. Berlin.

Kyrieleis, H. 2006b. "Paros und Olympia: zu den Skulpturen des Zeustempels in Olympia." ΓΕΝΕΘΛΙΟΝ: Αναμνηστικός τόμος για την συμπλήρωση είκοσι χρόνων λειτουργίας του Μουσείου Κυκλαδικής Τέχνης, edited by Ν. Σταμπολίδης, 183–201. Athens.

Lacroix, L. 1976. "La Légende de Pélops et son iconographie." *BCH* 100: 327–341.

Lapalus, E. 1947. *Le Fronton sculpté en Grèce: Des origines à la fin du IVᵉ siècle*. Paris.

Lapatin, K. D. S. 2001. *Chryselephantine Statuary in the Ancient Mediterranean World*. Oxford.

Lapatin, K. D. S. 2005. "The Statue of Athena and Other Treasures in the Parthenon." In *The Parthenon: From Antiquity to the Present*, edited by J. Neils, 260–291. Cambridge.

La Rocca, E. 1988a. "Der Apollo-Sosianus Tempel." In *Kaiser Augustus und die verlorene Republik*, edited by W.-D. Heilmeyer, E. La Rocca, and H. G. Martin, 121–136. Berlin.

La Rocca, E. 1988b. "Die Giebelskulpturen des Apollo-Sosianus-Tempels in Rom." *Gymnasium* 95: 129–140.

Larson, J. 1995. *Greek Heroine Cults*. Madison.

Lee, H. M. 1983. "Athletic Arete in Pindar." *AncW* 7: 31–37.

Linders, T. 1972. *Studies in the Treasure Records of Artemis Brauronia Found in Athens*. Stockholm.

Maass, M. 1993. *Das antike Delphi: Orakel, Schätze, und Monumente.* Darmstadt.

McInerney, J. 1997. "Parnassus, Delphi, and the Thyiades." *GRBS* 38: 263–283.

Mallwitz, A. 1972. *Olympia und seine Bauten.* Darmstadt.

Mallwitz, A. 1988. "Cult and Competition Locations at Olympia." In *The Archaeology of the Olympics: The Olympics and Other Festivals in Antiquity*, edited by W. J. Raschke, 79–109. Madison.

Mallwitz, A., and H.-V. Herrmann. 1980. *Die Funde aus Olympia.* Athens.

Mansfield, J. M. 1985. *The Robe of Athena and the Panathenaic Peplos.* Ph.D. diss., U. of California, Berkeley.

Marconi, C. 2007. *Temple Decoration and Cultural Identity in the Archaic Greek World: The Metopes of Selinus.* Cambridge.

Mark, I. 1993. *The Sanctuary of Athena Nike in Athens: Architectural Stages and Chronology.* Princeton.

Markle, M. M. 1981. "Demosthenes' *Second Philippic*: A Valid Policy for the Athenians against Philip." *Antichthon* 15: 62–85.

Marksteiner, T. 2002. *Trysa: Eine zentrallykische Niederlassung im Wandel der Zeit.* Vienna.

Martin, R. 1976. "Bathyclès de Magnésie et le 'Trône' d'Apollon à Amyklae." *RA*: 205–218.

Metzger, H. 1951. *Les représentations dans la céramique attique du IVe siècle.* Paris.

Miller, S. G. 1995. "Old Metroon and Old Bouleuterion in the Classical Agora of Athens." In *Studies in the Ancient Greek Polis*, edited by K. Raaflaub and M. H. Hansen, 133–156. Stuttgart.

Moreno, P. 1974. *Lisippo* 1. Bari.

Moreno, P., ed. 1995. *Lisippo: L'Arte e la Fortuna.* Florence.

Morgan, C. 1962a. "The Sculptures of the Hephaisteion I: The Metopes." *Hesperia* 31: 210–219.

Morgan, C. 1962b. "The Sculptures of the Hephaisteion II: The Friezes." *Hesperia* 31: 221–235.

Morgan, C. 1963. "The Sculptures of the Hephaisteion III: The Pediments, Akroteria, and Cult Images." *Hesperia* 32: 91–108.

Mostratos, G. 2004. "A Reconstruction of the Parthenon's East Pediment." In *The Parthenon and Its Sculptures*, edited by M. B. Cosmopoulos, 114–149. Cambridge.

Moustaka. A. 2002. "Zeus und Hera im Heiligtum von Olympia." In *Olympia, 1875–2000: 125 Jahre deutsche Ausgrabungen: Internationales Symposion, Berlin 9.-11. November 2000*, edited by H. Kyrieleis, 301–315. Berlin.

Müller, K. O. 1873. "Die erhobenen Arbeiten am Friese des Pronaos von Theseustempel zu Athen, erklärt aus dem Mythus von den Pallantiden." In *Kunstarchaeologische Werke* 4: 1–19. Berlin. Originally published in 1833.

Nagy, G. 1979. *The Best of the Achaeans.* Baltimore.

Neer, R. 2004. "The Athenian Treasury at Delphi and the Material of Politics." *ClAnt* 23: 63–93.

Neils, J. 1987. *The Youthful Deeds of Theseus.* Rome.

Neils, J. 1992. *Goddess and Polis: The Panathenaic Festival in Ancient Athens.* Hanover and Princeton.

Neils, J. 2001. *The Parthenon Frieze.* Cambridge.

Neils, J. 2005. "'With Noblest Images on All Sides': The Ionic Frieze of the Parthenon." In *The Parthenon: From Antiquity to the Present*, edited by J. Neils, 198–223. Cambridge.

Neumann-Hartmann, A. 2004. "Der Paian des Philodamos an Dionysos und der Ausbruch des 4. Heiligen Krieges." *MusHelv* 61: 9–31.

Nicholls, R. 1970. "Architectural Terracotta Sculpture from the Athenian Agora." *Hesperia* 39: 115–138.

Oakley, J. H., and R. H. Sinos. 1993. *The Wedding in Ancient Athens*. Madison.

Oberleitner, W. 1994. *Das Heroon von Trysa*. Mainz.

Ohnesorg, A. 1993. *Inselionische Marmordächer*. Berlin.

Osborne, R. 1998. *Archaic and Classical Greek Art*. Oxford.

Palagia, O. 1998. *The Pediments of the Parthenon*, 2nd ed. Leiden.

Palagia, O. 2000. "Meaning and Narrative Techniques in Statue-Bases of the Pheidian Circle." In *Word and Image in Ancient Greece*, edited by N. K. Rutter and B. A. Sparkes, 53–78. Edinburgh.

Papaspyridi-Karusu, S. 1954–1955. "Alkamenes und das Hephaisteion." *AM* 69–70: 67–94.

Parke, H. W. 1939. "Delphica." *Hermathena* 53: 59–78.

Parke, H. W. 1981. "Apollo and the Muses, or Prophecy in Greek Verse." *Hermathena* 130–131: 99–112.

Parker, R. 2005. *Polytheism and Society at Athens*. Oxford.

Patay-Horváth, A. 2004. "Pausanias und der Ostgiebel des Zeustempels von Olympia." *ActaArchHung* 44: 21–33.

Patay-Horváth, A. 2005. "Die Frisuren der weiblichen Protagnoisten im Ostgiebel des Zeustempels von Olympia." In *Otium: Festschrift für Volker Michael Strocka*, edited by T. Graschow and M. Steinhart, 275–283. Remshalden.

Pederson, P. 1989. *The Parthenon and the Origin of the Corinthian Capital*. Odense.

Perysinakis, I. N. 1990. "The Athlete as Warrior: Pindar's *P*.9.97–103 and *P*.10.55–59." *BICS* 37: 43–49.

Pfuhl, E., and H. Möbius. 1977–1979. *Die ostgriechischen Grabreliefs*. Mainz.

Picard, C., and P. de la Coste-Messelière. 1931. *Fouilles de Delphes IV: Monuments figurés sculpture, III: Art archaïque (fin): Sculptures des Temples*. Paris.

Picard, O. 1991. *Guide de Delphes: Le Musée*. Paris.

Pimpinelli, M. A. 1994. "Eracle ad Olimpia: Le metope del tempio di Zeus." *Ostraka* 3: 349–416.

Pleket, H. W. 1992. "The Participants in the Ancient Olympic Games: Social Background and Mentality." In Πρακτικά Συμποσίου Ολυμπιακών Αγώνων, 5–9 Σεπτεμβρίου 1988 (Proceedings of an International Symposium on the Olympic Games, 5–9 September 1988) edited by W. Coulson and H. Kyrieleis, 147–152, Athens.

Pollitt, J. J. 1972. *Art and Experience in Classical Greece*, Cambridge.

Pollitt, J. J. 1997. "The Meaning of the Parthenon Frieze." In *The Interpretation of Architectural Sculpture of Greece and Rome*, Studies in the History of Art 49, edited by D. Buitron-Oliver, 51–65. Washington D.C.

Pollitt, J. J. 2000. "Patriotism and the West Pediment of the Parthenon." In *Periplous: Papers on Classical Art and Archaeology Presented to Sir John Boardman*, edited by G. R. Tsetskhladze, A. J. N. W. Prag, and A. M. Snodgrass, 220–227. London.

Pouilloux, J. 1976. *Fouilles de Delphes III: Epigraphie IV: Les Inscriptions de la terrasse du temple et de la region nord du sanctuaire.* Paris.

Pouilloux, J., and G. Roux. 1963. *Énigmes à Delphes.* Paris.

Queyrel, A. 1984. "Scènes Apolloniennes et Dionysiaques du Peintre de Pothos." *BCH* 108: 123–159.

Raschke, W. J. 1988. "Images of Victory: Some New Considerations of Athletic Monuments." In *The Archaeology of the Olympics: The Olympics and Other Festivals in Antiquity,* edited by W. J. Raschke, 38–54. Madison.

Raubitschek, A. 1940. "Two Monuments Erected after the Victory of Marathon." *AJA* 44: 53–59.

Raubitschek, A. 1949. *Dedications from the Athenian Akropolis.* Cambridge.

Raubitschek, A. 1974. "Zu den zwei attischen Marathondenkmälern in Delphi." In *Mélanges helléniques offerts à Georges Daux,* 315–316. Paris.

Reber, K. 1998. "Das Hephaisteion in Athen: ein Monument für die Demokratie." *JdI* 113: 31–48.

Rehak, P. 1998. "Unfinished Hair and the Installation of the Pedimental Sculptures of the Temple of Zeus at Olympia." In *ΣΤΕΦΑΝΟΣ: Studies in Honor of Brunilde Sismondo Ridgway,* edited by K. J. Hartswick and M. C. Sturgeon, 193–208. Philadelphia.

Ridgway, B. S. 1981. *Fifth Century Styles in Greek Sculpture.* Princeton.

Ridgway, B. S. 1992. "Images of Athena on the Akropolis." In *Goddess and Polis: The Panathenaic Festival in Ancient Athens,* edited by J. Neils, 119–142. Hanover and Princeton.

Ridgway, B. S. 1997. *Fourth-Century Styles in Greek Sculpture.* Madison.

Ridgway, B. S. 1999. *Prayers in Stone: Greek Architectural Sculpture ca. 600–100 B.C.E.* Berkeley.

Ridgway, B. S. 2005. "'Periklean' Cult Images and Their Media." In *Periklean Athens and Its Legacy: Problems and Perspectives,* edited by J. M. Barringer and J. M. Hurwit, 111–118. Austin.

Robertson, M. 1975. *A History of Greek Art.* Cambridge.

Robertson, M. 1984. "The South Metopes: Theseus and Daidalos." In *Parthenon-Kongress Basel, Referate und Berichte, 4. bis 8. April 1982,* edited by E. Berger, 206–208. Mainz.

Robertson, N. 1983. "The Riddle of the Arrhephoria at Athens." *HSCP* 87: 241–288.

Robertson, N. 1985. "The Origins of the Panathenaea." *RhM* 128: 231–295.

Robertson, N. 1998. "The City Center of Archaic Athens." *Hesperia* 67: 283–302.

Rolley, C. 1999. *La Sculpture grecque* 2. Paris.

Rotroff, S., and J. Oakley. 1992. *Debris from a Public Dining Place in the Athenian Agora, Hesperia Suppl. 25.* Princeton.

Roux, G. 1979. *L'Amphictionie, Delphes, et le temple d'Apollon au IVe siècle.* Lyon and Paris.

Säflund, M.-L. 1970. *The East Pediment of the Temple of Zeus at Olympia.* Göteborg.

Scanlon, T. 1984. "The Footrace of the Heraia at Olympia." *AncW* 9: 77–99.

Scanlon, T. 1988. "Combat and Contest: Athletic Metaphors for Warfare in Greek Literature." In *Coroebus Triumphs: The Alliance of Sports and the Arts*, Proceedings of the First Annual Meeting of the Sport Literature Association, edited by S. J. Bandy, 230–256. San Diego.

Scanlon, T. 2002. *Eros and Greek Athletics*. Oxford.

Schauenburg, K. 1963. "Athletenbilder des vierten Jahrhunderts v. Chr." *AntP* 2: 75–80.

Scheffer, C. 1996. "Return or No Return: The So-Called *Ephedrismos* Group and the Hephaisteion." *OpAth* 21: 169–188.

Scholl, A. 1995. "ΧΟΗΦΟΡΟΙ: Zur Deutung der Korenhalle des Erechtheion." *JdI* 110: 179–212.

Schörner, G., and H. R. Goette. 2004. *Die Pan-Grotte von Vari*. Mainz am Rhein.

Schultz, P. 2001. "The Akroteria of the Temple of Athena Nike." *Hesperia* 70: 1–47.

Schultz, P. 2007. "Leochares' Argead Portraits in the Philippeion." In *Early Hellenistic Portraiture: Image, Style, Context*, edited by P. Schultz and R. von den Hoff, 205–233. Cambridge.

Schwab, K. 2005. "Celebrations of Victory: The Metopes of the Parthenon." In *The Parthenon: From Antiquity to the Present*, edited by J. Neils, 158–197. Cambridge.

Sekunda, N. V. 1990. "The *Lampadephoroi* of the Tribe Aiantis." *ZPE* 83: 149–182.

Serwint, N. 1993. "The Female Athletic Costume at the Heraia and Prenuptial Initiation Rites." *AJA* 97: 403–422.

Shapiro, H. A. 1989. *Art and Cult under the Tyrants in Athens*. Mainz.

Shapiro, H. A. 1994. *Myth into Art: Poet and Painter in Classical Greece*. New York.

Shapiro, H. A. 1995. *Art and Cult under the Tyrants in Athens, Supplement*. Mainz.

Shapiro, H. A. 1996. "Athena, Apollo, and the Religious Propaganda of the Athenian Empire." In *Religion and Power in the Ancient Greek World*, edited by P. Hellström and B. Alroth, 101–113. Uppsala.

Shapiro, H. A. 1998. "Autochthony and the Visual Arts in Fifth-Century Athens." In *Democracy, Empire, and the Arts in Fifth-Century Athens*, edited by D. Boedeker and K. A. Raaflaub, 127–151. Cambridge.

Shapiro, H. A. 2005. "The Judgment of Helen in Athenian Art." In *Periklean Athens and Its Legacy: Problems and Perspectives*, edited by J. M. Barringer and J. M. Hurwit, 47–62. Austin.

Shapiro, H. A. 2006. "Scythians in Greek Vase Painting: History, Myth, or Symbol?," abstract, http://www.archaeological.org/webinfo.php?page=10248&searchtype=abstract&ytable=2006&sessionid=5C&paperid=822, accessed 4 June 2006.

Shear, J. 2001. "Polis and Panathenaia: The History and Development of Athena's Festival." Ph.D. diss., University of Pensylvania.

Shear, T. L. Jr., 1975. "The Athenian Agora: Excavations of 1973–1974." *Hesperia* 44: 331–374.

Shear, T. L., Jr. 1994. "Ἰσονόμους τ' Ἀθήνας ἐποιησάτην: The Agora and the Democracy." In *The Archaeology of Athens and Attica under the Democracy*, edited by W. D. E. Coulson et al., 225–248. Oxford.

Simon, E. 1968. "Zu den Giebeln des Zeustempels von Olympia." *AM* 83: 147–166.

Simon, E. 1975. "Versuch einer Deutung der Südmetopen des Parthenon." *JdI* 90: 100–120.

Simon, E. 1983. *Festivals of Attica: An Archaeological Commentary.* Madison.

Simon, E. 1998. *Die Götter der Griechen*, 4th ed. Munich.

Sinn, U. 1991. "Olympia: Die Stellung der Wettkämpfe im Kult des Zeus Olympios." *Nikephoros* 4: 31–54.

Sinn, U. 1994. "Apollon und die Kentauromachie im Westgiebel des Zeustempels in Olympia: Die Wettkampfstätte als Forum der griechischen Diplomatie nach den Perserkriegen." *AA*: 585–602.

Sinn, U. 2000. *Olympia: Cult, Sport, and Ancient Festival.* Translated by T. Thornton. Princeton.

Sourvinou-Inwood, C. 1991. *"Reading" Greek Culture.* Oxford.

Sourvinou-Inwood, C. 2005. *Hylas, the Nymphs, Dionysos and Others.* Stockholm.

Spivey, N. 1996. *Understanding Greek Sculpture.* London.

Splitter, R. 2000. *Die "Kypseloslade" in Olympia.* Mainz.

Stähler, K. 1991. "Zum sog. Marathon-Anathem in Delphi." *AM* 106: 191–199.

Stehle, E., and A. Day. 1996. "Women Looking at Women: Women's Ritual and Temple Sculpture." In *Sexuality in Ancient Art*, edited by N. B. Kampen, 101–116. Cambridge.

Steiner, D. 1998. "Moving Images: Fifth-Century Victory Monuments and the Athlete's Allure." *ClAnt* 17: 123–149.

Stewart, A. 1977. *Skopas of Paros.* Park Ridge, NJ.

Stewart, A. 1982. "Dionysos at Delphi: The Pediments of the Sixth Temple of Apollo and Religious Reform in the Age of Alexander." In *Macedonia and Greece in Late Classical and Early Hellenistic Times*, Studies in the History of Art 10, edited by B. Barr-Sharrar and E. Borza, 204–227. Washington DC.

Stewart, A. 1983. "Pindaric Dike and the Temple of Zeus at Olympia." *ClAnt* 2: 133–144.

Stewart, A. 1990. *Greek Sculpture: An Exploration.* New Haven.

Stewart, A. 1993. *Faces of Power: Alexander's Image and Hellenistic Politics.* Berkeley.

Stewart, A. 1995. "Imag(in)ing the Other: Amazons and Ethnicity in Fifth-Century Athens." *Poetics Today* 16: 571–597.

Stewart, A. 1997. *Art, Desire, and the Body in Ancient Greece*, Cambridge.

Stewart, A. 2000. *"Pergamo Ara Marmorea Magna*: On the Date, Reconstruction, and Functions of the Great Altar of Pergamon." In *From Pergamon to Sperlonga: Sculpture and Context*, edited by N. T. de Grummond and B. S. Ridgway, 32–57. Berkeley.

Stewart, A. 2004. *Attalos, Athens, and the Akropolis: The Pergamene "Little Barbarians" and their Roman and Renaissance Legacy.* Cambridge.

Stibbe, C. M. 1992. "Dionysos mit einer Kithara?" In *Kotinos: Festschrift für Erika Simon*, edited by H. Froning et al., 139–145. Mainz.

Stilp, F. 2006. *Die Jacobsthal-Reliefs.* Rome.

Strauss Clay, J. 1996. "Fusing the Boundaries: Apollo and Dionysos at Delphi." *Metis* 11: 83–100.

Szemethy, H. D. 2005. *Die Erwerbungsgeschichte des Heroons von Trysa*. Vienna.

Taeuber, H. 1997. "Ein Inschriftenfragment der Pulydamas-Basis von Olympia." *Nikephoros* 10: 235–243.

Tersini, N. D. 1987. "Unifying Themes in the Sculpture of the Temple of Zeus at Olympia." *ClAnt* 6: 139–159.

Themelis, P. 1976. "Κεντρικὴ μορφὴ ἀπὸ τὸ ἀνατολικὸ ἀέτωμα τοῦ ναοῦ τοῦ Ἀπόλλωνος τῶν Δελφῶν." *ArchEph*: 8–11.

Themelis, P. 1979. "Contribution à l'étude de l'ex-voto delphique de Daochos." *BCH* 103: 507–520.

Thompson, H. A. 1937. "The American Excavations in the Athenian Agora, Eleventh Report." *Hesperia* 6: 1–226.

Thompson, H. A. 1949. "The Pedimental Sculpture of the Hephaisteion." *Hesperia* 18: 230–268.

Thompson, H. A. 1962. "The Sculptural Adornment of the Hephaisteion." *AJA* 66: 339–347.

Thompson, H. A. 1966. "Activity in the Athenian Agora 1960–1965." *Hesperia* 35: 37–54.

Thompson, H. A., and R. E. Wycherley.1972. *The Athenian Agora 14, The Agora of Athens*. Princeton.

Trianti, I. 2002. "Neue technische Beobachtungen an den Skulpturen des Zeustempels von Olympia." In *Olympia 1875–2000: 125 Jahre Deutsche Ausgrabungen*, Internationales Symposion, Berlin 9–11. November 2000, edited by H. Kyrieleis, 281–300. Mainz am Rhein.

Tulunay, E. T. 1998. "Pelops statt Apollon? Ein neuer Deutungsvorschlag für die mittlere Figur im Westgiebel des Zeustempels in Olympia." *IstMitt* 48: 453–460.

Vanderpool, E. 1942. "An Archaic Inscribed Stele from Marathon." *Hesperia* 11: 329–337.

Vidal-Naquet, P. 1967. "Une Énigme à Delphes: A propos de la base de Marathon (Pausanias, X, 10, 1–2)." *RHist* 91: 281–302.

Vidal-Naquet, P. 1981. "Athens and Atlantis: Structure and Meaning of a Platonic Myth." In *Myth, Religion, and Society*, edited by R. L. Gordon and R. G. A. Buxton, 201–214. Cambridge.

Villanueva Puig, M-C. 1986. "À Propos des Thyiades de Delphes." In *L'Association Dionysiaque dans les sociétés anciennes*, Actes de la table ronde organisée par l'École française de Rome, Rome 24–25 mai 1984, 31–51. Rome.

Vogt, S. 1998. "Delphi in der attischen Tragödie." *A&A* 44: 30–48.

Vollgraf, W. 1927. "Le péan delphique à Dionysos." *BCH* 51: 423–468.

Von Bockelberg, S. 1979. "Die Friese des Hephaisteion." *AntP* 18: 23–50.

Von den Hoff, R. 2001. "Die Posen des Siegers: die Konstruktion von Überlegenheit in attischen Theseusbildern des 5. Jahrhunderts v. Chr." In *Konstruktionen von Wirklichkeit: Bilder im Griechenland des 5. und 4. Jahrhunderts v. Chr.*, edited by R. von den Hoff and S. Schmidt, 73–88. Stuttgart.

Von den Hoff, R. 2003a. "Der Tatenzyklus." In *Theseus: Der Held der Athener*, edited by M. Flashar, R. von den Hoff, and B. Kreuzer, 17–21. Munich.

Von den Hoff, R. 2003b. "Theseuskult." In *Theseus: Der Held der Athener*, edited by M. Flashar, R. von den Hoff, and B. Kreuzer, 33–35. Munich.

Von den Hoff, R. 2003c. "Theseus und Skiron." In *Theseus: Der Held der Athener*, edited by M. Flashar, R. von den Hoff, and B. Kreuzer, 23–25. Munich.

Von Wilamowitz-Moellendorff, U. 1922. *Pindaros*, Berlin.

Wesenberg, B. 1983a. "Parthenongebälk und Südmetopenproblem." *JdI* 98: 57–86.

Wesenberg, B. 1983b. "Perser oder Amazonen? Zu den Westmetopen des Parthenon." *AA*: 203–208.

Wesenberg, B. 1995. "Panathenäische Peplosdedikation und Arrhephorie: Zur Thematik des Parthenonfries." *JdI* 110: 149–178.

Wesenberg, B. 1998. Review of I. Mark, *The Sanctuary of Athena Nike in Athens: Architectural Stages and Chronology in Gnomon* 70: 235–240.

Wetzel, H. 1996. "Das Hephaisteion in Athen und seine Umgebung: Studien zur Funktion eines Peripteros im 5. Jh. v. Chr." In *Kult und Funktion griechischer Heiligtümer in archaischer und klassischer Zeit*, edited by F. Bubenheimer et al., 31–42. Mainz.

Williams, D. 1983. "Herakles, Peisistratos and the Alcmeonids." In *Image et céramique grecque*, Actes du colloque de Rouen, 25–26 novembre 1982, edited by F. Lissarrague and F. Thelamon, 131–140. Rouen.

Woodford, S. 1971. "Cults of Heracles in Attica." In *Studies Presented to George M. A. Hanfmann*, edited by D. G. Mitten, J. G. Pedley, and J. A. Scott, 211–225. Mainz.

Wyatt, W. F., Jr., and C. N. Edmonson. 1984. "The Ceiling of the Hephaisteion." *AJA* 88: 135–167.

Ziro, D. 1994. *Μελέτη Αποκαταστάσεως του ναού της Αθηνάς Νίκης* 1a. Athens.

INDEX OF ANCIENT CITATIONS

Aelius Aristides
  38.480, 55
Aischines, 161
Aischylos
  Eum. 13, 22–26, 128, 133,
    155
Andokides
  Against Alkibiades 29, 49
  De mysteriis 40, 137
Anth. Pal. 6.280, 107
Apollodoros
  2.4.5, 196
  Epit. 5.10, 44
Aristophanes
  Clouds 603–606, 155
  Lysistrata 642–647, 106,
    108
  Peace 1183–1184, 130
Augustine
  De civ. D. 18.9, 66

Bacchylides
  16, 155
  18, 116

Cicero
  Nat. D. 1.83, 127
Clement of Alexandria
  Protr. 4.54.5, 55

Demosthenes
  60.8–10, 83
Dio Chrysostomus
  11.45, 22
  31.95–97, 50

Diodorus Siculus
  12.9.6, 47
  16.92.5, 55

Euripides, 155
  Ion 20–24, 102
  Ion 267–274, 102
  Lykymnios, 155

Harpokration
  Kolonetas, 137
  Lexicon, s.v. Polygnotos, 192
Herodotos
  5.47, 50
  5.62, 159
  5.102, 43
  7.61, 196
  8.47, 43
Hesiod
  Theogony, 71
  Theogony 570–591, 93
  Works and Days 57–105, 93
Homer
  Iliad 1.265, 116
  Iliad 23, 199
  Odyssey, 44

IG I³ 82, 134
IG I³ 131, 49
IG I³ 472, 126

Lucian
  Pro eikonibus 11, 51
Lysias
  2.4–47, 83

Pausanias
1.3.1, 135
1.3.2–3, 136
1.14.6, 112
1.15.2, 73
1.15.2–3, 135
1.17.2, 192
1.17.3, 77
1.18.1, 189
1.18.2, 192
1.2.1, 83
1.22.7, 190
1.23.7, 190
1.24.1, 81
1.24.5, 66, 69
1.24.7, 91
1.25.2, 206
1.27.3, 101, 103
1.27.8, 81
2.20.5, 188
2.27.2, 190
3.12.1–2, 46
3.13.6, 46
3.14.3, 49
3.18.14, 187
3.18.9–3.19.5, 54,
   186
4.17.9, 43
5.6.7, 30
5.7.6–10, 9, 30
5.7.7, 22, 46
5.8.2, 9
5.8.4, 46
5.8.10, 43
5.10.2, 13
5.10.3, 20
5.10.4, 13, 16
5.10.6–8, 13, 33
5.10.9, 28
5.12.5, 44
5.13.2, 22
5.13.4–6, 44
5.13.8, 22
5.14.6–7, 43
5.15.4, 30
5.15.7, 30
5.15.12, 49
5.16.2–4, 30
5.17.4, 55
5.17.7, 34
5.17–19, 22
5.20.3, 44
5.20.9–10, 54
5.21.2–3, 36

5.21.4, 36
5.24.5, 45
5.24.9, 35
5.25.8–10, 37, 49
6.5, 50
6.5.4–6, 47
6.5.7, 47
6.11.2, 50
6.11.5, 50
6.11.8–9, 50
6.20.9, 30
8.45.5–7, 189
9.4.2, 190
10.4.3, 160
10.10.1–2, 161
10.10.3–4, 188
10.11.5, 163
10.19.4, 150
10.25.1, 73
Pherekydes, 33
   FGrH 3 F 37, 10
Philochoros
   FGrH 328 F115, 159
Philodamos of Skarpheia,
   168
Pindar
   frag. 123.10–12, 45
   Isth. 1.51–53, 44
   Ol. 1, 33
   Ol. 1.1–7, 48
   Ol. 1.40–45, 45
   Ol. 1.67–88, 9, 10,
      40
   Ol. 1.97–99, 49
   Ol. 2, 51
   Ol. 3.16ff., 22
   Ol. 6.64–67, 30
   Ol. 6.67–69, 9
   Ol. 8.1–17, 35
   Ol. 9.94, 45
   Ol. 10.24–25, 9, 22,
      57–59
   Pyth. 1.83–84, 52
   Pyth. 8, 169
   Pyth. 9.97–100, 30
Plato
   Kritias 109c–d, 140
   Kritias 112a–c, 140
   Ti. 24e–25d, 141
Pliny
   HN 34.16, 51
   HN 34.57, 190
   HN 36.18–19,
      91

Plutarch, 160
  Ant. 60.4, 206
  Lyc. 22.4, 43
  Per. 12, 63
  Quaest. Conv. 2.5.2,
    43
  Thes. 27.4–5, 83
Pseudo-Aristotle
  Ath.Pol. 15.4, 82
Sophokles
  Antigone 1146–1152, 155
  frag. 844, 137

Strabo
  8.3.30, 35

Thukydides
  2.13.5, 91

Valerius Maximus
  8.11, est. 3, 127

Xenophon
  Hell. 3.2.21–22, 35
  Hell. 4.7.2, 35

OBJECT INDEX

Amsterdam, Allard Pierson Museum
  1588, 198
Athens, Akropolis Museum
  145, 82
  370, 82
  631, 72
  1358, 96
Athens, National Museum
  179, 151
  180, 151
  595 (CC968), 34, 40
  664, 1664a, 81

Basmahane, Museum
  4338, 185
Berlin, Staatliche Museen
  F2273, 126
  F2294, 126
Brussels, Musées Royaux d'Art et d'Histoire
  2314, 126

Eleusis, Archaeological Museum
  MA 51, 185

Florence, Museo Archeologico
  4209 (François Vase), 116
  81 600, 126

Göttingen, Georg-August-Universität
  J22, 34, 40

Istanbul, Archaeological Museum
  369, 198

Mykonos, Museum
  2240, 73

Naples, Museo Nazionale
  5026, 201
  6015, 206
  81669 (2422) (Vivenzio hydria), 83
  G103–104, 24, 111
New York, American Numismatic Society
  1944.100.12983, 200
  1944.100.12983, 56

Olympia, Archaeological Museum
  45, 47
  B1010, 42
  B2600, 41
  B5100, 41
  T2, 45

Paris, Musée du Louvre
  B370, 199

Rome, Vatican
  344, 141

St. Petersburg, Hermitage
  St. 1807, 154

SUBJECT INDEX

abduction, 45, 176, 183, 189, 190, 193,
    196–198, 204. *See also* Leukippos,
    daughters of
Achaians, 37, 44, 83
Achilles, 9, 53, 69, 84, 133, 138, 141, 178,
    200
Actium, Battle of, 211
Aglauros. *See* Athens, Akropolis, Shrine of
    Aglauros; Kekrops, daughters
    of
agon, 9, 17, 46, 52. *See also* battle and warfare,
    games
Agon (personification), 44
Agora. *See* Athens, Agora
Aigeus, 81, 116, 182
Aigina
    Temple of Aphaia, pediments, 27
Aineias, 74, 210, 212
Aithra, 74
Ajax, 53, 141
Akropolis, 78. *See* Athens, Akropolis
akroteria, 16, 45, 46, 53, 121, 135, 188, 190,
    193
Alexander the Great, 54–56, 199–202, 209,
    210
Alkamenes, 96, 127
Alkmaionidai, 159, 169
Alpheios River, 35
Amazonomachy, 4, 53, 67–69, 73, 79, 82–85,
    91–92, 94–95, 108, 111, 114, 118, 151,
    175, 181, 186, 187–188, 191, 192, 197,
    198, 203–205, 211
Amazons, 31, 83, 95, 121, 135, 188, 206, 207.
    See also Amazonomachy, Antiope,

Herakles, labors; Hippolyta,
    Penthesilea
    and Bellerophon, 198
Amphictyonic League, 149, 159, 161,
    164
Amyklai, 54
    Throne of Apollo, 186–187, 188,
    189
anakalypteria, 45
Anchises, 74
Andokides, 137
Androsthenes, 151
Antiope, 69, 83
Apaturia, 133
Aphaia. *See* Aigina, Temple of Aphaia;
    pediments
Aphrodite, 1, 53, 74
    and Arrhephoria, 101, 102
    and birth of Pandora, 93
    and Hephaistos, 133
    birth of, 94
apobatai, 86, 91
Apollo, 4, 15, 19, 23, 30, 32, 51, 53, 80, 142,
    144, 151, 153, 154–157, 158, 159, 160,
    161, 162, 164, 165, 168, 169. *See also*
    Amyklai, Throne of Apollo; Delphi,
    Temple of Apollo; Herakles: and
    Apollo; Rome, Temple of Apollo
    Sosianus
    and Python, 144
    Paian, 155, 169
Apollonia, 186
apotheosis. *See* immortality
apotropaic, 183

259

apples. *See* Herakles; labors; Atlas and
    Hesperides
Archidamian War, 40
archon basileus, 101
Areopagos, 138
Ares, 10, 41, 44, 133
arete, 19, 20, 44, 52
Argos, 20, 161, 188, 196
    Agora of, 188
aristocracy, 5, 51, 103–105, 107, 138, 199
Aristogeiton. *See* Tyrannicides
Aristophanes, 6
Arkadia, 161
Arkteia, 105–107, 108
Arktoi. *See* Arkteia
armor and weapons, 5, 25, 34, 40–44, 68, 77,
    94, 110, 124, 133, 139, 140, 141, 163,
    170, 182, 203, 204. *See also* votives
    axes, 23
    boulders, 124, 139, 140, 141
    cuirass, 40
    daggers, 23
    helmets, 40, 41, 45, 49
    shield bands, 42
    shields, 13, 34, 40, 104, 136, 160, 161
    spears, 10, 34, 40
    swords, 23, 182
Arrephoroi. *See* Arrhephoria
Arrhephoria, 91, 101–103, 106, 107, 108
Artemis, 1, 53, 104, 151, 159, 178
    Brauronia, 104, 105–107
    Limnatis, 107
Asia Minor, 170, 171–202
Assyrian reliefs, 199
Atalanta, 178
Athena, 4, 26, 60–62, 66–67, 71, 79, 81, 82,
    83, 85, 87, 94, 95, 103–104, 107–108,
    110, 111, 133, 137, 138, 141, 162, 163,
    169, 207. *See also* Delphi, Sanctuary of
    Athena Pronaia
    and Arrhephoria, 102
    and birth of Erichthonios, 102–103
    and birth of Pandora, 93, 94
    and Hephaistos, 124–128, 137–138,
        140–141, 142, 143
    and Herakles, 21, 114, 118, 132, 136
    and Theseus, 118
    birth of, 69–71, 98, 108
    Ergane, 100–101, 103, 137–138
    fights Giants, 95
    Hephaisteia, 138
    Limnatis, 107
    palladion of, 74
    Parthenos, 53, 103
    Polias, 103, 104, 137

Athens, 4, 8, 28, 40, 45, 49, 66, 67, 70, 73, 79,
    84, 91, 96, 112, 133, 140–141, 142,
    143, 205. *See also* autochthony
Academy, Altar of Hephaistos, 134
Agora, 60, 108
    Bouleuterion, Old (Old Metroon), 130,
        131
    Eponymous Heroes Monument, 110,
        130
    Hephaisteion, 3, 109–143, 162, 187,
        198, 204, 205; cult statues, 53,
        126–128, 137, 138, 140, 143; east
        frieze, 122, 124, 131, 138–142, 143;
        friezes, 128–130; metopes, 113–122,
        128–130, 131–132, 135, 136, 142, 143,
        162; pediments, 124–126; west frieze,
        122–124, 131, 140, 141, 142–143, 203
    Kolonos Agoraios, 112, 131, 134, 136,
        137, 140
    Metroon, Old. *See* Athens: Agora,
        Bouleuterion, Old
    Orchestra, 131
    Stoa Basileios, 130, 136, 188
    Stoa Poikile, 73, 111, 135–136, 143,
        188
    Stoa of Zeus Eleutherios, 130, 136
    synedrion, 130, 136
    Tholos, 130
Akropolis, 3, 59–82, 108, 109, 113, 140,
    203, 204
    Altar of Athena, 62, 97
    Beule Gate, 60
    Building III, 101
    Erechtheion, 72, 76, 80, 81, 86, 105;
        caryatids, 98, 105, 108; Shrine of
        Pandrosos, 103
    Lesser Attalid Dedication, 206–207
    Pandrosion, 80
    Parthenon, 3, 5, 6, 58, 96, 97, 101, 105,
        107, 108, 112, 113, 135, 159, 187, 198,
        205, 206–208; cult statue (Athena
        Parthenos), 53, 69, 71, 91–95, 187,
        203; east frieze, 102, 105, 124; east
        metopes, 71–73, 82, 85, 92, 95; east
        pediment, 69–71, 73; frieze, 6, 63–65,
        79, 85–91; metopes, 65–66, 79, 94;
        north metopes, 73–74, 83–85, 94, 95;
        pediments, 6, 65; south metopes,
        74–85, 91, 95, 122, 142, 203, 204; west
        frieze, 81; west metopes, 67–69, 73,
        79, 82–85, 91–92, 94–95, 205; west
        pediment, 66–67, 71, 73, 79, 95
    Propylaia, 60, 190
    Sanctuary of Artemis Brauronia, 104,
        106

Shrine of Aglauros, 192
Shrine of Athena Ergane, 100–101
Shrine of Pandion, 80
temple inventories, 20, 105
Old Temple of Athena, 62, 72, 76, 158
votives, 103, 108. *See also* Alkamenes,
    korai, Prokne, Theseus
and Delphi, 144–170
Dipylon gate, 60
and Herakles, 118
and Pergamon, 206–208
Sanctuary of the Dioskouroi, 189, 192
Theseion, 28, 77, 82, 136, 138, 142, 186,
    187, 192
and Theseus, 116
athletes and athletics, 3, 5, 14, 15, 16, 17, 19,
    20, 29–32, 40–52, 54, 56, 57, 80, 133,
    136, 137, 204, 205. *See also* games,
    Heraia
Atlantis, 140–141, 143
Atlas, 114. *See* Herakles, labors
Atreus, 34
Attalids, 206, 207, 209. *See also* Athens,
    Akropolis, Lesser Attalid Dedication;
    Pergamon
Attika, 143, 187, 205
Augean stables. *See* Herakles, labors
Augustus, 210, 212
Aulis, 106
autochthony, 101–103, 107, 127–128, 133,
    140

bacchai, 5, 155. *See also* Thyiades
Bacchic rites, 97
Bacchos. *See* Dionysos
banquets, 49, 174, 176, 178, 182–183, 185,
    193–195, 196–198
Bassai
    Temple of Apollo, 188, 198, 203
Bathykles of Magnesia, 54, 186
battle and warfare, 5, 9, 26, 40–44, 47, 111,
    124, 138–142, 163, 175, 178–181,
    193–195, 196–198, 199. *See also*
    Actium, Battle of; Archidamian War;
    Chaironeia, Battle of; city siege;
    Marathon, Battle of; Peloponnesian
    War; Persian Wars; Plataia, Battle of;
    Tanagra, Battle of; Third Sacred War
    training, 40–44, 45
Belevi
    Mausoleion, 198
Bellerophon, 178, 181, 187, 190, 191, 192,
    193, 195–196, 198, 205
Bes, 183, 193
Black Sea, 203

Brauron, 106
Bromios. *See* Dionysos
building accounts, 126, 149

Caria. *See* Halikarnassos
Carrey, Jacques, drawings by, 66, 69, 77, 80
caryatids. *See* Athens, Akropolis, Erechtheion
Centauromachy, 2, 3, 4, 15, 22–30, 32, 51, 53,
    57, 58, 59, 74–85, 91, 95, 108, 109,
    116, 122–124, 130, 131, 140, 141,
    142–143, 159, 175, 181–182, 186,
    187–188, 191, 192, 196, 198, 203–205
Centaurs, 79, 83, 203. *See also*
    Centauromachy; Chiron; Herakles,
    and Pholos
Chaironeia, Battle of, 55, 164, 165
Chalkeia, 101, 137
chariot race, 9, 16, 32–46, 57, 66, 205
Charites, 53
cheating, 13, 19, 33–40
childbearing. *See* childbirth, mothers
childbirth, 1
Chimaira. *See* Bellerophon
Chiron, 83
chryselephantine, 16, 53, 54–55, 91, 166
citizens, 5, 60
    Athenian, 3, 95–96, 98, 108, 109–143
city siege, 178–181, 193–195, 196–198,
    205
civic ideology, 131
    Roman, 211
Claudius, 210
coins, 55, 91, 200, 209
comedy, 6
competition, 30, 57. *See also* agon
Corcyra, 40
Corinth, 40
craftsmen, 100, 134, 137, 138, 139, 140,
    159
Cretan bull. *See* Herakles, labors
Crete, 116
Croissant, F., 151, 152, 155
cults. *See* religion and rituals

Daidalos, 79
Daochos of Pharsalos, 164–168
Darius II, 47
dedications. *See* votives
Deidameia, 32
Delian League, 62–63
Delos, 62
Delphi, 68
    Akanthos column, 166–168, 193
    and Athens. *See* Athens, and Delphi
    Argive Dedication, 188

Delphi (*cont.*)
  Athenian base near Treasury, 163
  Athenian Treasury, 114, 116–121, 143,
    153, 162–163, 198, 204, 205
  Charioteer, 49
  Corycian cave, 155
  Daochos Monument, 168
  gymnasion, 170
  hoplotheke, 170
  Lesche of the Knidians, 73
  Marathon Base, 161–162, 165
  Mt. Parnassos, 149, 155, 160
  oracle. *See* oracle, at Delphi
  Sacred Way, 117, 145, 161
  Sanctuary of Athena Pronaia, 144,
    170; Tholos, 54, 198
  Sikyonian Monopteros, 189
  Sikyonian Treasury, 189
  Siphnian Treasury, 26, 72, 189; east
    pediment, 153; frieze, 153
  Stoa of the Athenians, 163–164,
    170
  Temple of Apollo, 3–4, 144–170; east
    pediment, 26; fourth century B.C.,
    metopes, 149, 150; fourth century
    B.C., pediments, 146–160, 168–169;
    fourth-century B.C., east pediment,
    151; fourth century B.C., west
    pediment, 151; metopes, 160; sixth
    century B.C., east pediment, 26; sixth
    century B.C., pediments, 158–159,
    160; sixth century B.C., west
    pediment, 72, 153
Demeter, 1, 110
  Chamyne, 30
Demetrios Poliorketes, 201
democracy, 3, 80, 110, 130, 131, 132, 133,
  136, 137, 141
Democracy (personification), 136
Demos, 136
Demosthenes, 83, 161
dike, 19, 45–46, 51, 52
Diomedes. *See* Herakles, labors, horses of
  Diomedes
Dionysia Greater, 91
Dionysius I of Syracuse, 159
Dionysos, 4, 144, 148, 151, 154–157, 159,
  160, 168, 169, 201, 207
Dioskouroi, 178. *See also* Leukippos,
  daughters of
divinization, 172, 199–202
donors. *See* patrons and patronage
Dorian, 45
Doryphoros of Polykleitos, 200
drama, 6, 155

Egesta, 50
Eleans. *See* Elis
Eleusinian Mysteries, 109, 110, 136
Eleusis, 91
Elgin, Lord, 66
Elis, 13, 16, 17, 20, 29, 34–40, 44, 46, 49, 53,
  57, 58, 80, 203
ephebes, 130, 132, 133, 134, 135, 137,
  141
Ephialtes, 137
Ephialtic reforms, 138
Epidauros
  Temple of Asklepios, 151, 190
  Tholos, 54
Epimetheus, 94
epinician, 6, 40, 50–52. *See also* Pindar
epiphany, 152, 154, 159
Erechtheus, 79, 90
Ergastinai, 101
Erichthonios, 133, 140
  birth of, 53, 102–103, 127–128, 138, 140,
    141
Eros, 74
Erymanthian boar. *See* Herakles, labors
ethos, 19
Euripides, 6, 38, 94
Eurydike, 54, 55
Eurymedon, 162
Eurystheus, 20
Exekias, 141

females. *See* women
festivals. *See* Apaturia; Eleusinian Mysteries;
    games; Hephaisteia; Panathenaia;
    religion and rituals; Theseia
François Vase, 116
funeral cult, 173, 182, 197

Gaia (Ge), 102
games
  for Herakles at Marathon, 143
  funeral, 9, 43–44
  Isthmian, 9
  Nemean, 9
  Olympian, 3, 8–13, 14, 16, 17, 19, 20, 22,
    30, 32, 40–52, 53, 54, 57, 142,
    145
  Panathenaic, 62, 110, 133
  Panhellenic, 43–44, 46–52
  Pythian, 3, 9, 49, 144, 170
Gauls, 206, 207
Ge. *See* Gaia
gender, 5, 7, 30–32, 44–46
Geryon. *See* Herakles, labors
Giants, 138, 207. *See* Gigantomachy

Gigantomachy, 4, 27, 58, 60, 71–73, 85, 92, 95, 108, 138, 153, 154, 158, 190, 206–208
Gilgamesh, 196
Gjölbaschi-Trysa. *See* Trysa
Gorgon, 183
gymnasion, 45

Halikarnassos, Mausoleion, 171, 198, 199
Harmodios. *See* Tyrannicides
Hektor, 49
Helen, 53, 73, 74, 84–85, 94, 95, 103, 108
Hellenistic period, 206–209
Henrichs, A., 160
Hephaisteia, 134–135
Hephaisteion. *See* Athens, Agora
Hephaistos, 111, 113, 124–128, 133–135, 137–141, 142, 143, 169
    and Athena Ergane, 101
    and birth of Athena, 70, 71
    and birth of Erichthonios, 102–103
    and birth of Pandora, 93, 94
Hera, 20, 30, 31, 53, 107, 133. *See also* Heraia
Heraia, 20, 30–32, 44–46, 53, 54, 107
Heraion. *See* Olympia, Temple of Hera (Heraion)
Herakles, 9, 22, 41, 43, 46–50, 52, 53, 54, 55, 82, 112, 113–122, 130, 135, 136, 141, 143, 162–163, 195, 200, 201, 203. *See also* Amazonomachy
    and Amazons, 69
    and Apollo, 26, 153
    and Gigantomachy, 71
    and Pholos, 22, 163, 182, 187
    labors, 3, 16, 51, 57, 109, 128, 130, 132, 136, 153, 162, 204
        Amazon, 21, 114, 121, 204
        Atlas and Hesperides, 21, 22, 52–53, 114, 162
        Augean stables, 21, 22, 114, 162
        Cretan bull, 21, 46, 162
        Erymanthian boar, 21, 113, 162
        Geryon, 21, 22, 114, 118, 163
        horses of Diomedes, 21, 114, 117
        Hydra, 21, 22, 46, 113, 162
        Kerberos, 21, 114, 162
        Keryneian hind, 21, 46, 117, 162
        Kyknos, 163
        Nemean lion, 21, 42, 46, 47–48, 53, 113, 117, 162
        Stymphalian birds, 21, 114, 162
    Parastates, 43
Hermes
    and birth of Pandora, 94

hero, 20. *See also* Herakles, heroes, Pelops, Perithoos, Theseus,
hero cult, 5, 54, 199, 205, 206, 209. *See also* heroon
heroes
    eponymous, 86, 161–162
    Homeric, 199. *See also* Achilles, Ajax, Hektor, Menelaos, Paris, Patroklos
heroization, 4, 5, 56, 58, 170, 171–202, 204, 205
heroon, 49, 50, 54. *See also* Amyklai, Throne of Apollo; Athens, Theseion; Delphi, Sanctuary of Athena Pronaia, Tholos; Limyra, Heroon of Perikles Limyra, Ptolemaion; Olympia, Pelopion; Trysa, Heroon
Herse. *See* Kekrops, daughters of
Hesperides. *See* Herakles, labors
Hieron of Sicily, 45
Hippias, 159
Hippocratic corpus, 107
Hippodameia, 9, 15, 19, 30, 32–46, 53
Hippolyta, 69, 83, 211
Hoff, R. von den, 132
Homer, 25, 44
hoplites, 9, 40–44, 88
Horai, 53
hubris, 19, 46, 51–52, 83
hunt, 181–182, 193, 196–198, 199. *See also* Kalydonian boar hunt
    and battle, 199
    eastern, 199
Hyakinthia, 186
Hyakinthos, 186–187
Hydra. *See* Herakles, labors
Hyperboreans, 22

iconography, 45, 47, 76, 138, 190
    Lycian, 175
    Near Eastern, 175
Idas. *See* Leukippos, daughters of
Ikarios, 46
Ikaros, 79
Ilioupersis, 73–74, 83–85, 94, 95, 151, 181, 205, 210
immortality, 22, 46, 47, 48–52
influences
    Egyptian, 193
    Near Eastern, 171–193, 195–196, 199, 202
initiation, 31, 106
inscriptions, 6–7, 22, 36, 37, 55, 102, 103, 126, 146, 149, 163, 164, 168, 172
Iphigeneia, 106. *See also* Arkteia
Ithaka, 178

Itys. *See* Prokne
Ixion, 79

Kadmos Painter, 154
Kaineus, 25, 124, 141, 143, 175, 182, 198,
    203, 204
Kalydon. *See* Kalydonian boar hunt
Kalydonian boar hunt, 178, 187, 188–189,
    191, 196
Kassandra, 52–53, 83
Kastor. *See* Dioskouroi; Leukippos,
    daughters of
Kekrops, 67, 82, 98, 105
    daughters of, 101–103, 168
Kerberos. *See* Herakles, labors
Keryneian hind. *See* Herakles, labors
Kimon, 82, 162, 163
Kladeos River, 35
Kleopatra, 211
Kleophrades Painter, 83
kleos, 20, 48–52, 56
korai
    from Athens, Akropolis, 103, 108
Korres, M., 79
Kos, 187
Kreousa, 74
Kroisos of Lydia, 145
Kronos, 9, 70
Kypselos. *See* Olympia, Chest of Kypselos

Lakedaimonians. *See* Sparta and Spartans
Lapiths. *See* Centauromachy, Kaineus,
    Perithoos
Lemnos, 133
Leochares, 54
Leto, 151
Leukippos, 192
    daughters of, 181–182, 187, 189–190, 191,
        192, 193, 196, 204
Libon of Elis, 20
Limyra
    Heroon of Perikles, 196, 199
    Ptolemaion, 198
Lycia, 4, 205, 212. *See* Limyra, Trysa,
    Xanthos
Lykourgos of Athens, 156
Lynkeus. *See* Leukippos, daughters of
lyric poetry, 6
Lysias, 83
Lysippos, 50, 200

Macedonia and Macedonians, 4, 54, 149,
    157, 160–161, 164–166, 171, 182, 199,
    201, 202. *See also* Alexander the Great,
    Philip II

Magna Graecia, 14, 50, 189
Marathon, 81. *See also* Theseus
    Battle of, 81, 111, 114, 121, 135, 136, 143,
        161–164, 188, 204, 205
    marriage, 19, 30, 31, 32, 46, 51, 53, 85, 95–98,
        102, 106, 107, 108, 204
Medes. *See* Persia and Persians
Medusa, 13, 178, 187. *See also* Perseus
Meleager, 178
Melian reliefs, 188, 190
Menelaos, 74
metics, 5, 60, 96, 134
Metis, 69–70
metopes, 189, 190, 198
Milo of Croton, 47
Miltiades, 41, 161–162
Minotaur. *See* Theseus
mothers, 95–98, 102, 103, 107, 204
Mt. Olympos, 45
Muses, 151, 155, 160, 168
Mykonos, 73
Myron, 190
Myrtilos, 33, 34

Nemea. *See* games; Herakles, labors
Nemesis, 53
Neoptolemos, 74, 83
Nereids, 193
Nestor, 49
Nikai. *See* Nike
Nike, 16, 46, 52, 53, 91. *See also* Olympia;
    Nike of Paionios
Nikias
    Peace of, 134
Niobe, 53

Oberleitner, W., 183
Octavian, 211
Odysseus, 44, 178, 190, 191, 192, 197, 210
offerings. *See* votives
Oibatos of Dyme, 50
Oinomaos, 9–13, 15, 16, 19, 32–46, 52, 205
Olympia, 3, 5, 19, 20, 59, 60, 68, 144, 170,
    205
    Achaian Monument, 37, 49, 54
    Altis, 14, 15, 29, 30, 43, 48–52, 54, 55, 79
    ash altar of Zeus, 14, 22, 49, 54
    Chest of Kypselos, 22, 34, 35, 54, 57, 186
    Echo Hall, 47
    Megarian Treasury, 27, 54, 72, 158
    military votives, 20
    Nike of Paionios, 41
    oracle. *See* oracle, at Olympia
    Pelopion, 14, 44, 45, 49, 54, 55, 56, 171
    Philippeion, 54–56, 58, 166

Poulydamas base, 47–48, 50
Stadion (III), 42
Temple of Hera (Heraion), 14, 22, 30, 44, 49, 53, 54
Temple of Zeus, 3, 8, 53, 58, 65, 142–143, 198, 203; cult statue, 16–22, 46, 52–54, 55, 56, 57, 94, 186, 188; east pediment, 13, 16, 19, 32–46, 52; metopes, 16, 19, 20–22, 42, 43, 46–50, 51, 109, 114, 115, 150, 162, 205; west pediment, 15, 19, 20, 22–30, 32, 51, 53, 58, 77, 79–80, 116, 122, 159, 188
  treasuries, 14, 145
  Zanes, 35–37, 54
Olympias, 54, 55
Onasias, 190
oracle, 35, 43, 50, 205
  at Delphi, 3, 144–145, 153, 155, 157, 159, 161, 162
  at Olympia, 3, 30, 145
Ouranos, 70

paian, 168
Paionios, 41
palladion. See Athena, palladion of
Pallantids, 138, 141
Pallas. See Pallantids
Panathenaia, 5, 60–62, 73, 87–91, 98, 101, 105, 108, 109, 133, 136, 137
Pandion, 67, 80, 96
Pandora, 53, 95, 102, 103, 108
  birth of, 92, 94, 98
Pandrosos, 102. See also Kekrops, daughters of
Panhellenic, 57
  hero. See Herakles
  politics, 145, 156
  sanctuaries, 4. See Delphi, Olympia
  victors, 43–44, 46–52, 209
Pankrates of Argos, 168
Paris, 95
parthenoi, 105, 107
Parthenon. See Athens, Akropolis
Patroklos, 9, 43, 44, 199
patrons and patronage, 4, 13, 16, 34–40, 44, 46, 54, 57, 60, 80, 82, 112, 130, 148, 159, 163, 168, 170, 173, 198
Pausanias, 2, 6
pederasty, 44–45
Pegasos, 178, 196
Peisistratids, 159
Peisistratos, 82
Peleus, 178
Peloponnesian War, 40, 91, 98, 113

Pelops, 9–13, 14, 15, 16, 17, 19, 28, 30, 32–46, 51, 52, 56, 57, 59, 171, 205. See also Poseidon
Penelope, 46, 178
Penthesilea, 53, 69, 84
Pergamon
  Altar of Zeus, 4, 66, 206–208
Perikles, 63, 98, 137
  funeral oration, 91
Perithoos, 15, 23, 27, 30, 32, 46, 51, 53, 80, 116, 124, 142. See also Centauromachy
Persephone, 110
Persepolis, 199
Perseus, 187, 190, 197
  and Medusa, 190, 191, 195–196
Persia and Persians, 4, 19, 46, 172, 193, 196, 199, 206, 207, 211. See also Marathon, Battle of; Persian Wars; Plataia, Battle of
Persian Wars, 8, 19, 41, 62, 66, 83, 207
personifications, 33, 35, 44. See also Agon, Democracy, Demos
Pheidias, 16, 52–54, 57, 65, 91, 94, 162. See also Athens, Akropolis, Parthenon, cult statue (Athena Parthenos); Olympia, Temple of Zeus, cult statue
Phellos, 186
Pherekydes, 40
Philip II, 54–56, 160–161, 164, 199, 202, 209
Philippos of Croton, 50
Philodamos of Skarpheia, 168–169
Philomela, 96–101
Phocis, 149, 161
Pholos. See Herakles, and Pholos
Pindar, 6, 50–52
Pisa, 9, 13, 44, 46
plague, 106
Plataia
  Battle of, 8
  Temple of Athena Areia, 190, 191
Plato, 140–141, 143
Pliny, 2, 6
Pollitt, J.J., 91
Polydeukes. See Dioskouroi; Leukippos, daughters of
Polygnotos of Thasos, 73, 189, 190, 192
  Circle of, 188
Polykleitos. See Doryphoros
Polyxena, 74
Pompeii, 210
Pompey, 210
Poseidon, 10, 33, 34, 44, 66–67, 71, 73, 95, 201. See also Sounion, Temple of Poseidon
  and Pelops, 45

Poulydamas, 47–48, 50
Praxias, 151
Priam, 83
Prokne, 96–101, 108, 127
Prokrustes. *See* Theseus, and Prokrustes
Prometheus, 53. *See* Zeus, and Prometheus
prophecy, 69
Pythia, 155
Pythiad, 166
Python. *See* Apollo, and Python

religion and rituals, 1, 3, 4, 7, 108, 112, 133, 155, 160. *See also* sacrifices, votives
Rhamnous
    Temple of Nemesis, cult statue, 53
Rhodes, 187
rite of passage, 31, 102, 199
rites. *See* religion and rituals
Roman copies, 82, 127, 206
Roman use of Greek myth, 211–212
Rome
    Temple of Apollo Sosianus, 211
ruler cult, 171–202, 209–210

sacrifices, 1, 14, 30, 34, 43, 49, 62, 86, 97, 98, 106, 134, 178, 180, 193, 199
sarcophagi, 184
    from Sidon, 198
    from Trysa, 174
    Roman, 210, 211
sarcophagus. *See* sarcophagi
Satyros of Elis, 49
Satyrs, 5
seers, 33, 34–35
Selinus
    Temple C, 190
    Temple E, 205
semiotics, 2
Seven against Thebes, 175, 188, 190, 191, 196
sexuality, 7, 84, 85, 95, 108
Silanion, 49
Silaris (Foce del Sele), Treasury of the Heraion, 189
Skythians, 83
slaves, 5, 139
Sophokles, 38
Sosius. *See* Rome, Temple of Apollo Sosianus
Sounion, Temple of Poseidon, 187, 198
Sparta and Spartans, 13, 31, 42, 43, 54, 55, 107, 159, 161, 186, 187
Sperlonga, 210
sphinx, 53
stadion, 13, 14, 50, 52

Sterope, 32, 33
Stesichoros, 95
Stewart, A., 96
Strabo, 6
Strauss Clay, J., 155
Stymphalian birds. *See* Herakles, labors
Sybaris, 47

Tanagra, Battle of, 13
Tantalos, 37, 40
technai. *See* techne
techne, 70, 94, 103, 128, 133, 137, 138, 141, 142, 168–169
Tegea, Temple of Athena Alea, 151, 189
Telephos, 207
Tereus of Thrace, 96
Thasos, 50
Theagenes of Thasos, 50
Thebes and Thebans, 53, 160–161, 164. *See also* Seven against Thebes
Theoxenia, 168
Theseia, 132–133
Theseion. *See* Athens, Theseion
Theseus, 15, 23, 28, 30, 41, 43, 46, 51, 53, 69, 80–82, 84, 100, 112, 113–122, 124, 128–130, 131–133, 135–136, 138, 141, 142, 153, 162–163, 182, 187–188, 191, 192, 197, 198, 204, 205, 211. *See also* Centauromachy
    and Kerkyon, 116, 117
    and Krommyon sow, 116
    and Marathonian bull, 81, 116, 117
    and Minotaur, 42, 81–82, 116, 117, 131, 132, 182, 187, 188
    and Periphetes, 116, 117
    and Prokrustes, 82, 115, 117
    and Sinis, 116, 117, 182
    and Skiron, 116, 135, 182, 188
Thessaly, 15, 23, 27, 29, 50, 58, 76, 80, 142, 164, 182, 203
Thetis, 74
Third Sacred War, 149, 161
Thrace, 96
Thrasymedes of Paros, 190
Thyiades, 149, 151, 155, 160, 168
Tiberius, 210
Timaios, 131
tombs, 170, 171–202. *See also* heroon
    at Taranto, 198
tragedy, 19, 37–40, 94
treasuries, 26, 198, 205. *See also* Delphi, Athenian Treasury; Delphi, Sikyonian Treasury; Delphi, Siphnian Treasury; Olympia, Megarian Treasury; Olympia, treasuries

Troizen, 116

Trojan War, 69, 73, 211

Troy and Trojans, 44, 69, 83, 95, 138. *See also* Ilioupersis, Trojan War

Trysa, Heroon, 4, 5, 171–202, 204, 205

Tyrannicides, 24, 28, 30, 80, 111, 122, 124, 130, 131, 136, 138, 142–143

vase painting, 68, 69, 71, 91, 116, 124, 132, 139, 154, 187, 188, 190, 192, 193, 205, 212

  Apulian, 38

  Attic, 34, 40, 72, 80, 98, 116, 126, 141, 143, 154, 186, 189

victory monuments. *See* votives

viewers and viewer perception, 1, 2, 3, 5, 17, 20, 29–32, 44–46, 51–52, 54, 57, 60, 79, 80, 84, 97, 98, 109, 111, 112, 122, 148, 203, 205, 207, 212

  eastern, 199

Villanueva Puig, M.-C., 160

Vivenzio hydria, 83

votives, 1, 7, 14, 22, 37, 46, 54, 55, 86, 95–98, 110, 117, 145, 149, 163, 182, 188, 205, 206. *See also* Athens, Akropolis, temple inventories; Athens, Akropolis, votives; korai, from Athens, Akropolis

  thank offerings, athletic, 16, 43, 48–49

  thank offerings, military, 13, 16, 20, 42, 43, 45, 48–49, 54–56, 57, 160–162, 163–168, 204, 207

wall painting, 28, 73, 186, 187, 188, 190, 191–192, 199. *See* Athens, Agora, Stoa Poikile; Athens, Agora, Stoa of Zeus Eleutherios; Athens, Theseion; Delphi, Lesche of the Knidians

  Roman, 210

warfare. *See* battle and warfare

weapons. *See* armor and weapons

weaving, 30, 72, 96, 100, 101, 102, 103, 137

wedding, 23, 25, 45, 78, 124, 142, 182, 204. *See also* Centauromachy

Wesenberg, B., 79, 91

western Greece, 2. *See* Magna Graecia,

white-ground lekythoi, 98

women, 3, 5, 23, 25, 30–32, 57, 59–108, 122, 124, 142, 175, 182, 203, 204, 205. *See also* Amazons, Centauromachy

Xanthos, Nereid Monument, 171, 187, 189, 193–195, 199

xoanon, 62, 72, 88, 101

Zeus, 1, 4, 19, 22, 27, 32–33, 35–37, 41, 48, 52, 53, 102, 55–56, 66, 67, 85, 126, 136, 140, 143, 159, 175, 207. *See also* Olympia; Pergamon

  Ammon, 201

  and birth of Athena, 71

  and Ganymede, 45

  and Prometheus, 93–94

  Areios, 43

  founder of Olympic games, 9